WIRED TO GROW

Harness the Power of Brain Science to Learn and Master Any Skill

Second Edition
Revised and Expanded

Britt Andreatta, PhD

7th Mind
Publishing

7th Mind
Publishing

Revised edition originally published 2016.
Second edition 2019.
7th Mind Publishing
Santa Barbara, California

The following are all registered trademarks of 7th Mind, Inc.: Change Quest™, Four Gates to Peak Team Performance™, Three Phase Model of Learning™, Growth Culture™, Learn Remember Do™, and Survive Belong Become™. Copyrighted images on pages 19, 21, 36, and 128 graciously shared with permission.

For orders or bulk purchases of this book, please write Orders@7thMindPublishing.com.

For training materials affiliated with this book, visit BrittAndreatta.com/Training.

For speaking engagements please contact Teresa Fanucchi at Speaking@BrittAndreatta.com, or visit BrittAndreatta.com/speaking.

ISBN: 978-0-9973547-7-5 (paper)
ISBN: 978-0-9973547-6-8 (ebook)

This book is printed on acid-free paper in the United States of America.

For Chris and Kiana.
You are my heart and soul. You help me learn and grow every day. I am the luckiest person on the planet to get to spend this life with you.

CONTENTS

IV. Learn: Where It All Starts

V. Design + Deliver Learning

VI. Create a Growth Culture of Learning

INTRODUCTION

"When you know better, you do better."
Maya Angelou, poet and author, *I Know Why the Caged Bird Sings*

So, I was wrong. Well, not wrong exactly but some things I wrote in the first edition of this book have shifted so dramatically that they are now out of date. I have written two books since the first edition of *Wired to Grow* and, frankly, I got better at it as I went. So, it felt like a good time to update—but honestly, I thought I would dig into the research and find a handful of things to rework for the revision. Not so. Neuroscience has come far in the past five years. Many more researchers are looking at learning, memory, and behavior change. New tools and big data are shifting what scientists know about the brain, and memory research has undergone radical transformation due to some groundbreaking studies. And medical doctors are leveraging recent findings in neuroscience to create new treatments that are producing astonishing results.

You might not know this, but the rule for a second edition of a book is that at least 20 percent must change. Well, you're getting a whole new book because this is not only a complete rewrite of the first edition, but I have added 50 percent more content and revised my Three Phase Model of Learning™ as well.

In addition to the science, and perhaps because of it, the learning industry has changed significantly too. New technologies have made learning much more accessible. Thanks to smart phones, people all around the world are following their interests, developing their skills, and learning from peers and experts, many regardless of their circumstances, education, or income. Technology has also made learning more scalable to large groups of people and also more impactful. This has enlivened a new learning hunger in people of every age. Deloitte's *2019 Global Human Capital Trends* report, a study done with 10,000 participants from 119 countries, found that "people now rate the 'opportunity to learn' as among their top reasons for taking a job," and that "the No. 1 reason people quit their jobs is the 'inability to learn and grow.'" This has forced organizations to prioritize learning and, in fact, it tops their list of top-10 trends, along with leadership development and reskilling the current workforce for new kinds of work and jobs. Learning has expanded far beyond childhood classrooms to become a lifelong journey on a path to becoming our best selves.

Learning is the most powerful and natural process in the world. It's at the heart of any transformation we have made or will ever make both as individuals and a society. I am not talking about education or training but the process of learning: how we start at one level of awareness, understanding, or skill and shift to a different—and better—level. We are biologically wired to learn. Our survival depends on our ability to learn from our environment and experiences. And therefore, intrinsically, several aspects of our central and peripheral nervous system are dedicated to the learning process.

Thousands of years ago, when all humans were living in tribes and subsisting off the land, our ancestors who survived were the ones who learned how to recognize when predators were nearby, to know which foods were poisonous, and to read signs of hostility in others. Today, our survival instinct still drives much of our learning but the context is vastly different. Instead of learning how to forage for food, we must successfully navigate our work environments. Survival is still the goal, since we use our paychecks to buy food, water, and shelter. But rather than learning to build fires and huts, we now need to know how to drive a car and use a computer.

Socially, we still need to learn how to read signs of hostility in others, as well as kindness, curiosity, and a host of other complex emotions, the process known as emotional intelligence. While that need hasn't changed, technology has connected the world, so we now need to do it beyond the familiarity of a shared language, culture, or geographic region. And we might even use emotional intelligence to understand words on a monitor, a voice on a device, or a face on a two-dimensional screen.

In addition to being the key to our survival, learning is also the path to fulfilling our potential—our capacity to become or develop into something more. Within each of us is unrealized ability waiting to blossom into the fullest expression of who we are. As individuals and as a species, we yearn to realize the highest and best version of ourselves. It's in our DNA, the strands of which even visually model the journey of an ever-upward climb. It's about transforming ourselves across the course of our lifetime.

And now, these advances in neuroscience have helped us identify the most effective way to learn. Instead of stumbling along, we have the ability to maximize our learning abilities, allowing us to more intentionally shape our growth and development. Transformative learning is a three-dimensional approach to learning that drives real behavior change. This means a person's understanding shifts through experiences and information about the "why" of things (psychological); their belief systems irrevocably shift through epiphanies, flashes of insight, and "aha!" moments (convictional); and their actions shift through observation, application, experimentation, and practice (behavioral). We'll learn more about how this fits in the bigger picture in section V, but for now just know that each dimension of transformative learning helps create and groove neural pathways and habits of the desired behaviors in yourself or others.

This revised and expanded edition of *Wired to Grow: Harness the Power of Brain Science to Learn and Master Any Skill* is designed to help you fully unlock your potential, incorporating recent discoveries in neuroscience to give you new ways to maximize your ability to learn and grow. You can apply this material to your own life immediately, starting today. If you have a role where you help others learn and grow, you will also gain new tools for unlocking their potential and becoming a more effective manager, parent, leader, educator, or health care worker.

This book is organized into six sections:

I.   We'll begin by looking at the big developments of the last five years in the neuroscience of learning.

II.   Next, we'll dive into the new findings about memory (there are nine types!) and how the type of memory determines how you set up learning.

III. We'll explore new research about skills, habits, and behavior change.

IV.   Next, we'll look at how to set up learning to maximize its effectiveness from the start.

V.   We'll turn our attention to the latest brain-based best practices in learning design and delivery.

VI.   We'll end with specific tips and strategies for creating a growth culture of learning in your organizations.

My Research Process

This book focuses on new developments since 2014 and, boy, there have been a lot of them. As a learning professional seeking cutting-edge information in learning and development, I have immersed myself in neuroscience research, which has forever changed how I approach learning design and delivery. Sadly, there is currently no centralized place to look for how brain science might inform learning professionals, so I began by diving deep into the latest studies.

I first focused on neuroscience, reading journals like *Neuron, The Journal of Neuroscience, Trends in Neuroscience and Education, Social Cognitive and Affective Neuroscience,* and *The Year in Cognitive Neuroscience.* Inevitably, these studies led me to other disciplines and recent studies in biology, psychology, business, and education. I also reached out and interviewed thought leaders in the field, like Dr. Mike Miller at the DYNS lab at the University of California, a coeditor of *The Year in Cognitive Neuroscience,* and Dr. Robert Clark, the co-author of *Behavioral Neuroscience of Learning and Memory*. I read books, watched TED talks, and listened to podcasts. Inevitably, key themes emerged as I connected dots between studies, disciplines, and scientists that are rather siloed from each other.

Another important part of my research process is mapping what scientists find in their labs to issues that impact today's workplaces. I leverage research by data giants like Gallup, Deloitte, and McKinsey as well as professional associations like the Association for Talent Development (ATD) and the Society for Human Resource Management (SHRM). To be clear, I am not a neuroscientist; my PhD is in education, leadership, and organizations, and I have done my own research on the science of success. Because I am an active practitioner, designing and delivering learning experiences out in the field, I can see where lab studies do and do not translate to how people experience learning in the real world.

Some of the studies confirmed things I had found through trial and error long ago; others completely shifted how I approach my craft. What I found not only changed how I design and deliver learning for others but also how I approach my own transformation. Now that I know and truly understand the neuroscience of learning, I have unlocked more of my own potential and the potential of participants in my sessions.

In addition, I used this research to build several new brain science–based training programs that are proving to be exceptionally effective in all kinds of organizations and industries. If you want to learn more, visit BrittAndreatta.com/Training.

In the first edition, I introduced my Three Phase Model of Learning and just five years ago, it looked like this:

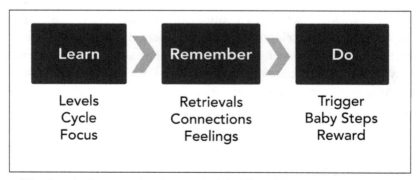

The first (and now outdated) version of the Three Phase Model of Learning

Enriched by new research and data, the revised model looks like this:

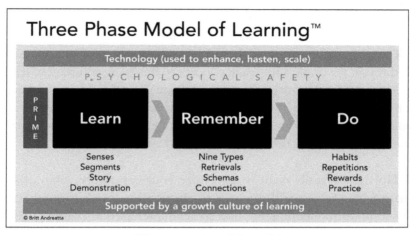

The new version of the model

It still includes the core phases of Learn, Remember, Do, but the elements within them have shifted. And in addition to the critical component of fostering psychological safety, this new version explores the importance of properly priming for learning, as well as technology's role in aiding learning, all of which rest upon a growth culture of learning.

I am eager to share with you my exciting discoveries on the many new developments in the neuroscience of learning. So, let's take a journey together. I'd like to introduce you to the fascinating miracle that happens inside you every day: learning. Once you understand this brain-based process, you'll be able to use it more effectively and efficiently in your own life. You'll also have the keys to help others learn better and faster.

Let's get started!

Take a Learning Journey

Before I wrote this book, I taught this content through workshops, keynote presentations at conferences and corporations, and in online courses. In a live presentation, I model these concepts so participants get the most out of the experience. I'd like to replicate that for you here, so before you read on, pick something that you'd like to learn. It could be something you are currently learning, or something you want to learn in the near future. It could be a new professional skill, like public speaking or mastering unfamiliar software. Or it could be something personal like playing an instrument, speaking a new language, or dancing the tango.

The only requirement: it should be truly meaningful to you. As you work through the book, apply each concept to this thing you want to learn—your learning goal—and by the end you will have a robust and exciting plan to help you realize your potential in this area. To help, I created a free downloadable PDF for you to print and fill out as you explore each concept (www.BrittAndreatta.com/Wired-to-Grow).

Tip: If you really want to maximize your experience, find a partner to share with. As you will discover in chapter 13, social learning actually boosts long-term retention. So, find a friend interested in chatting with you about what you learn in this book and your progress on your learning goal. Perhaps they might want to take this journey with you, comparing notes as they learn something new themselves.

NEW DEVELOPMENTS IN THE NEUROSCIENCE OF LEARNING

"The whole of life, from the moment you are born to the moment you die, is a process of learning."

Jiddu Krishnamurti, philosopher and author,
The Awakening of Intelligence

1. Advances in Neuroscience Research

Neuroscientists at top universities and institutes around the world are engaged in cutting-edge research about how we learn. All learning involves the brain and flows through neural pathways. While learning is something our bodies have done for over 200,000 years, we continue to discover new things about how this amazing process happens. Great progress has been made but I cannot emphasize enough how new this exploration into our brains really is because neuroscience itself is only 30 years old.

We are only just beginning and, like any scholarly pursuit, scientists start with the big picture and then eventually dig deeper, splitting off into thousands of explorations and all kinds of specializations. As competing theories and models arise, more studies seek to replicate and validate earlier results. In addition, innovations in technology create new methods for exploration, which can impact the comparability of findings. When I review the literature, I am astounded by the volume (breadth) of studies and also by the lack of depth, simply because this research is so new to the timeline of scientific study. That said, the findings I share here represent a bit of both: studies with enough replication and validation to know we're onto something as well as some new developments that sound exciting but may not stand the test of time.

Neuroscience, the study of the biological features of our central nervous system (CNS), is at the forefront of this exploration because advances in medical technology have opened a whole new frontier for understanding the human body. The CNS comprises the brain and spinal cord and connects to the limbs and organs through the nerves of the peripheral nervous system (PNS). The neuroscience of learning looks at how these systems work together to create and retain new knowledge and skills.

In addition to neuroscience, a host of other disciplines study how the brain shapes human thought and behavior, including psychology, psychiatry, and anthropology. Together they are crafting a detailed road map that we can all use to enhance our own learning and support the learning of others. Here's an overview of several key developments in the past five years in our understanding of how the brain learns, which set up the recommendations in the rest of this book (for those of you who read the first edition, this will jump-start your learning with the newest data up front):

- New technologies for viewing and analyzing the brain
- New neural proof of multiple intelligences
- New discoveries about how creativity happens in the brain
- New methods for manipulating the brain and nervous system

- New understandings of how to leverage artificial intelligence and virtual reality
- New discoveries in what memories are, how they are formed, and where they are stored

New Technologies and Big Data

Advances in medical technology now allow researchers to see inside brains and bodies in ways that were previously impossible. As of today, several distinct technologies are used for viewing brain activity. Computed tomography (CT/CAT) scans work like an x-ray and allow researchers to see gross features in the brain. Magnetic resonance imaging (MRI or fMRI) machines help scientists explore blood flow in the brain to identify activation in brain structures and regions when we engage in a variety of activities. Positron-emission tomography (PET) scans create detailed color and even 3-D images of internal tissues. All of these machines are quite large and require a person to lay within a tube-like device, so they are not conducive to certain activities like group interactions or even moving around.

Other new tools are smaller and transportable, allowing scientists to study people doing normal activities in their natural settings. These include the electroencephalography (EEG), which is a method for seeing the electrical activity within the brain, often displayed in the form of brain waves. In addition, magnetoencephalography (MEG) combines MRI and EEG technology into one device and merges the data into a more complete picture. Near-infrared spectroscopy (NIRS) allows researchers to see blood oxygenation levels as well as glucose burn, and transcranial magnetic stimulation (TMS) gives researchers the ability to stimulate regions of the brain by applying a non-invasive electrical current. Together, these tools give scientists the ability to look at the brain from various levels of analysis from general regions to specific structures to even individual neurons.

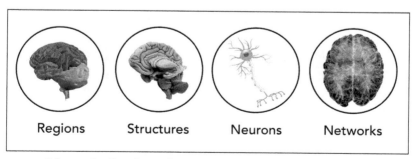

| Regions | Structures | Neurons | Networks |

New tools allow for studying the brain at many levels of analysis

In addition to these new technologies, scientists are leveraging big data to not only see across large groups of people but also to dig into the individual differences among them. One of the major shifts of the past five years is scientists combining live data from these various techniques to gain a more holistic view of the brain. This has brought forth a new understanding of the brain as a complex and highly networked organ. Scientists at the University of California in San Francisco have recorded some of this data in a video called *The Glass Brain* (find it on YouTube and Vimeo). This incredible footage shows just how active our brains are as the video pans from an external view to traveling inside the brain.

Cue image from my childhood favorite movie, *Fantastic Voyage,* when a blood clot threatens the brain of an important scientist, and a miniaturized medical team travels inside his body to repair his brain. As they zoom through his bloodstream, they see the inner workings of the scientist's body in larger-than-life Technicolor clarity. While that was truly the stuff of science fiction back in the 1960s, researchers now routinely use nanobots to travel through many of our systems, and neuroimaging is continually revealing new and exciting information about these bodies we inhabit.

But all this fabulous technology is not without its faults. Beware the dead salmon. Dr. Craig Bennett, a neuroscientist at Dartmouth University, was preparing an fMRI experiment involving people thinking about pictures they were shown. His team ran a rehearsal of the process and decided to use as a stand-in for a human subject a whole salmon one of them had just purchased at the market. They ran through their instructions and activated the fMRI machine with the salmon inside. To their surprise, the results showed activity in the dead salmon's brain, something that was not possible. It turns out that these machines can sometimes throw off false positive results and highlighted a need for researchers to not only employ statistical calibration to counter balance the effect, but also to rerun data on hundreds of previous studies to ensure accuracy. This 2009 incident created a buzz among scientists, because at the time, 25 to 40 percent were not using the corrected comparisons. Dr. Bennett went on to win the Ig Nobel Prize in Neuroscience, and was featured in a *Scientific American* article where the author states, "by the time this group won the Ig Nobel last week, that number has dropped to 10 percent. And who knows, it might, in part, be due to a dead fish."

2. Neural Proof of Multiple Intelligences

Rather significantly, there is now strong neural evidence for the theory of multiple intelligences, which was first proposed in the 1980s by Dr. Howard Gardner, a professor at the Harvard Graduate School of Education. He argued that people can be intelligent in a range of ways, not just the two measured by IQ tests and most school assessments: linguistic and logical-mathematical. Gardner describes the eight intelligences as follows.

1. **Linguistic:** The ability to learn languages, analyze information, or create products involving oral and written language. Writers, poets, lawyers, and speakers often have high linguistic intelligence.

2. **Logical-mathematical:** The ability to develop equations and proofs, make calculations, and solve abstract problems, as well as detect patterns, reason deductively, and think logically. This intelligence is most often associated with scientific and mathematical thinking.

3. **Musical:** The ability to produce, remember, and make meaning of different patterns of sound and the capacity to recognize and compose musical pitches, tones, and rhythms. People with this intelligence often have skills in performance and composition.

4. **Bodily-kinesthetic:** The ability to use one's own body to create products or solve problems, and to use mental abilities to coordinate bodily movements. Athletes and dancers exhibit this intelligence.

5. **Spatial:** The ability to recognize and manipulate large-scale and fine-grained spatial images. This can be with open space, like that used by navigators and pilots, as well as the patterns of more confined areas such as those used by sculptors, surgeons, chess players, artists, or architects.

6. **Intrapersonal:** The ability to recognize and understand one's own moods, desires, motivations, and intentions. In Howard Gardner's view it involves having an effective working model of ourselves, and to be able to use such information to regulate our lives.

7. **Interpersonal:** The ability to recognize and understand other people's moods, desires, motivations, and intentions. It allows people to

work effectively with others. Educators, salespeople, religious and political leaders, and counselors all need a well-developed interpersonal intelligence.

8. **Naturalist:** The ability to identify and distinguish among different types of plants, animals, and weather formations that are found in the natural world.

In 1999, Gardner put forth a candidate for a ninth intelligence: **Existential/spiritual**, which is the capacity to tackle deep questions about human existence, such as the meaning of life and death. However, this addition has not been formally included in the theory.

Do the different intelligences show up differently in the brain? The answer is yes. While the theory of multiple intelligences gained traction before the explosion in neuroscience research, recent studies have demonstrated its neurological legitimacy. In 2017, two researchers (Shearera and Karanian) published a study titled "The Neuroscience of Intelligence: Empirical Support for the Theory of Multiple Intelligences?" They reviewed the research, mapping the brain regions to each of the eight intelligences along three levels of neural analysis: primary brain regions, subregions, and particular brain structures within the subregions. (See Table 1.)

The results were quite astounding, showing a clear alignment for each intelligence. The authors concluded, "Based on the detailed analysis of over 318 neuroscience studies, it appears there is robust evidence that each of the eight intelligences possesses its own unique neural architecture." Future studies will likely illuminate more.

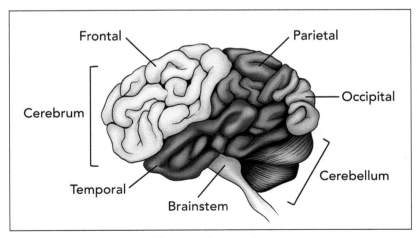

The major brain regions

Table 1. *Top neural structures affiliated with the multiple intelligences*

	Rank Order of Primary Neural Structures and Subregions
Linguistic	• Temporal Cortex: Superior Temporal Gyrus • Frontal Cortex: Broca's Area, Motor Cortex • Parietal: Inferior Parietal Lobule, Supramarginal Gyrus, Angular Gyrus
Logical-Math	• Frontal Cortex: Prefrontal Cortex, Inferior Frontal Gyrus • Parietal: Intraparietal Sulcus, Inferior Parietal Lobule, Angular Gyrus • Temporal Cortex: Medial Temporal Lobe
Musical	• Frontal: Motor Cortex • Temporal Cortex: Superior Temporal Sulcus, Primary Auditory Cortex • Subcortical: Basal Ganglia
Bodily-Kinesthetic	• Frontal Cortex: Motor Cortex, Primary Motor, Premotor, Supplementary Motor • Parietal Cortex: Posterior Parietal Cortex • Subcortical: Basal Ganglia, Thalamus • Cerebellum
Spatial	• Frontal Cortex: Motor Cortex • Parietal Cortex: Intraparietal Sulcus, Superior Parietal Lobe • Temporal Cortex: Medial Temporal Lobe • Occipital Cortex
Intra-personal	• Frontal Cortex: Prefrontal Cortex • Cingulate Cortex: Anterior Cingulate Cortex • Temporal Cortex: Medial Temporal Lobe, Amygdala, Superior Temporal Sulcus • Parietal Cortex: Medial Parietal Cortex, Inferior Parietal Cortex • Subcortical: Basal Ganglia, Brainstem
Inter-personal	• Frontal Cortex: Prefrontal Cortex • Temporal Cortex: Medial Temporal Lobe, Amygdala, Superior Temporal Sulcus • Cingulate Cortex: Anterior Cingulate Cortex • Parietal Cortex
Naturalist	• Temporal Cortex: Superior Temporal Sulcus, Amygdala • Subcortical: Brainstem, Thalamus, Basal Ganglia • Frontal Cortex • Occipital Cortex • Parietal Cortex

From Shearer, C.B. & Karanian, J.M. (2017). The neuroscience of intelligence: Empirical support for the theory of multiple intelligences? *Trends in Neuroscience and Education, 6,* 211-223.

Many teachers and schools embraced Gardner's work and actively sought ways to honor the diversity of children's intelligence, so often overlooked or undervalued. This has been especially true for children who are labeled or diagnosed with a learning deficit or disability. (I encourage educators to read *Multiple Intelligences in the Classroom* by Thomas Armstrong.) Despite efforts to change, standardized assessments have and still do focus primarily on linguistic and logical-mathematical intelligences, which naturally advantages some children and disadvantages others. This sets kids up to create beliefs about how smart they are and what they are capable of, and it also influences access to college and certain careers.

Here's the main thing I take away from it: none of us should define ourselves or others by what "smart" looks like in school. We all have talents to bring to the table and if we only look at who is successful in school, we miss 75 percent of the real talent and gifts. So many of us suffer from scars we got in school because none of us escaped scrutiny and judgment. I have a PhD, so people would think that I represent educational excellence, but the truth is that I was turned away from my true passion of marine biology my first year in college because I struggled in calculus and chemistry. It made me feel stupid for a long time and perhaps that partially contributed to me pursuing a PhD. This quote by Albert Einstein is so relevant, "Everybody is a genius. But if you judge a fish by its ability to climb a tree, it will live its whole life believing that it is stupid." I wonder how many geniuses, right now, are feeling like they are dumb and how much we are losing as a society without their true gifts and talents.

3. New Understanding of Creativity

This is another significant development since the first edition of this book: understanding creativity and how it happens in the brain. The old belief of the left brain being analytical and the right brain being creative has been debunked. Creativity, it turns out, is a networked activity simultaneously involving many regions of the brain and is a four-phase process:

1. **Preparation.** This is the time a person spends trying to solve an issue or come up with an idea. It includes things like researching, prototyping, and tinkering.

2. **Incubation.** This phase, also called percolation, starts when you have exhausted your options and set it aside for a bit, intentionally not working on it. Taking a break lets the preparation stew.

3. **Illumination.** This phase is the actual "aha!" moment, when the solution suddenly appears.

4. **Verification.** The final phase when you make sure that your insight actually works and solves the problem.

Dr. Scott Kaufman, a researcher at Columbia University and coauthor of *Wired to Create: Unraveling the Mysteries of the Creative Mind*, identified three networks involved with creative cognition. The first is the executive attention network, which gets involved when you're concentrating on something and trying to figure it out through focused attention. This network includes the prefrontal cortex along with posterior parietal lobe. The second is the imagination network or default mode network (DMN), which activates when we engage in considering alternative perspectives or outcomes, like musing about the present and daydreaming about the future. This involves deeper regions of the prefrontal cortex as well as the medial temporal lobe and post cingulate. Finally, there is the salience network, which Kaufman states, "constantly monitors both external events and the internal stream of consciousness and flexibly passes the baton to either the executive attention or imagination network depending on whatever information is most salient to solving the task at hand." The salience network involves the anterior insula and the anterior cingulate cortices.

Doctors John Kounios and Mark Beeman, neuroscientists at Drexel University, have captured images of the "aha!" moment in action. Neural imaging shows that one-third of a second before the "aha!" moment, there is a burst of gamma waves above the right ear in the anterior temporal gyrus, as well as a rush of blood into that part of the brain. Gamma waves are the highest brain waves, oscillating at 38 to 42Hz and are affiliated with insight, peak focus, and expanded consciousness. Even more surprising, the MRI showed a burst of alpha waves in the right occipital cortex one full second before that. Alpha waves oscillate at 8 to 12Hz and are associated with relaxation, visualization, and creativity. Essentially, the brain is suppressing vision right before the "aha!" moment occurs. Scientists call this a "brain blink."

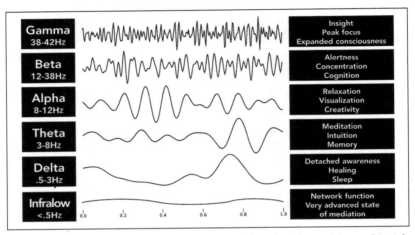

Properties of gamma and alpha brain waves affiliated with creativity and insight

Kounios and Beeman, authors of *The Eureka Factor: Aha Moments, Creative Insight, and the Brain*, think this is why we get so many good ideas in the shower—there is not a lot of visual stimulation and you have the white noise of the water, which essentially replicates this brain blink and sets us up for insight. They have gone on to research different forms of creativity, finding that some people get to their "aha!" moments somewhat intuitively while others get there through an analytical process. They found a person's resting brainwaves predict which she or he uses more, indicating this is actually a neurological trait, not a choice.

Collectively, this research is giving us a playbook for enabling creativity in ourselves and in others. Studies suggest that if you want to boost creativity, remember Kaufman's process:

- **Preparation:** Prepare your brain by exposing yourself to information outside of your primary sources. When you want to have an idea about something, seek out the new and different, and even the uncomfortable as you explore or study your area of interest. Think of it as reading lots of books in the library and from different subject areas—this sets your brain up to connect the dots and have those "aha!"moments.

- **Incubation:** Next, give your brain a break. Let your mind wander and do a little daydreaming. Some find it helpful to take that shower or be near water in nature, like a stream, lake, or ocean. This is called the resting neocortex and is part of how you induce insight.
- **Illumination:** Revisit the problem while you engage in what scientists call sensory gating. You intentionally shut down some of the five senses so you can toggle your focus between the topic and awareness of your environment. Close your eyes, or meditate for a bit and see what comes to you.
- **Verification:** Finally, check that your insight works.

As I read that, I realized this is exactly the process I follow when I write a book (this one included) or build a presentation or training. I first expose myself to research across a wide range of disciplines and different sources. After I've exhausted all the sources I can think of, I let it all stew around in my head. This is when I take lots of walks on the beach, swim at my gym, and just try to trust the process because, inevitably, something starts to take shape. Because of the nature of this research, I am increasingly intentional with the process. Before, I would take breaks when I felt stuck but felt guilty about slacking off when I had work to do. But now, when I'm stuck, I happily take a break knowing that insight will eventually follow.

Few of us reach adulthood with our innate sense of creativity intact. In his book *Orbiting the Giant Hairball,* Gordon MacKenzie, a cartoonist at Hallmark, describes visiting schools and asking children, "How many artists are there in the room? Would you please raise your hands?" He saw this consistent pattern, "First grade: en mass the children leapt from their chairs, arms waving wildly, eager hands trying to reach the ceiling. Every child was an artist. Second grade: about half the kids raised their hands, shoulder high, no higher. The raised hands were still. Third grade: at best, 10 kids out of 30 would raise a hand. Tentatively. Self-consciously. And so on up through the grades. The higher the grade, the fewer children raised their hands. By the time I reached sixth grade, no more than one or two did so and then only ever-so-slightly–*guardedly*–their eyes glancing from side to side uneasily, betraying a fear of being identified by the group as a 'closet artist'."

In her research on shame and vulnerability, Dr. Brené Brown has seen the impact this has on adults, "I found that 85 percent of the men and women who I interviewed remembered an event in school that was so shaming, it changed how they thought of themselves for the rest of their lives. But wait–this is good–fifty percent of that 85 percent, half of those people: those shame wounds were *around creativity*. It was shut down in them as children.

For those folks, when I say *'unused creativity is not benign,'* what I really mean is it metastasizes into resentment, grief, heartbreak."

Creativity matters, especially in today's organizations where "thinking outside the box" and innovation often distinguish the top performers from the rest. Training in creative thinking can make a big difference. One study by Dr. Trisha Stratford and Corinne Canter found that 80 percent of participants in a creative thinking training improved their creative thinking and nearly two-thirds (63 percent) generated more viable solutions to problems. All participants showed an increase in gamma waves in their brain scans.

Finally, I want to introduce you to a view of creativity that's a bit unusual, so please hang in there with me.

I'm a bit of a foodie, so I have read all of Dr. Michael Pollan's bestselling books on the subject, including *Food Rules, In Defense of Food, The Omnivore's Dilemma*, and *Cooked*. This is my pleasure reading, so when his new book came out last year, I immediately got a copy without even really looking at the subject, expecting another wonderful foodie journey. While the book does feature mushrooms, it was certainly not at all what I expected. Titled, *How to Change Your Mind: What the New Science of Psychedelics Teaches Us about Consciousness, Dying, Addiction, Depression, and Transcendence*, Pollan takes the reader into a deep exploration of the medical and neuroscience research on psychedelics (namely mushrooms and LSD) and it blew my mind.

Pollan delves deep into all the numerous studies on the therapeutic benefits of psychedelics, as well as exploring the natural and political history, and botanical properties of these substances. He includes a deeply researched section on the neuroscience of psychedelics, which are nontoxic and nonaddictive. Because so many people who use them describe similar experiences, neuroscientists wanted to see what is happening in the brain. Enter the default-mode network (DMN). First discovered in 2001 by Dr. Robin Carhart-Harris, DMN is seen as the seat of our ego or sense of self. It's involved in a host of activities like metacognition and self-reflection, and it lights up when our mind wanders.

Most importantly, the DMN serves as an orchestra conductor, filtering and controlling thousands of neural activities in the brain. There are so many neurons firing at any one time, and the DMN's role is to contain that so we don't feel constantly overwhelmed. The DMN comes online during childhood, which is why babies and young children have that sense of wonder and awe. Dr. Alison Gopnik, an expert on the cognitive development of children, states, "… babies and children are basically tripping all the time."

Neuroscientists like Carhart-Harris and doctors Mendel Kaelen and David Nutt have discovered that when adults take psychedelics the DMN goes offline, allowing all kinds of data from the different parts of the brain to surface. This is responsible for the merged sensations (called synesthesia) that people describe on psychedelics, where they can taste color or see music. It also allows for a flood of creativity as diverse parts of the brain connect and talk with each other in ways that don't happen without the substance. According to research by Pollan, many Silicon Valley engineers participated in the acid trip culture of the 1960s and credit the invention of the microchip to the new insights they had while taking psychedelics. Even today, several Bay Area companies have "microdosing Fridays" to support and expand innovation. Pollan himself tried psychedelics as part of his research process and says, "A psychedelic experience has the power to shake the snow globe, disrupting unhealthy patterns of thought and creating a space of flexibility."

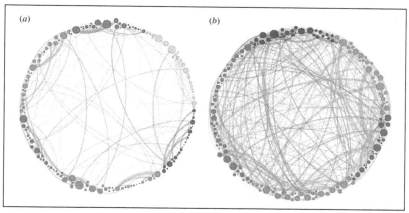

Usual lines of communication in the brain (a) expand when DMN goes offline (b)

The DMN going offline is also what creates that sense of "oneness" or spiritual experience that is part of the overwhelming majority of psychedelic trips, where people see the connectedness of all living things. And it's this aspect that creates the astounding therapeutic results for people with addiction and depression as well as those with terminal diagnoses like late-stage cancer. Numerous and convincing studies demonstrate the benefits of psychedelics, which is why as of this writing two states in the US, Oregon and Colorado, have ballot initiatives legalizing the use of psychedelics for therapeutic use.

As we consider the ways of promoting or enhancing creativity and innovation, it appears we can add psychedelics to the box of possible tools. It's certainly not for everyone, and I'm not promoting this practice, but I do encourage you to read Pollan's book and consider the evidence and its implications.

4. New Methods for Manipulating the Brain and Nervous System

Perhaps the most amazing new development is how much medical doctors and brain researchers can now manipulate the brain and nervous system to produce astounding levels of healing.

I'll focus on medical developments first, as they may offer some hope to you or people you know and love. All these treatments are leveraging what neuroscientists call neuroplasticity and neurogenesis. Neuroplasticity is the nervous system's ability to change over our lifetime and neurogenesis is the body's ability to birth and grow new neurons. Dr. Norman Doidge has written two books on neuroplasticity: *The Brain That Changes Itself* and also *The Brain's Way of Healing*. In each, he details amazing case studies of how the brain has healed itself, even overcoming severe injuries and damage. Dr. Jill Bolte Taylor, a neuroanatomist at Harvard, used these principles to recover from a massive stroke, which she details in her book (and TED Talk) *My Stroke of Insight: A Brain Scientist's Personal Journey*.

First, doctors and scientists are now using virtual reality to regrow neurons and help people regain movement after injuries. Virtual reality headsets allow patients to look down and "see" their legs walking or arms moving. This mimics how we originally learned to move our bodies and how the brain first wired those neurons of movement. This same process helps patients with prosthetic limbs learn how to move those limbs and regain mobility more quickly. Researchers have even seen neural growth in paraplegics by having them watch their legs moving in a virtual reality (VR) headset for an hour twice a week. Several patients have been able to feel their limbs after consistent treatment.

Second, doctors use robots to facilitate healing in patients with strokes, Parkinson's disease, and spinal cord injuries. Neural growth and muscle rehabilitation is all about repetition; it often takes hundreds to get results. This can be extremely difficult for patients who fatigue easily or can't control their movements enough to achieve consistent repetitions. Many hospitals and rehabilitation centers now offer robotic training where a patient is strapped to a machine that facilitates numerous repetitions of the correct forms, resulting in significant mobility gains, even when the original injury or illness occurred many years ago.

Third, doctors have discovered ways to change core aspects of the brain through neurostimulation. Neurostimulation, the purposeful modulation of the nervous system using invasive and noninvasive methods, shows promise for treating intractable pain, Parkinson's disease, multiple sclerosis, seizures, and other common disorders. Noninvasive methods include transcranial magnetic stimulation (TMS) or transcranial electric stimulation (tES/tDCS/tACS), which has been shown to have outcomes as good or better than prescription drugs, without the side effects. Invasive methods include techniques such as deep brain stimulation (DBS), involving microelectrodes implanted in specific regions of the brain itself.

Fourth, we have reached the point where we can control robots with our minds. Doctors John K. Chapin and Miguel A. L. Nicolelis have successfully created brain–machine interfaces (BMIs), or neuroprostheses, that can be moved by the brain patterns or thoughts of rats, monkeys, and humans. This work is already helping people regain mobility by controlling a robotic limb; eventually the technology will be able to reanimate biological limbs.

Finally, and perhaps most astounding of all, neuroscientists have helped paralyzed people stand up and walk again. One group of scientists at the Neurorehabilitation Laboratory in São Paulo, Brazil, worked with eight patients who had been paralyzed for 3 to 13 years. Using a year-long protocol of virtual reality training and walking with brain wave (EEG) controlled robotic exoskeletons, the patients exhibited new neural growth that created significant improvement in both sensation and movement. Half of the patients were rediagnosed with partial rather than complete paraplegia.

Photo: © 2019 EPFL / Jamani Caillet

New forms of neurorecovery leverages neuroplasticity and neurogenesis

Doctors Grégoire Courtine and Jocelyne Bloch have gone even further, enabling paralyzed patients to actually stand up and walk on their own. They implanted an electrode that produced electrical stimulation to the spinal cord below the point of the injury and instead of using continuous stimulation, like many previous researchers had done, they instead mimicked the fluctuating stimulation that occurs with normal walking. Patients were able to regain control over their muscles to the point of standing and walking without assistance or electrical stimulation. The YouTube video (https://www.youtube.com/watch?v=XFXWR4b9iVA) moved me to tears. I highly recommend it!

These studies all demonstrate the power of neuroplasticity and neurogenesis, and how much we still have to learn about the body and its ability to heal with the right support. It made me realize that we are wired to learn—and relearn—throughout our lifetimes. Our biology is incredibly powerful. If we can help a paralyzed person walk again, there really is no limit to human potential.

5. New Ways to Leverage Artificial Intelligence and Virtual Reality

As the previous chapter demonstrates, virtual reality plays a major role in neurorecovery—but that's not the only development along these lines.

It turns out that virtual reality (VR) is powerful because it replicates the first-person point of view (POV) in our own bodies, which allows for deep immersion in an experience. It's not perfect, but it's realistic enough to elicit biological responses in the body. I experienced this firsthand when my family got a VR headset over the holidays. I watched the video of climbing El Capitan in Yosemite National Park and felt the adrenalin rush as if I was really standing on a ledge looking down thousands of feet to the ground below. I startled when I looked over my shoulder to find a lion sniffing me while watching the African Safari. And I felt real motion sickness riding a virtual roller coaster, to the point that I had to take off the set before I lost my lunch. While my rational brain knew these were filmed images, because I could turn my head and see in all directions, my brain and body responded as if I was really there.

I wasn't imagining things. Studies are showing that VR experiences code in the body like a lived experience. In other words, we can use VR to create realistic embodied memories. In a 2019 study, several researchers at the Laboratory of Cognitive Neuroscience in Geneva, Switzerland, discovered that VR experiences in which people see some aspect of "their" body, like an arm or leg, have better and longer recall of those events, statistically similar to a lived experience.

VR codes in the brain as a personal memory

Studies indicate that VR codes in the brain as a lived experience, creating memories

Originally, the researchers were interested in whether VR could be used as a reliable tool in scholarly memory studies; they concluded that, in fact, VR can be a stand-in for a real experience.

In a study at Stanford University's Virtual Human Interaction Lab, similar findings show that children know the difference between their own lived memories and stories told to them about an experience they could have. In this case, researchers described how a child swam with two friendly orcas. Later, the children clearly stated that it did not happen in real life. However, children are less certain when they put on a VR headset and virtually swim with the orcas. Later, when asked if they have ever done that, some "remembered" the experience as if it really happened.

We can surmise that VR creates experiences that the human body perceives as real and stores as a memory. (As a parent, I need to comment here that we should all be careful of allowing children to play violent games on VR sets. Until the research is more clear, I am concerned that there seems to be a real possibility of children having "memories" of harming people.) The upside is that VR is being used to drive all kinds of new advances in professional learning. Companies are training employees in virtual settings, giving them real memories of places and skills.

For example, one oil company has filmed their deep-sea ocean rigs so that employees can become familiar with these dangerous work environments before arriving. A cruise liner is training servers in a virtual dining room since the windows of time to do so in person is limited. As a result, the wait staff are able to deliver exceptional service from the first encounter with customers. Similarly, a plane manufacturer is using VR to give new employees the experience of riveting the fuselage, incorporating footage of a top-performing employee. When the trainees look down, they see "their" hands doing the correct actions. Obviously, VR cannot replace doing real work in real time, but it can jumpstart an employee's skills.

Virtual reality has also been shown to make people more empathetic and compassionate. Dr. Jeremy Bailenson has done a series of studies on this topic. In one, some participants were taken through a VR experience, called *Becoming Homeless* (a control group did not). Later, the group who did the VR were more empathetic toward the homeless and more likely to sign a petition supporting affordable housing than the other participants.

In other studies, Bailenson took people through a virtual experience of racial discrimination and they became less biased to people of color; likewise, people who virtually experienced aging became less ageist. Another series of four studies of different age groups shows that VR can even make people more curious and committed about issues like climate change.

For clarity, VR is one of many tools that exists on the virtual continuum, also known as extended reality or XR. On one end, you have the real environment, the tangible world that we see, touch, and engage with in real time. At the other end is the virtual environment, a three-dimensional computer-generated place, which can either mimic or replicate something real or be a fantastical creation. A person can interact with this virtual world in real time but, while wearing the headset, they are not aware of or able to interact with their real environment. Next, there is augmented reality or AR. According to a 2018 report titled *Technologies with Potential to Transform Business and Business Education*, "AR enhances real-world experiences by adding virtual, computer-generated components, such as digital images, data, or sensations as a complementary new layer to create enhanced interactions." A person using AR, for example Google Glass, would be aware of the real world and able to interact with both real and virtual elements in real time. Finally, there is mixed reality or MR that combines elements of AR with VR. The person can see the real world but can simultaneously see virtual objects that are anchored to the real environment so can be interacted with. Both the Microsoft product HoloLens and the world lenses on Snapchat are examples of MR technology.

In addition to VR, scientists are leveraging artificial intelligence (AI) to boost learning. When practicing social skills, we must often engage with other people. But doing so in real life may be difficult or even harm a relationship. AI can drive algorithms that hear what we say and offer up realistic responses or engagement in the form of computer-generated avatars. For example, one company has created a realistic training experience for restaurant servers in responding to various customers' needs and attitudes. AI relies on machine learning (where computers learn independently of specific programming) and deep learning (where computers make inferences based on data they have encountered before). I have witnessed these in action, and they can be surprisingly accurate and effective.

Interestingly, researchers who work with AI and robots are taking a page from child development theory and programming machines to learn like children. According to Diana Kwon, in a *Scientific American* article titled "Intelligent machines that learn like children," "Since the beginning of the twenty-first century, roboticists, neuroscientists, and psychologists have been exploring ways to build machines that mimic such spontaneous development. Their collaborations have resulted in androids that can move objects, acquire basic vocabulary, and even show signs of social behavior." AI and VR are already being applied in numerous ways and we're only just beginning to explore how they can enhance education and learning.

6. New Discoveries about Memory

One of the biggest shifts in what we now know about learning is coming from the latest research on memory. Our understanding of memory has greatly expanded in the last decade, as technology has allowed for deeper analysis of the brain and more realistic studies.

Older studies relied on human subjects in labs doing tasks like memorizing long strings of numbers or nonsensical words. Today, scientists are studying the brain while people are doing daily activities in real time. We can now see what happens in students' brains while they're sitting in their classrooms learning concepts and taking exams, or what happens when working professionals engage in daily work and problem-solving with their colleagues. Scientists are even able to see where specific memories are stored in individual neurons. As UCLA neuroscientist Dr. Alcino Silva states, "Memory research has undergone a revolution: new technologies image the activity of individual neurons and even turn the cells on and off at precise moments, allowing brain scientists to perform experiments that were thought of as science fiction just a few years ago."

We now can distinguish between several different kinds of memory and where they are processed and stored in the brain, something that has changed our definition of memory and what it means to remember and forget. Since we'll be diving into more details on memory in section II, I'll just give you a quick overview here. Memory falls into two broad categories, short-term and long-term, with subsets within each:

Short-term memory comprises sensory memory and working memory. Sensory memory is short-lived and includes what you notice with your senses, like an image you see, an odor you smell, or a touch like the warmth of your coffee mug. Even if you are not aware of it, your sensory memory processes thousands of sensations per day but the brain is designed to only process what might be useful in the future. Sensory memory degrades very quickly (200 to 500 milliseconds) and is essentially there to give the brain time to perceive that information or let it pass by. Right now, your senses are taking in all kinds of data, but it will all disappear unless something makes it notable and moves it into working memory.

Working memory (WM) begins when you focus on something. This might happen because you're trying to learn (for example, reading this book or taking a course) or because something or someone draws your attention.

Try this right now: Just tune in to the sounds in the room around you. What do you hear? A hum from a machine or appliance? Outside sounds, like traffic or birds? What about your heartbeat or breathing? Can you get quiet enough to hear them? Tuning into the sounds in the room activated your working memory, but WM begins to decay after 15 to 30 seconds; it's meant to hold temporary information, to be forgotten or moved into long-term memory.

Short-term memory is the first stop to long-term memory. Long-term memories are made up of sensory memories that are moved into our working memory. Let's look at how some of these become a long-term memory.

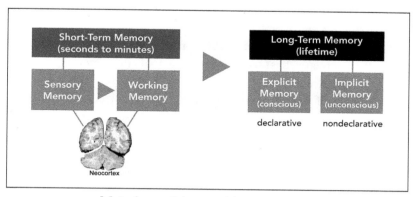

Main forms of short- and long-term memory

Long-term memories are stored in the brain in a way that is retrievable over time. While short-term memory has a shelf-life of minutes, long-term memory can literally last for a lifetime. According to neuropsychologist Dr. Richard Mohs, studies show that long-term memory decays very little and that the brain is capable of storing an unlimited amount of information. (Because long-term memories involve the firing of neurons in much wider regions of the brain than short-term memories.)

In fact, recent studies have shown that different types of long-term memory fire in specific structures and even individual neurons. Within long-term memory, we have declarative (explicit) memory and nondeclarative (implicit) memory. According to Dr. Boris Suchan, a professor of neuropsychology at Ruhr University in Germany, declarative or explicit memory is knowledge you are aware or conscious of having and can share with others. In contrast, nondeclarative or implicit memory is not conscious and includes things like classical conditioning and habituation. For example, if you take a training on time management, you'd have an explicit memory of the experience. But you likely have several unconscious habits about how you use time, like how you calendar meetings or when you take breaks. These are implicit memories. We'll explore memory in more detail in the next section.

Your Learning Journey

At the end of each section, take the opportunity to apply the concepts to your own life and the thing you want to learn. Use these questions to help you identify possible strategies to support your learning goal.

- What would you like to learn in the coming months? By engaging in this learning, what are you hoping to gain or shift in your self, work, or life overall?
- Consider the six new developments described in this section. Which relates best to your learning goal and how might you leverage them?
- Which of the eight intelligences are your strengths? How might you more intentionally use your intelligences for your learning goal?
- How might you use the new understanding of creativity to boost your own opportunities for insight?
- What is an enduring belief about yourself that perhaps holds you back a little? Given the power of neuroplasticity and neurogenesis, how might you develop new neural pathways to shift your current belief into a new state?
- How might you try using VR/AR/XR technology to support you with the thing you want to learn? Do a little research to see what options exist.

REMEMBER:
THE MEMORY MATRIX

"Has it ever struck you...that life is all memory except for the one present moment that goes by you so quickly you hardly catch it going? It's really all memory."

Tennessee Williams, playwright,
Cat on a Hot Tin Roof

7. Nine Types of Memory

As you recall, the three phases of the learning model are Learn, Remember, and Do. We're going to wait on Learn and start with the middle phase, Remember, because the type of memory you want to create dictates how you set up the learning. This phase is all about types of memory, retrievals, schemas, and connections.

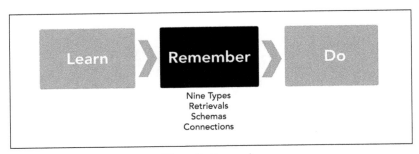

Phase 2: Remember

All learning becomes a memory, so in order to best understand learning we start with an in-depth exploration of the nature of memories and how they form. Recent studies have identified nine types of memory and each involves different areas of the brain. According to Helen Shen, author of *How to See a Memory*, the brain leaves a physical trace of a specific memory, called an engram. She states, "Only in the past decade have new techniques for labeling, activating, and silencing specific neurons in animals allowed researchers to pinpoint which neurons make up a single memory." We also have new understandings of forgetting and the vital role it plays in learning.

A memory begins as an experience that we encode into our brain through our senses. That memory is then stored in the brain until we engage in some act of recall or recollection and then it comes back into our conscious awareness.

As we learned in the last chapter, everything begins with short-term memory, and specifically sensory memory, which is all the data your sensory nerves process every minute of your life. Sensory memory is fleeting, only lasting milliseconds unless something occurs that causes us to notice or focus on our senses, and then it's moved to working memory where we can attend to it. Working memory is a bit like a bulletin board—it's a place to pin something for a moment so you can take a look and decide whether it's something to worry about, before discarding or filing it into long-term memory.

Recent developments in what scientists know about working memory have upended old beliefs, like human short-term memory being limited to "seven, plus or minus two" things. First identified by Dr. George Miller at Harvard University, this was thought to represent the human capacity for accurately processing information in short-term memory. Known as Miller's Law, this view held for decades and was long believed to occur in the prefrontal cortex region of the brain. But several recent studies have shown that our working memory has much more size and flexibility than originally thought and is now seen as more of a resource model that responds to demands, rather than having a rigid capacity.

In fact, Doctors Derek Nee and Mark D'Esposito argue that the brain uses both the prefrontal cortex as well as the posterior sensory cortices depending on the task, with more conceptual or abstract processing relying on the prefrontal cortex. And a study by Dr. David Giofrèa and his colleagues demonstrates that working memory differs depending on whether subjects are engaged in mathematical (visuospatial working memory) or reading tasks (verbal working memory). It's clear that working memory is not as static as once believed.

We all have experiences with a flexing working memory. Our brains can often feel "full" when we are juggling several different tasks or have just learned some complex material. We might not have much ability to take on new information since our brain is already processing several things—the bulletin board is jammed and has no room to add one more note. But if we are doing something that we're very familiar or comfortable with, there can be room to take on more because you stacked some of your notes together, creating more space.

Our bulletin board can also flex with the time of day. Daniel Pink, in his recent book *When: The Scientific Secrets of Perfect Timing*, found that most of us have a natural cycle, periods when we feel sharpest, because our cognitive abilities fluctuate over the course of the day. Studies show that nearly 75 percent of people experience the day in these three phases:

- **A peak in the morning** when we feel most focused. This is the best time to tackle analytical work and often our most productive time of the day.
- **A "trough" after lunch,** when we can feel sluggish and find it difficult to concentrate. This is the time we are likely to make the most mistakes.
- **A rebound in the late afternoon or early evening**. This is the best time to innovate or do insight-based work where our lowered inhibition and resolve set us up for "aha!" moments.

Pink also found that about one quarter of people experience this in reverse order, coming into their highest performance time in the evening. These folks—the quintessential "night owls"—do their best work after most workplaces shut down. (I'm married to a night owl and he's just hitting his stride when I'm fading.) Oxford University neuroscientist Dr. Russell Foster states, "The performance change between the daily high point and the daily low point is equivalent to the effect on performance as drinking the legal limit of alcohol." Wow.

While working memory is not an easily quantifiable thing, Miller's (seven-plus-or-minus-two) Law is still useful to us because organizing lots of information into smaller segments or chunks can make it easier to remember information. This is why phone numbers come in short blocks (a three-three-four configuration in the United States, for example) and why good learning is broken down into smaller lessons. It's also why I believe in short chapters in my books and keeping my training videos to five minutes or less.

The Senses and Survival

I want to emphasize that a memory is actually just a bundle of sensations forever tied together. Almost like strings, the brain encodes what we see with our eyes, hear with our ears, etc., as part of the memory. Pull any one of the strings with a similar sight, sound, etc., and the memory comes rushing back to our conscious awareness.

The more senses involved, the more data we have and the more strings that can be pulled to retrieve it. This is why it's important to include many senses when learning—they enhance memory creation. The quality of that original sensory data impacts the quality of the memory. If you attended a lecture that relied heavily on visual supports and couldn't see the presentation, then the quality of your memory would be compromised, as it would if you could see the presentation but couldn't hear the speaker.

If you think about your sensory receptors, you have two for visual data (eyes), two for auditory data (ears), and while you have one nose, it contains 350 olfactory nerves that connect directly to the amygdala in the brain. Smell is ten times more sensitive than taste, which is why it can evoke such visceral memories. Some are positive and evoke strong emotions of love and comfort, like the smells of holiday baking or the fragrance worn by a romantic partner. But they can evoke negative memories too. When my friend was a child in 1956, she lost her father to a flood, and to this day the smell of rain makes her feel anxious. It was especially triggering for her when our Santa Barbara community was devastated by mudslides that killed 23 people.

Taste can elicit memories because we have 2,000 to 4,000 gustatory senses—taste buds—on our tongue that renew themselves every week. About a quarter of people are "super tasters" who have a heightened sense of taste. We also have thousands of nerves in our gut brain, making that "gut feeling" a real thing that can also elicit past memories. Finally, we have our skin, with 300 million skin cells (19 million per square inch) that register pressure, temperature, texture, pain, etc. The human adult has 21 square feet of skin, making it our largest sensory organ.

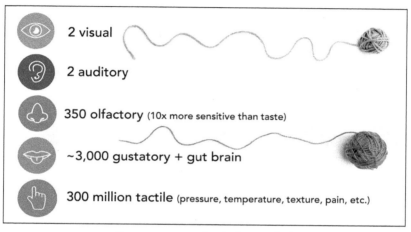

2 visual

2 auditory

350 olfactory (10x more sensitive than taste)

~3,000 gustatory + gut brain

300 million tactile (pressure, temperature, texture, pain, etc.)

Sensory receptors in the human body

What we process with our senses can also create a layer of emotion because the sensory nerves in our head attach directly to the amygdala. The amygdala is most known for its role in our survival because it's the source of the fight-flight-freeze response. While emotional intensity may range from weak to strong and from negative to positive, experiences with strong emotions, such as fear or joy, create long-lasting memories. The body's default setting interprets strong emotions as something worthy of remembering. As a result, emotion becomes its own kind of string that can retrieve memories, so feeling joy can recall other times of joy, and fear or grief can elicit other memories of fear or grief.

8. The Expansion of Long-Term Memory

Over the past few years, scientists' understanding of long-term memory has shifted. As we learned in the previous section, long-term memories fall into two main types, explicit memory (also known as declarative) and implicit memory (nondeclarative). We are most familiar with explicit memory because we are conscious of these memories—we know we have them.

There are two categories of declarative memory, semantic and episodic, which occur in the medial temporal lobe, involving the hippocampus and entorhinal cortex. Semantic memory is factual: bits of knowledge you picked up without having any personal experience of it, like learning multiplication, the capitals of countries around the world, or what conjunctions are. This might include sensory data like seeing a graphic of the multiplication table or a picture of the map of France or images from Paris.

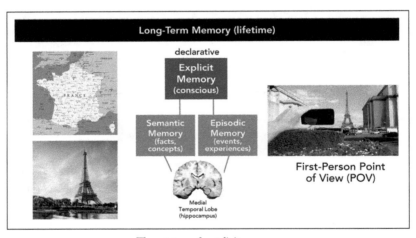

Two types of explicit memory

In contrast, episodic memory is autobiographical and filled with rich sensory data from your own personal point of view. These memories are more like video recordings, with you as the star of the show. If you have ever travelled to Paris, France, you can recall the sights, sounds, smells, and textures of your time there. I vividly remember the wonderful smells coming from a bakery near our hotel, as well as the pungent aroma from the cheese shop by the subway station. It was raining the day I went to the Louvre, so my memory of the *Mona Lisa* includes the sound of my rain jacket and the dampness of my hair.

When most of us think of memory conceptually, we think of declarative memories because we have clear knowledge of making and retrieving them. Think of this as "knowing what." But we also rely on our nondeclarative or implicit memory every day, to do things like use a tool, move our bodies, avoid a danger, or perform a skill. Think of this as "knowing how." We gain these memories through sensorimotor experiences; they can be acquired quickly (burning your hand on the stove) or through repetitions (tying your shoe or driving a car).

According to UC San Diego's Dr. Richard Clark, nondeclarative memory "is a collection of different memory abilities that depend on different and discrete brain structures. We do not have conscious access to the content of nondeclarative memory. Rather, these forms of memory are expressed through experience-based changes in performance."

There are four specific types of nondeclarative memory:
1. procedural
2. priming
3. nonassociative
4. classical conditioning

Procedural memory is how we learn to do skills or habits that eventually become automatic behaviors, like riding a bike or using a smart phone. We'll explore this further in section III, as much of adult learning and professional development involves procedural memory.

Priming is our ability to connect the dots with something we have encountered before, and it involves the neocortex. For example, several studies have shown that if you show students information or content they have not yet learned, it aids their ability to remember when they do. It's like showing someone a map of Paris before they go for a visit. While the map means nothing at the time of viewing, it becomes relevant when physically walking along the Champs-Élysées and realizing that it leads to the Arc de Triomphe. Priming can be utilized to make learning experiences more effective, and it's often used in marketing and sales campaigns as well.

Nonassociative memory uses the brain's reflex pathways and drives both habituation and sensitization. Habituation is becoming less responsive to a stimulus with exposure. For example, if you move to a new office and are bothered by the sound of the air conditioning, it's likely that habituation will kick in and you won't even notice it after a few weeks. On the other hand, sensitization is becoming more responsive to a stimulus with exposure. An example would be noticing that your manager takes credit for your work or that a coworker makes racial comments. You will likely become more annoyed over time, rather than less.

The last type of long-term memory is classical conditioning, of which there are two types: somatic and emotional. Most of us remember learning about Pavlov's dogs whereby ringing a bell before serving the dogs their food caused the dogs to begin salivating at the sound of the bell. It's an example of somatic conditioning, because salivation is a physical response and it occurs in the cerebellum, whereas emotional conditioning occurs in the amygdala. A stimulus is used to condition a specific emotion, such as fear or happiness, to a location, sound, etc. Post-traumatic stress disorder (PTSD) is an example of emotional conditioning. Classical conditioning shapes us every day, from when and how we wake up in the morning, to when and where we eat our lunch, to when and how we interact with our manager or colleagues.

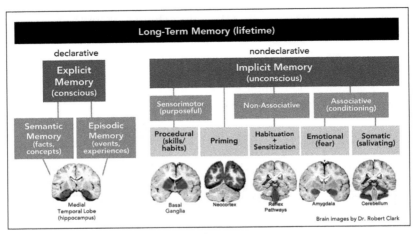

Seven types of long-term memory

While scientists have been able to neatly separate and study these different kinds of memory, our daily experience of them is much more interwoven and complex. Today, you might have woken just minutes before your alarm was set to go off (conditioning), driven to work (procedural), logged on to your computer (procedural), before heading off to a staff meeting where you recalled something relevant (priming) from a report you read last week (semantic). At lunch with a friend, you might have read a few menu items (working) before you made your selection and then shared a story from your weekend or recent vacation (episodic). In the afternoon, you might have avoided an annoying colleague (sensitization) and then listened to a podcast on your way home, not bothered by the noisy traffic around you (habituation).

We can use what scientists are learning about memory to become more successful. I find it helpful to think of memory as a range of tools our brain uses in service of our core needs to survive, belong, and become. That process is biological and automatically programmed in us from before our birth to the moment of death.

Several scientists have found that fetuses as young as 33 weeks show signs of memory in utero, habituating to external noises and vibrations, remembering them not only days but weeks later. Other studies have shown that newborns recognize their mother's voice and can tell the difference between their native language and another, showing a preference for it even when spoken by people other than the mother. But we can also intentionally use those systems to greater effect and for our own benefit.

As we age, memory can seem to fail us. We joke about having "senior moments" and forgetting things can create worries about the onset of Alzheimer's disease or other age-related mental decline. But Dr. Christiane Northrup, a medical expert on health and aging, says that we are experiencing the effect of having exponentially more data and memory networks to traverse to find what we are looking for. A 60-year old has far more memories than a 20-year old, and an 80-year old has even more, so some age-related slowness is not only normal but a sign of a life well-lived. However, declining memory can be a sign of more serious issues and should be diagnosed by a professional. A study by Dr. Robert Wilson at Rush University Medical Center, found that memory decline sped up 8 to 17 times more during the two to three years prior to death. Another study by Wilson found that elderly people who maintain their mental activity through reading, writing, and playing games, and so on, have stronger cognitive health, and that a reduction in these activities predated declines in memory function.

Fortunately, because of neuroplasticity, we are also capable of forming new memories up until the moment of death. Any hospice worker will tell you that the dying often have new insights even as their body breathes its last breath. I certainly witnessed this in my own mother and have heard similar stories from friends and colleagues. I'm heartened by the eulogy delivered by Steve Jobs's sister, Mona Simpson. She reported that his last words were, "OH WOW. OH WOW. OH WOW." His body might not have been around long enough to use that new memory but I am confident that his brain made one.

9. The Importance of Remembering and Forgetting

I'm going to focus now on declarative memory (we'll dive more into non-declarative memory in section III). While it's clear that our brains are built to make a wide range of memories, it doesn't mean we can always recall what we want, when we want.

Remembering is really about re-activating or retrieving a memory that already exists. It's there in your skull somewhere but the trick is to find the right link (or string) to bring it back.

And we have an infinite capacity to store memories. As Dr. Paul Reber of Northwestern University states, "Neurons combine so that each one helps with many memories at a time, exponentially increasing the brain's memory storage capacity to something closer to around 2.5 petabytes (or a million gigabytes). For comparison, if your brain worked like a digital video recorder in a television, 2.5 petabytes would be enough to hold three million hours of TV shows. You would have to leave the TV running continuously for more than 300 years to use up all that storage."

So if it's not an issue of storage, then how do we forget? And does forgetting indicate failed memory, something that we should try to overcome? Scientists and philosophers have been asking this question for years. In the 1880s, Dr. Hermann Ebbinghaus, used himself as the subject and created his famous "forgetting curve" charting how quickly newly learned information fades from memory.

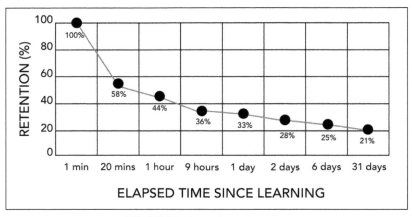

The Ebbinghaus forgetting curve

Ebbinghaus was curious about memory and wanted to see if there was a concrete formula or equation to quantify how fast people forget. You'll still find this chart today in education and learning textbooks, seminars, conferences, and product brochures. But here is what's interesting: the data represents a sample of one, Ebbinghaus himself, and his ability to retain nonsensical, single-syllable words that he created like RUR, DUS, MEK, BES, HAL, and SOK. So, really, the forgetting curve is a chart of semantic memory—but not even for real words. This design was intentional; he wanted to test pure memory and didn't want it clouded by meaningful words that might therefore activate other parts of the brain. But this chart is often taken out of context to represent how quickly all information fades from memory. But it doesn't.

UCLA professors, Doctors Robert Bjork and Elizabeth Bjork, have proposed the New Theory of Disuse. They argue that every memory has both a storage strength and a retrieval strength. Storage strength indicates how well you learned something and it increases with studying and use. For example, when you were little, you learned your alphabet and your numbers. At first you might have just been memorizing these concepts but now, you have used them throughout your life so often that their storage strength is huge. Comparatively, retrieval strength refers to how quickly or easily something you learned comes to mind. Studying and use also increase retrieval strength but if we stop using the information, it does fade over time. While most of use learned our country's leaders and the capitals of the states, we have probably largely forgotten all but the most often-used pieces. The TV game show *Are You Smarter than a 5th Grader?* is based on this principle—11-year olds often beat the grownups because the questions elicit high retrieval strength for their memories but it's nearly zero for the adults.

One of the biggest breakthroughs in understanding the reason we forget occurred in 1953, when a young man named Henry Molaison (or Patient HM) underwent brain surgery to ease intense epileptic seizures. At the time, doctors thought that removing his hippocampus would help (they also removed his amygdala and entorhinal cortex). It did, but, tragically, this is how neurosurgeons discovered that the hippocampus is where we form new declarative memories. From the moment he woke up, Molaison lived in the perpetual present, unable to recall anything after five minutes—not people, nor information, nor experiences. From that day, he had to live in an institution. He became the star subject of over 50 years of memory research until his death in 2008.

His brain was preserved and continues to be studied today. The primary researcher, Dr. Suzanne Corkin, partnered with many scientists over the years. Some key findings:
- While Molaison couldn't form new memories, he could remember things from up until two years *before* the surgery.

- Henry's working memory was intact, so he could retain information for a few minutes before it faded.
- His procedural memory still functioned so he could do things he had learned prior to the surgery (like playing the piano), and he could also learn new physical skills/habits and keep them.
- Molaison could complete crossword puzzles using his pre-1953 semantic memories but he could also update those memories with post-1953 information as long as he had an original memory to attach it to. (For example, he was able to attach Jonas Salk to the knowledge he already had about polio.)
- As he aged, he experienced faster decline of his semantic memories, forgetting words he'd once known but didn't use often.

The last finding in this list is from research by Dr. Donald MacKay, a professor at UCLA, who studies language. He shares insights from several studies he did with Henry Molaison in a *Scientific American* article titled "The Engine of Memory." Interestingly, learning language can be an example of both implicit and explicit memory. Children under age seven easily learn languages because they use procedural memory to pick up vocabulary and usage (it's essentially a skill or habit that was coded through the basal ganglia). This is why exposing young children to new languages is so powerful. Even if they don't speak a language regularly, their brain still encodes it, making it easy for them to understand and speak that language later in life. In contrast, when adults learn a new language, they use declarative/semantic memory to actively learn the rules and words of a new language.

Today, scientists are discovering that forgetting is a vital part of learning. As Benedict Carey, author of *How We Learn: The Surprising Truth about When, Where, and Why It Happens* states, "Without a little forgetting, you get no benefit from further study. It is what allows learning to build, like an exercised muscle." Forgetting is a form of filtering since we can't possibly hold everything we have learned at the ready to be remembered at any moment. It's when we recall or recollect information that we strengthen that memory's neural pathway.

Remembering also alters memories. Every day we add new memories to our brain, and every year we mature as new experiences shape our knowledge, values, beliefs, and actions. We have all had the experience of a childhood memory popping up in our adult minds, only to see it in a new light. For example, visiting your former elementary school can make everything there seem smaller than you remember because you've added a couple feet to your height. Or how memories of your "mean" parents shift when you find yourself faced with parenting challenges and you're doling out similar consequences to your own kids. Updates to your knowledge and awareness change your memories too.

As we grow, remembering alters our memories as we filter through new perspectives

I have a personal example of just how powerful this process can be. When I was 18 years old, I had an amazing job working at a marine park in Canada. Every day, I took care of the octopus, fed the orphaned harbor seal pups, and played with the orcas in between shows to keep them from getting bored. I'd kneel at the edge of their pool, scratching their skin, giving them simple commands, and rewarding them with fish. Fast forward 25 years and I'm up late, unable to sleep, and channel surfing until I land on a documentary about orcas titled *Blackfish*. It seemed like a great thing to watch, until they started to show images of the very marine park where I once worked. I found myself watching news footage about the death of another 18-year old, Keltie Byrne, who had my same job. She was pulled down and drowned by one of the orcas, who went on to kill two other people. I started to hyperventilate, cry, and shake violently as my body merged my old memory with this new information and perceived me to be in danger. This went on for nearly 30 minutes even though I was sitting in my living room thousands of miles from the park that had closed years before.

Sadly, that event has changed my memories of that job even though I had positive experiences. I cannot think of it without feeling some anxiety—even now, typing this, my hands are shaking just a little. In addition, I was not aware of the brutal practices that were used in capturing the animals, so I also feel guilt that I was part of a cruel industry. While this is an extreme example, it underscores that memories, particularly episodic memories, are inevitably altered in the remembering of them. Sometimes it's a slight shift and sometimes it's dramatic.

10. Retrievals, Not Repetitions

One of the biggest insights from brain science has to do with how our memories are made. We used to think it was repetition, which many of us experienced during our education, forced to write or recite things again and again. But it turns out that it is retrieval, not repetition, that makes the difference. For conceptual learning, the evidence is clear: it is the act of retrieval—having to recall something we've learned—that makes learning memorable.

The difference between retrieval and repetition is subtle but powerful. Let's take what you learned about types of memory as an example. Rereading that section or going over your notes would be repetition, because you are taking the information *in* again. A retrieval would be asking yourself to name the nine types, like a mini-quiz. In other words, you have to look inside your mind and get what you learned *out* of there. If you got them correct, that would be one successful retrieval (or recall). You could ask yourself to define each type, and that would give you another successful recall.

Many studies have proven this, such as one at Kent State University where Doctors Katherine Rawson and John Dunlosky compared several groups of students that learned the same information and then were tested on that information 46 days later. The first group just learned the information once. The second group did one retrieval session with correct recalls and the third group did three retrieval sessions with correct recalls. The retrieval session groups performed significantly better than the first group, which seems kind of obvious. But note that they were asked to retrieve what they had already learned, not learn it again. Being able to recall the information correctly, and then spacing out those retrievals, significant improved both retention and accuracy.

They also tested whether more retrievals led to even better results but the students only showed minimal improvements after three. So, the researchers suggest learners do three correct recalls per retrieval session and then space out three retrieval sessions over time. The level of specificity depends on the situation and what the learner needs to be successful.

And retrievals are not only tests and quizzes. Retrieval can occur through a variety of methods like sharing what you learned with someone else, reflecting on how it relates to a past experience, doing a hands-on activity, quizzing yourself (like recalling answers to flashcard questions), and a host of other typical learning activities. Learning designers can easily build those kinds of retrievals into learning events as well as empower learners to do that for themselves.

Here's another fascinating study on retrievals: Doctors Rohrer and Taylor at South Florida University assigned college students learning math to one of two groups. Group A learned math and, that same day, did 10 problems using that math. Group B learned the same math but only did 5 problems. Seven days later Group B did 5 more problems. In other words, both groups had the same instruction and same total number of problems, but they were spaced differently. Then both groups took the same test. Group A, who did the 10 problems on Day one got 75 percent right; Group B got 70 percent right. At this point you might think that doing the 10 problems together is the better way to go right? But wait . . . the researchers tested the students again four weeks later, and this time Group A performance dropped to 32 percent while Group B held up to 64 percent—twice the performance of Group A.

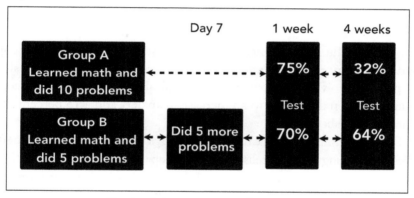

Retrievals boost retention of information

Researchers at Santa Clara and York Universities looked at the timing of the spacing to see if it mattered. They asked a group of students to learn Swahili and English word pairs and then split the students into four groups. All were given the same long-term memory test. The first group didn't do a retrieval session and later did a long-term memory test; they remembered 50 percent of it. The second group had one retrieval session on the same day they learned the material, but it was 12 hours later (like 8 a.m. to 8 p.m.); on the long-term memory test, they retained 55 percent. The third group also had a 12-hour span of time from learning to retrieval but it was overnight (8 p.m. to 8 a.m.). This group retained 65 percent. And finally, the fourth group had 24 hours between their learning and the retrieval session. And they retained 75 percent of the learning. What's going on here? What's causing this significant difference? The answer: it's sleep!

Brain scientists have discovered all kinds of fascinating things about the sleeping brain, including the fact that our day's learning moves into long-term memory during sleep. While we sleep, our brain does a little housecleaning, dumping the bits of information and experiences that were not relevant and then moving the most relevant bits into the various regions of our brain, integrating what we already know with what we just learned. If you have not yet seen Pixar's animated movie *Inside Out*, you should. They do a great job depicting this nightly process. Scientists have also discovered that all of this mainly happens during the stage of sleep called REM, for rapid eye movement. In fact, it turns out that last hour of sleep is the most important. The hour right before we wake up is when most of this happens.

Before I learned about this research, I used to set an alarm and I relied on it to wake up. But using an alarm often cuts off that last hour of sleep, shortchanging this important brain process. If possible, try to structure your schedule so you wake up naturally, without the aid of a device. Most adults need seven to nine hours of sleep each night, according to a 2019 article titled "The New Science of Sleep." A study of over 10,000 people found that memory and cognition were impaired by shortchanging sleep, with problem solving, reasoning, and verbal abilities the most impacted. In addition, sleep debt leads to an increase in anxiety and a 15 percent drop in our pain threshold.

Besides helping with learning, sleep provides other amazing benefits. Bodies heal during sleep as cells and tissues repair themselves and the body sweeps out toxins like smoke, pesticides, and other carcinogens we have been exposed to during the day. Some medical doctors believe that the buildup of those toxins over time lead to cancer, Alzheimer's disease, and other disorders. A study at Duke University identified that lack of sleep was associated with diabetes, heart disease, and elevated stress levels.

Harvard Medical School has an entire division dedicated to sleep medicine and the profound effect sleep has on mood, focus, and mental performance among other things. Dr. Michael Roizen, the Chief Wellness Officer at the famous Cleveland Clinic states that sleep is the most under-utilized health habit.

Further, a study published in *Science* magazine estimated that even one extra hour of sleep can boost happiness, especially for people who are not getting enough. Better sleep has been associated with weight loss, enhanced creativity, and better performance. In her book *Thrive: The Third Metric to Redefining Success and Creating a Life of Well-Being, Wisdom, and Wonder*, Arianna Huffington details her own journey through exhaustion to a serious medical incident that served as her wake-up call (no pun intended). She now is a major proponent of sleep, offering her employees the opportunity to use nap pods on site at the *Huffington Post*. "I am paying people for their judgment, not their stamina," she stated. Companies like Zappos and Google also offer employees opportunities to nap because research shows that in as little as 15 to 20 minutes, employees can bounce back to high performance.

In their book *Nurture Shock: New Thinking about Children*, authors Bronson and Merryman synthesize several important studies about children and they dedicate an entire chapter to sleep. Children today actually get one less hour of sleep than they did 30 years ago and researchers believe it correlates with lower IQ (intelligence quotient), strained emotional well-being, and obesity. Teens in particular need more sleep as their brains undergo a massive restructuring that changes one-third of their neuro-connections and shifts their melatonin release by two hours. Biologically, teens are wired to stay up later (11 p.m.) and wake later (9 a.m.) but school schedules mean that most suffer from chronic sleep debt. Several studies show that teens need 12 hours per night and when they get less than 8, are more likely to use alcohol and drugs as well as contemplate or attempt suicide.

Clearly, sleep is important to our overall health and well-being at every age. Take time to learn more about the benefits of sleep, and focus on getting more, and better quality, sleep. Remember, from a learning perspective, you'll boost your memory if you space each of the three recommended retrievals after one of those nights of quality sleep. And retrievals help with long-term retention, at least for semantic memories of facts and concepts. The learning sticks because the neurological path to get to the information is more travelled. Essentially, retrievals reshape the forgetting curve, increasing our retention of the material for longer.

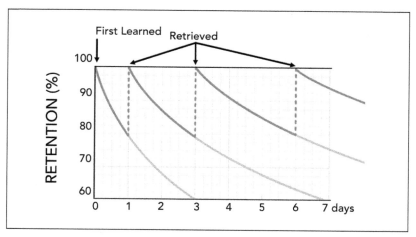

Boost retention by doing three retrievals spaced with sleep

11. Leverage Existing Schemas

Besides retrievals, another powerful tool for moving learning into long-term memory is connecting it to something we already know. Again, research on the brain has illuminated a natural process that already exists: the human brain has a method in place for categorizing what we learn. Much like an elaborate filing system, our brains have "folders," where related material gets stored. Scientists call these folders "schemas" and they are essentially clusters of information, or neural networks, that get bigger and stronger as we add to them over time, through experience. For example, think of a banana and up will pop its color, shape, taste, smell, whether you like them or not. Because I traveled in Venezuela, my schema for banana includes the smaller, sweeter *cambur*. And Jack Johnson's song "Banana Pancakes" is part of my schema too, along with fond memories of baking with family. But Jack Johnson doesn't just live in my banana folder—he also attended my college so he's in the UCSB folder, along with the folder of folksy male musicians and people who live in Hawaii. Venezuela has its own folder too and is filled with lots of memories of my visits there as well as its history, economy, and now its current human rights crisis under the regime of Nicolás Maduro.

Unlike real file folders, these schemas in our brain can hold an infinite amount of information and make unlimited connections between them, linked by memories and the strings of sensations. So, when I learn something that could be attached to several schemas, it can be added to all of them simultaneously, creating a rich web of information. This is also why I can be eating a banana, and the next thing I know, I am humming a few bars of a Jack Johnson song or thinking about people I know in Venezuela.

As we live and learn, we continue to grow this neural network and update our schemas whether we want to or not (like when I saw the movie *Blackfish* and several of my schemas were irrevocably altered). And this schema process is accelerating with technology. Of the world's population, 68 percent (5.135 billion) are mobile device users. According to Nielsen, adults are now spending nearly half of their day interacting with electronic media. The average adult spends approximately 136 minutes per day on social networking sites where new content is continually being pushed via articles, videos, posts, and tweets. And that's just one day! By the end of the week, we can and often do feel overloaded and overwhelmed.

As we focus on the learning process, learning professionals can intentionally leverage our natural wiring by attaching new learning to schemas that already exist in the learner's brain. This accomplishes two things. First, you can create an insight or an "aha!" moment when people see the connection to something they already know. The best teachers instinctively do this. Whether teaching calculus, software, or leadership, they explain the abstract in concrete ways that connect to learners' existing schemas. Having been a dean at a major research university, I noticed that this was what distinguished the best math and science instructors from the rest. They were gifted at connecting to schemas that existed in the minds of young adults in a way that made the complex not only accessible, but easy. Second, once learning is linked to an existing schema it is difficult to forget it. What's learned becomes part of that stronger neural network instead of being a small, isolated piece of information floating around in the brain.

So, how do you activate your learners' schemas? To begin with, you must step into the perspective of your learner. An example that works for Baby Boomers will probably generate blank stares with Millennials. Any learning design or facilitation should start with you asking yourself, *Who is in the room? How can I make meaningful connections to something they already know?* Knowing your audience should give you some clues.

Personally, I also try to share a few different conceptual models or examples instead of just one. This broad approach allows me to activate the schemas of more people in the room since I know that at least one is likely to hit the target. And this approach creates an added benefit of allowing learners to connect the dots between those models. For example, when I teach my change management training, I use the Greiner Curve of organizational development, research on the neuroscience of resistance, and Dr. Brené Brown's research on vulnerability. Taught together, these models offer the broader "why and how" change is both necessary and difficult. More importantly, they collectively tap into the participants' schemas, helping them see the intersections at play.

But nothing is more powerful than tying learning to the schema of personal experience, with its rich episodic memory and bundle of sensory data. If your audience happens to share an experience, you can certainly leverage that schema. But I find that this is harder to do as the workforce gets more diverse and the pace of hiring increases. So instead, I shift the focus to be from *an* experience to *their* experience. In my change training, I ask my audience to remember two times that they experienced change, one that went smoothly and one that was difficult. This exercise activates their specific memories and their individual schemas of change without me having to know what they are. By pairing this with hands-on activities for effectively leading change, I see powerful, long-lasting results because I am tapping into the pool of enduring connections that already exist in my participants' brains.

12. Six Powerful Connections

Research has revealed six types of powerful connections that can help move your learning into long-term memory. I like to use a mix of these in my learning events but each may be used individually and tailored to specific needs. Consider how you would use them with the thing you want to learn.

Metacognition

Metacognition is a fancy word for thinking about thinking. Right now, you're thinking about learning and how you can enhance your learning process. Another type of metacognition is reflection, when we review a past experience. Metacognition also occurs when we take an assessment because it helps us see our behavior in a new way. I agree with Peter Brown and Derek Sivers, coauthors of *Make it Stick: The Science of Successful Learning*, who state, "Reflection is a form of practice."

They also talk about the value of elaboration, which is the process of giving new material meaning by expressing it in your own words and connecting it with what you already know. In essence, you use elaboration to activate your own schemas.

I love to use a type of metacognition called appreciative inquiry. It's a guided form of reflection where you ask people to focus on their peak performances. You could ask them a time when learning was easy and fun. Or a time when they successfully worked through challenging material. Or even a time they overcame an initial failure. The goal is to light up the neural pathways of success rather than failure. When we ask people to review times they failed we light up the failure pathways, which isn't exactly productive and it often activates negative emotions like anxiety or embarrassment.

By focusing on peak performances, you can look at what made those times work and build upon those successes. You can ask questions like, *What made that situation different? What worked about it? How can we translate that to a new situation?*

If you want to learn more, I recommend visiting the Center for Appreciative Inquiry's website or reading the book *Appreciative Leadership: Focus on What Works to Drive Winning Performance and Build a Thriving Organization* by Diana Whitney and others.

Wordplay

Our second most powerful connection is wordplay. Let me demonstrate by asking you to finish these sentences.

I before E, _____.

Thirty days hath September, _____.

Or, for those of you who took music classes: Every good boy _____.

These little phrases help us remember things like which months have 30 days or the notes on the musical scale. (See answers on page 51.) They are a type of wordplay.

Wordplay moves things into long-term memory because you activate the language centers of the brain, connecting learning to the abundant schemas of words. The examples I just gave are from the English language but there are examples of wordplay in every language and culture.

Mnemonic devices are also connections based on wordplay. They're fantastic because they take a lot of information and package it into something easy to remember. I experienced this as a senior in high school, when I was studying for the AP biology exam. We had to learn thousands of pieces of information, so my friend Ian and I started to create mnemonic devices to give ourselves a fighting chance with all that material. To this day (many years later), I still remember that the names of fungi can be unlocked with this device: Orange Zebras Always Bite Dried Fruit. It stands for "oomycetes, zygomycetes, ascomycetes, basidiomycetes, deuteromycetes = fungi." And to this day I remember how much we laughed as we came up with it. That thing is still in my brain all these years later, even though I don't need that information. But my mnemonic device unlocks it every time because it's tapping into my brain's rich language center.

Acronyms are forms of wordplay where (usually) the first letter of every word combines to make a new word. For example, SCUBA (self-contained underwater breathing apparatus), SONAR (sound navigation ranging), and SWAT (special weapons and tactics. Here's one I definitely want you to remember: FAIL stands for "first attempt in learning." We'll dive more into why this is important in section III.

As a learning designer, use wordplay to create fun ways for your learners to remember information. Or, more importantly, teach them the value of this type of connection so that they can create their own, which will be even more powerful in the long run.

"My Wife and My Mother-in-Law" by Willam Hill

Insight

Have you seen this optical illusion before? Some people immediately see an older woman and others see a young one. They are both in this image. Can you see them?

When I do this activity with a live audience, you can actually hear little gasps, oooohs, and comments around the room as people see the missing piece. If you want to experience more of this, search for optical illusions online (I recommend BrainDen/optical-Illusions.htm).

That thing that happens when you see the image in the new way is called insight. It's the "aha!" moment, when you gasp or say "ooooh!" as the synapses in your brain connect.

In a 2018 study, neuroscientists from Austria and the United Kingdom worked together to explore what happens when people solve puzzles, which represents a kind of "aha!" moment. Thirty participants completed nearly 50 puzzles and the study showed that during the moment of insight, a rush of dopamine into the nucleus accumbens creates that brief sense of excitement or joy and relief. This adds a chemical reward as well as positive emotions, both which facilitate long-term memory storage.

Insight is powerful because once it happens it cannot be undone—that moment of learning cannot be lost. You will never be able to look at the image again and not see the hidden picture. Flashes of insight are indestructible. It reminds me of the movie *The Matrix*, and Neo's choice to take the red pill. Once he sees through the illusion, he can never go back to seeing the world the old way.

So how can we use insight as a learning tool? Dr. Josh Davis suggests "Instructional design should perhaps shift from content delivery to creating the space for insight." This is an important shift in learning. As educator Alison King famously noted, instructors need to move from being "the sage on the stage to the guide on the side." This means that if we have a choice between taking 5 minutes to tell someone information or designing a 15-minute experience for them to have their own "aha!" moment, we should always choose the latter. Their learning will be much longer lasting because the shift of perspective is permanent.

In my own work, I now consider these four ways to create opportunities for insight:

1. **Introduce a range of concepts.** This increases the chance of creating moments where learners can connect the dots.

2. **Create opportunities for people to learn on their own.** When people seek their own answers, it is much more likely to stick. This is where the advent of technology and smart phones can be a great boon because you can give folks a few minutes to seek for themselves.

3. **Build experiential activities that take learners to the "aha!" moment.** Instead of thinking, *What can I say to help them understand this idea?* it becomes, *What can I have them do that will show them this idea in action?*

4. **Give people down time from the learning.** This might be achieved through longer breaks or time between connected learning events. Yes, breaks from learning actually *create* moments for insight.

I have a question for you: Typically, where are you and what are you doing when you have moments of insight, those "aha!" moments? When I ask this question, people say things like, "In the shower," or "On a walk," or "Cooking." No one ever says, "Sitting at my desk, concentrating." As we covered in chapter 3, this is because the brain needs to move attention away from the learning for the connections to happen. Taking a break is critically important for insight so don't ever underestimate the power of a long break or time off between learning events. Some of your best work will happen when you are not working or with your learners.

Answers from p. 49:
I before E except after C
Thirty days hath September, April, June, and November.
Every Good Boy Does Fine.

13. Social Engagement and Maps

The next two connections are social engagement and maps. We are wired to be social creatures. I cover this in great detail in my book, *Wired to Connect: The Brain Science of Teams and a New Model for Creating Collaboration and Inclusion.* A big portion of our nervous system is dedicated to reading emotions in others and forming meaningful connections. This skill is part of our survival, so it also has biological components. If we think about the history of our species, our chances of survival were better if we banded together to gather food and fight the saber-toothed tigers. Even today, people who live in communities live longer than people who are isolated. And studies have shown that having a couple of close friends is an important component of happiness.

We are innately social creatures, and social learning helps us maximize that aspect of our biology. When we learn in a group, a couple important things happen. The social part of our brain turns on simply because we are in the room together. This is the part of the brain that scans facial expressions, tone of voice, body language, and subtle cues. By learning in community, we naturally activate all those neural pathways. In addition, we know that, emotionally, most people experience positive emotions when they have engaging and interactive learning experiences. This is why we gravitate to and respond well to stories. Even when we hear a story about someone we don't know or may never meet, stories naturally bring together our social wiring with the rich language information our brain holds. Finally, when we learn in community, our brain connects that learning with those specific people. When you run into each other later, you are likely to see that schema activated. For example, my friend Ian is forever in my brain's Biology folder and anything biology makes me think of Ian. When schools and workplaces intentionally anchor learning moments to peers, it causes constant reactivation of the material.

When I teach this material in person, I pair up folks to discuss how they can apply the concepts to the thing they want to learn. Those discussions give me and them several neuroscience goodies. First, the social wiring of the brain lights up as they talk, even if it's via remote technology like video or audio. Side note here: visual is always more stimulating than just audio so I highly recommend using video calls. Second, when they see their discussion partner later, they will naturally check in about how that learning is going. There will be a built-in reactivation and a retrieval of the material. Finally, if the subject in question requires learners to use the information or skill in concert or collaboration with other people, then they can practice that as well.

Not all learning can be made social, but I have yet to find a topic or skill that wouldn't benefit from adding some human interaction to the mix.

Maps

The fifth type of learning connection is making maps. Our brain is designed to navigate geography. It's tied to our survival as a species because we had to be able to both find food and water and make our way back to those sources in the future. We also had to find our village and, depending on our tribe, perhaps trek many miles as the seasons changed. Inside the hippocampus is a structure called the entorhinal cortex and it serves as our internal global positioning system (GPS). Doctors May-Britt Moser and Edvard Moser won the Nobel Prize for their research on the entorhinal cortex and their discovery of a sphere of cells, organized in a grid-like pattern, that create 3-D mental maps as we navigate space. This brain structure continually builds and edits our mental maps.

It turns out that the entorhinal cortex also helps map our memories in space and time. It's how, when you recall an event, you know where you were and roughly when it happened. Interestingly, the Mosers' research is shedding light on why patients with Alzheimer's disease become disoriented. It turns out that this cluster of grid cells gets damaged early in the course of the disease, thus disabling their mental maps of the places they should know. Even though they are navigating places they have been hundreds of times before, the internal map has disappeared and along with it, their recognition of a place as familiar.

People who navigate geographically often have a larger hippocampus than others. Neuroscientist Dr. Eleanor Maguire, at the University College London, spent five years studying the cab drivers of London, a city notorious for its confusing and complex geography. Brain scans have showed that the taxi drivers, who spent years memorizing the streets of their city, consistently had a much larger hippocampus compared with others.

This could be why the mapping technique used by memory champions is so effective. Yes, there are competitions for semantic memory. Competitors might be asked to memorize the exact order of 12 decks of cards or a 2,000-digit number. One memory champion, Boris Konrad, was born with normal memory but over time trained himself to do things like memorize 195 names and faces in fifteen seconds. He used a technique called the method of loci or "memory palace," dating back to ancient Greece, in which people picture a location in their mind such as a room or a building and then visualize each piece they need to memorize around that location. In other words, they engage the natural map-making function of their entorhinal cortex to help them memorize materials.

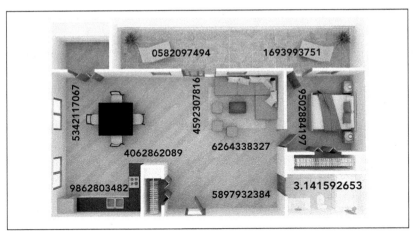

Memorizing the digits of Pi using the method of loci

Neuroscientist Dr. Martin Dresler, at the Radboud University Medical Center in the Netherlands, partnered with Konrad to see if the brains of memory champions are different than average people's and whether better memory can be taught. Not surprisingly, the brains of the memory champions were different, with more connections between the visual, medial temporal lobe, and default mode network. But when the average participants learned and practiced the mapping technique, Dresler found measurable differences in the brain scans as well as significant improvement in their memorization abilities. These were not short-lived changes either, with gains lasting for several months.

You, too, can learn techniques to boost your semantic memory. As neuroscientist Dr. Lars Nyberg puts it, "The finding that training can shape the brain in a similar way in non-experts supports the view that expert performance is really the result of training—not any particular abilities." Consider how this technique might be effective for the thing you want to learn or to help others improve their memory.

14. The Magic of Music

The last of the powerful connections is music. Have you ever wondered why you can remember the lyrics to thousands of songs? I know I can sing every Madonna song ever written, verbatim, from beginning to end. Music touches many regions of the brain to the point that musical memory is nearly indestructible. You can even sustain brain damage and you won't lose the musical part because it's connected to so many different lobes and regions.

If you're American and of a certain age you probably remember *Schoolhouse Rock*. My generation grew up watching those animated lessons set to a catchy tune. When I give talks on learning, I can sing just the first words of "Conjunction Junction…" and a room full of people will immediately sing back, "What's your function?" *Schoolhouse Rock* was brilliant. To this day, I can tell you how a bill becomes a law, what conjunctions are, and how adverbs work because the songs are still in my brain and easily retrievable.

Musician Bobby McFerrin knows that the human brain is wired for music and he often turns the audience into a musical instrument where, without using words, he guides them to sing an unknown melody in unison. You can watch a short video of this amazing process, called improvised pentatonic collaboration, on TED.com. It's part of *Notes and Neurons: In Search of the Common Chorus*.

Music is a global phenomenon. Every culture in the history of the world has had music, and it can be a powerful connector between people. While choral singing has always been popular—for example, over 20 million American adults sing in community-based performance choirs—there has been a recent upsurge in community singing, where people get together in small groups. As Kelsey Menehan states, "A community sing is about ordinary people joining their friends and neighbors in a public place to sing, just for the fun of it." There is no audition, no performance, not even any written song lists or lyrics. It's about our innate, tribal way of communicating and being together. I am a member of a community singing group and it's one of the most joyful things I do.

Researchers have found many benefits to singing with others, including better cognition and alertness, the release of endorphins and oxytocin that create positive feelings, better sleep, improved immune system, lowered blood pressure and stress, enhanced cooperation, and even longer life!

Tying learning to music is so powerful that it has been harnessed as a tool for a variety of therapies, and there are some incredible success stories with military veterans with traumatic brain injury, stroke victims, and people with autism. Here are just a couple of these amazing stories:

Arizona Congresswoman Gabrielle Giffords sustained severe brain trauma from a gunshot wound in 2011. The injury caused her to lose her ability to speak but music therapists started working with her because they knew that while she couldn't speak, she would still be able to sing. They used song to rewire the language part that had been damaged, rebuilding, refiring, and, therefore, regrowing, the neural pathways through uninjured tissue. So musical learning can help us with more than just remembering actual songs. It literally can help rewire damaged parts of the brain.

Music touches every region of the brain and is shared among cultures around the world

Music is even unlocking the memories of people with Alzheimer's disease and dementia. The documentary *Alive Inside: A Story of Music and Memory* shows how Dan Cohen, a social worker, used music to unlock memory in nursing home patients. The film is filled with examples of people who seem lost in their own minds but become animated after a few minutes of listening to familiar music. In the film, neurologist Dr. Oliver Sacks states, "Music is inseparable from emotion so it's not just a physiological stimulus. It will call the whole person through many different parts of their brain and the memories and emotions that go with it." Once the music "awakens" them, these people stay present and animated for quite a bit of time afterwards. Each song is like a key that opens the door to their whole being again. I was moved to tears while watching this film because my family has been touched by both dementia and Alzheimer's disease. We can all use music to help our loved ones stay connected to their real selves.

Music therapy is a useful tool that has been used for centuries around the world. Today, neuroscientists can better measure its effects and are verifying its benefits to help lots of people with brain injuries, diseases, movement disorders, and processing challenges. Doctors William Forde and Gottfried Schlaug have written a detailed article in *Scientific American* titled "The Healing Power of Music."

But how is this related to learning? Well, we can make learning nearly unforgettable by connecting it to music. One obvious way is to turn the content into a song, much like *Schoolhouse Rock* did. Once the song is learned, the content is embedded in the tune.

You can also affiliate the learning with a song that already exists. For example, you might find a song in which the lyrics perfectly underscore specific content or the tone of the experience you're creating. You can make that song an intentional part of the learning experience. Maybe you ask your learners to identify how the lyrics relate or have them tweak the lyrics to fit.

Think of it like creating a soundtrack for learning. For example, when I teach change management, I often use the Beatles' song "Yesterday" to illustrate the emotional transition that people go through with change and the resistance that usually arises during the early stages of the change. You could also be more subtle and simply play the song at breaks, creating an almost subconscious connection between the learning and the song. I think the first choice is more powerful and leaves less room for your learners to miss the connection. But people who make movies and television use music all the time to alter our emotions without us really being aware of it.

In an interview with Trevor Noah, Oscar-winning actor Mahershala Ali described a period where he was playing four roles at one time (*House of Cards, Luke Cage, Moonlight,* and *Future Relic*). To help himself manage the complexity of playing four different people, he created a music playlist for each one. "I began to curate playlists for each character because music influences your energy…and how you move through the world, so I'd listen to each different playlist depending on who I was working on at that time."

Finally, when teaching, empower your learners to use the power of music for themselves. Ask them to create their own personal songs or playlists to anchor learning and make information easier to recall later. When I teach leadership skills, I ask people to create a playlist of songs that recall a time when they were their best or inspires them to be their best. This not only connects the concepts to those songs but also creates an opportunity to retrieve or recall the content later as they put the playlist together.

These six types of learning connections will help you drive learning into long-term memory. Not every connection works for every kind of learning or learner, so try them out and pick and choose the ones that feel like natural fits for you and the learning you want to do.

15. Grow Your Remembering Skills

As we wrap this section on the Remember phase of the model, the key components are types of memory, schemas, connections, and retrievals.

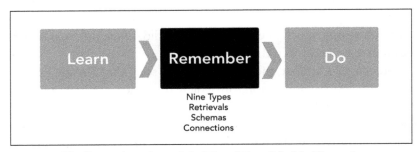

The Remember phase of the Three Phase Model of Learning

Since there are nine different kinds of memory so you have to tailor your actions to the type of memory you want to create. Here are some tips you can use for semantic and episodic memories (we'll cover procedural memories in section III).

For semantic memories, make sure you are using as many senses as possible and getting the best sensory data you can. In addition, intentionally activate your schemas, linking learning to something you already know. Be sure to leverage several of the following connections (you don't need to use all six simultaneously):

- Metacognition/elaboration
- Wordplay
- Insight
- Social engagement
- Mental maps
- Music

Following your learning, set up three retrieval sessions, spaced with sleep. If possible, leverage virtual reality to turn a semantic memory into an episodic one with you as the star of the scene.

Doctors Henry Roediger, III, and Jeffrey Karpicke are the researchers who first identified the benefit of retrievals, also known as the testing effect. They authored the book *The Power of Testing Memory: Basic Research and Implications for Educational Practice*. Roediger partnered with doctors Adam Putnam and Victor Sungkhasettee to author an article titled "Optimizing Learning in College: Tips from Cognitive Psychology," in which they offer several suggestions, providing the scientific evidence behind each:

Before class

- Organize your time by calendaring not only due dates for tests and assignments but the working sessions you'll need to meet those due dates.
- Buy new books so you're not tempted to use the previous owner's notes and highlights (especially since they might be wrong).
- Find a quiet place to study so that you can eliminate distractions and engage in the deep focus needed to learn.
- Answer comprehension questions about material before you learn. According to the authors, "It may seem counterintuitive to answer questions about topics you have not studied yet, but research suggests that…answering questions beforehand activates any related knowledge you have about the topic and makes it easier to connect new information to what you already know."
- Generate your own questions about the important concepts, as it helps you think about the content and also connect it to your existing knowledge.
- Instead of summarizing material, recall what you remember and then review the content, noting what you missed and what you had correct. They call this technique "read-recite-review."

During class

- Attend lectures, even if they just repeat what is in the reading. Hearing the content a different way creates another memory, which strengthens your knowledge and retention.
- Write your notes, don't use a computer. Several studies show that handwriting generates more comprehension and recall than typing.
- If you can, get a copy of the lecture slides beforehand and take notes directly on them during class. That way, you use your notetaking to elaborate on ideas rather than copying each slide's contents.

After class

- Study a little bit every day as it creates the spaced retrievals that are scientifically proven to boost retention. Rereading doesn't seem to help, so only reread when you are still confused and need clarity around some point.
- Use tools like flash cards and quizzes to create retrievals rather than repetitions.

- Engage in "successive relearning" where you strengthen your knowledge of the content through mnemonic devices, mind maps, and so on.
- For episodic memories, you'll also want to get the best sensory data that you can, using schemas and connections. Where possible, heighten your emotion so the amygdala can get involved.

Your Learning Journey

At the end of each section, take the opportunity to apply the concepts to your own life and the thing you want to learn. Use these questions to help you identify possible strategies to support your learning goal.

- Consider your own natural pattern each day and identify your peak (when it's easiest to focus), your trough (when it's difficult to concentrate), and your rebound. What is the best window to work on your learning goal?
- When you've recalled memories lately, what sensation tugged on a memory "string" and brought it up? How might you intentionally use the five senses so that your memory optimally supports your learning goal?
- Review the diagram in chapter 8 on the nine types of memory: sensory, working, semantic, episodic, procedural, priming, habituation/sensitization, emotional, and somatic. Identify an example of each from your own life. Which types of memory will you be creating with your learning goal?
- How can you use three retrievals spaced with sleep with your learning goal?
- Learning is "stickier" when we attach them to things we already know (schemas). How can you attach your learning goal to schemas you already have?
- Identify which of the six types of connections you can intentionally leverage for your learning goal: metacognition/elaboration, wordplay, insight, social engagement, mental maps, music.

DO:
BUILDING SKILLS + DESIGNING HABITS

"You don't learn to walk by following rules. You learn by doing, and by falling over."

Sir Richard Branson, founder,
Virgin Group, Ltd.

16. Understanding Skills and Habits

Most adult learning seeks behavior change, usually in the form of developing skills or creating habits. The third phase of the model is about changing behavior: Do. To this end, we're going to explore designing habits, repetitions, rewards, and practice.

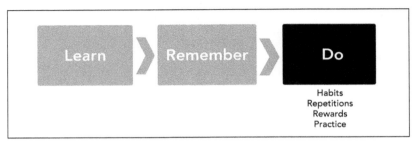

Phase 3: Do

Skills, behaviors, and habits are all examples of procedural memory, one of the four types of implicit memory. As we learned in section II, this is the "knowing how" aspect and involves how to do things like use a tool, move your body, avoid a danger, or perform a skill. We gain or build these memories through sensorimotor experiences. As memory research Dr. Richard Clark states, "These forms of memory are expressed through experience-based changes in performance."

As you recall, procedural memory is how we learn to do tasks that eventually become automatic behaviors, like driving a car or using a computer. Once learned, it's there to access in the future. This type relies on repetitions and ongoing feedback in the form of rewards. Procedural memories involve the basal ganglia, striatum, and motor cortex. According to neuropsychologist Dr. Boris Suchan, these structures are buried deep in the skull, protected by the cerebral cortex and, as a result, are rarely compromised, even with traumatic brain injury. This is why famous patients like Henry Molaison and Clive Wearing (another man who could not make long-term memories) not only maintained their pre-injury skills, but developed new ones, even though they could not create new semantic or episodic memories.

I grew up in Colorado, so my childhood sports were downhill skiing and ice skating. I became a competitive ice skater, doing triple jumps and complex spins, logging thousands of hours of practice. Even though I stopped skating at 18, my body still remembers. Muscle memory is a real thing and I can still do some moves even though I haven't skated in years. The good news is that I have muscle memory, the bad news is that I don't have the muscles (LOL!) so now it's single jumps. But it still surprises me how deeply ingrained procedural memories like these can be.

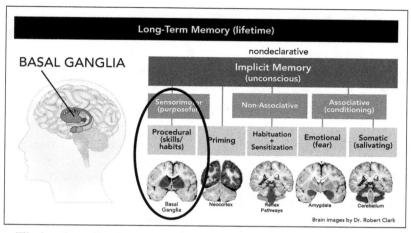

The basal ganglia plays a central role in the forming of procedural memories

As we grow up, we develop more procedural memories as we learn and hone a range of skills for our jobs and careers. All working adults rely on both skills and habits so it's useful to know what they are and how to maximize your effectiveness with each. What is the definition of a skill? It is proficiency, facility, or dexterity, acquired or developed through training or experience. Skills are conscious behavior we intentionally seek to improve.

Because of technology, this is now an unending cycle because the half-life of any learned skilled is about 5 years while our working years have extended to 60 or more, according to authors Lynda Gratton and Andrew Scott in *The 100-Year Life: Living and Working in an Age of Longevity*. As we climb the levels of any career or organization, our skills improve through experience and sheer repetition. (At this point in my life, I have built so many PowerPoint presentations, I could do it in my sleep.) The average person has 5 careers over their lifetime and on average, 11 to 12 jobs. The younger generation changes jobs more often, averaging four jobs in the first 10 years after graduation. Changing careers often requires developing completely new skills, which can be awkward after having some level of competence and then returning to a beginner level again.

I think it's helpful to think about levels of mastery ranging from beginner to expert, with levels in between like novice, intermediate, and advanced. Job recruitment and interviews are all about finding the person with the right skills that match the needs of the position or project. Hire someone too inexperienced and they can struggle to succeed; hire someone too advanced and they will likely suffer from boredom, easily lured away to a another position that offers a better match to their skill and experience.

Many studies show we do our best when we have the appropriate level of challenge and success. First observed by Mihaly Csikszentmihalyi, author of *Flow: The Psychology of Optimal Performance.* He defines flow as "a state in which people are so involved in an activity that nothing else seems to matter; the experience is so enjoyable that people will continue to do it even at great cost, for the sheer sake of doing it." The concentration or focus is so great that we have no attention for problems or anything else. You lose yourself in the activity and time passes quickly. This flow state is what produces happiness and even ecstasy.

Think of flow as the balance between your skill level and the challenge level of the task or job. If the challenge level is too high for your skill, you might experience anxiety and frustration, and if the challenge level is too low, you'll likely be bored. Humans hunger to grow and improve so getting in the flow is about increasing the level of challenge at the right time so you improve your skills. (Learn more by watching Csikszentmihalyi's TED talk.)

Neurologically, studies by Dr. Arne Dietrich have shown that during the flow state the prefrontal lobe exhibits decreased activity, which allows more brain regions to connect, enhancing creativity. Other researchers believe that the flow state is related to the brain's dopamine reward circuitry since curiosity is highly amplified during flow.

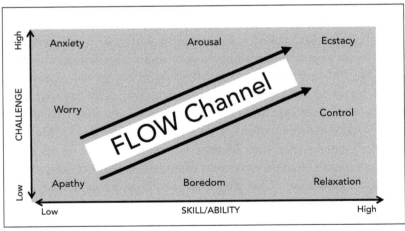

Flow occurs with the right balance of skill (or ability) to challenge

Many skills are also habits: recurrent, often unconscious patterns of behavior acquired through frequent repetition. Skills can contain many habits and habits can also be skills. Let's look at an example. I'm an author and have developed the skill for researching and writing a book. This skill relies on several habits—unconscious behaviors like reading articles and typing, as I don't have to try to read or type—it happens without thinking. But I do have to think about how to write a book. It's an intentional act and I have improved over time, especially with the help of my editor, Jenefer Angell. There is a bit of a chicken-and-egg thing here so don't get too wrapped up in the differences because, honestly, for working adults they are deeply intertwined on a daily basis.

From a scientific perspective habits are well-grooved neural pathways. We form habits when we do something so many times that it becomes automatic. Think about how you currently log onto your computer or get to work. You probably don't even have to think about it because your brain is running it as a habit loop. Learning something new, like how to drive a car or how to use new software, takes a lot of cognitive energy. Remember learning to drive? Making sure the mirrors were right, remembering the pedals, learning how to shift gears, keeping an eye on the other cars, remembering to signal. It required a lot of attention and focus, which requires the brain to spend a lot of energy. Our bodies have this wonderful biological weapon called the habit, which allows us to take behaviors that we do again and again and move them to a different part of the brain so that they take less energy, freeing up the parts of our brain that do the heavy lifting with new learning.

It's all the work of the basal ganglia, the structure in the brain that controls movement and reward. Things that we do again and again are condensed into a small energy package, where they can run on autopilot. Researchers at MIT have even been able to see the change in brain activity when this transition happens because the glucose burn in the brain drops significantly.

Habits are powerful and they are long lasting. Charles Duhigg's book *The Power of Habit* changed the way I see my work: I now consider myself a habit designer. He synthesized the research of many scientists who study habits and discovered that they can be broken down into three parts, known as the habit loop. First, there is the trigger or cue for starting a certain behavior. For example, getting in your car is the trigger or cue to begin the behavior of driving. Or walking into your kitchen in the morning is the cue to begin making coffee. The second part is the behavior routine itself. It's the act of driving—looking in mirrors, turning the steering wheel, stepping on the brake—or of starting the coffee maker and pulling a mug out of the cabinet. The third part, and perhaps most important, is the reward we get from doing a behavior. With driving it's getting to our destination. When I was a teenager the reward also included an enormous sense of independence. And for the coffee routine, the rewards might be a delicious Arabica bean plus the caffeine!

Here's the catch: The basal ganglia needs a sense of reward to form a habit loop, so the behavior routine must be compelling in some way. Isn't that interesting? If you want to form a new habit or change an old one, be sure to attach a compelling and immediate reward. When you don't, well, this is why so many of us fail at well-intentioned goals like starting to exercise or changing eating patterns. The reward is too distant for it to compel the basal ganglia to create the habit so we revert back to our old ways.

17. Designing a Habit: Repetitions, Not Retrievals

When we try to create behavior change, we need to think about the habits currently in place and how to design new, better habits that are more compelling than sticking with the comfort of the old ones.

Since I now think of myself as a habit designer, all my learning design starts with identifying the desired habit loop and working backwards from there. To do this, I ask myself these questions:

- What words and actions do I want to elicit from people?
- In what context will they need to use them?
- Are any habits currently in place?
- How can I make this new habit easier and more compelling than the old one?

As you recall, habits have three parts: a cue, a routine or behavior, and a reward. When you are building a habit, for yourself or someone else, here are some important things to know about all three.

A habit loop is composed of a cue, a routine, and a reward

To be consistently remembered, the cue or trigger needs to be something obvious, something that people will see or hear. Symbolically, the cue is like a giant "act now" button. A cue should not be an emotion, since those can vary too much in terms of intensity and timing. If you can, it's best to attach the new habit to a habit that already exists. For example, if you wanted to be better about flossing your teeth, the cue could be setting down your toothbrush. It's something that you can see, and brushing your teeth is already a well-grooved habit, so hooking onto it is more likely to be effective.

Cues can be all kinds of things, such as time of day, meals, or a regular activity like arriving at work or turning on your computer. The possibilities are endless and really depend on what you are trying to do. When I help leaders learn new behaviors for managing their people, we tie the cue to Mondays and preparing for their one-on-one meetings with their employees. If you are shifting software systems, the cue might be turning on the computer (now launch Google mail instead of Outlook) or processing an order (now go to SalesForce instead of Dynamics).

When shifting behavior, it's important to break the routine into baby steps. Routines are often long and complex. Think again about learning to drive. If you were teaching someone, giving them all the steps at once would be a recipe for disaster. The brain gets overwhelmed and they are likely to make mistakes. Each portion of the longer complex routine should be broken down into a small, doable step. In fact, the step should be so simple and so easy that it's impossible to fail. *First, adjust the mirrors so that you can see. Great! Next, position the seat so that you can easily reach the pedals. Nicely done.* And so forth. Notice the encouragement after completing each one?

Every correct step in the sequence should have a reward, no matter how small. The reward can be praise, a high five, or even a sound, like a "ding" from a game or a click like we often seen used with animals. To see a great example of this in action, watch this three-minute video of a nine-year-old girl learning to high jump (found at https://tagteach.com /TAGteach_track_and_field/). Though this is her first attempt, in fifteen minutes of instruction she executes a perfect high jump. As you watch the video, notice how the teacher uses cues, baby steps, and rewards (in this case a clicking sound) to build a habit from start to finish.

The instructor has facilitated the building of a new neural pathway using habit design that clearly illustrates Hebb's Law, "Neurons that fire together, wire together." Donald Hebb, a neuroscientist, noticed that when a behavior or movement is repeated, the neurons along that pathway begin to fire faster and faster. And, of course, that neural pathway will get stronger with further repetition.

As we learned in chapter 10, repetition is not an effective way to move learning into memory, but retrievals are. With habits, it's the reverse—habits are all about repetition. An old adage says it takes 21 days to form a habit. While they got the idea right, the details are wrong. Studies are showing that it takes about 20 repetitions of a behavior to start a neural pathway; and *40 to 50* repetitions to create a habit—provided the right cue and rewards are in place. By 66 repetitions, scientists can see and measure the neurons getting thicker on that neural pathway. The high jump instructor would want to bring the girl back and run the habit loop again and again, adding repetitions to create a well-grooved habit. Another adage—"You can't teach an old dog new tricks"—is also wrong. With enough repetitions, you most certainly can. Many of the advances in neurorecovery with stroke and spinal injury patients are due to sheer repetition in new ways that mimic or support how our nervous system naturally operates.

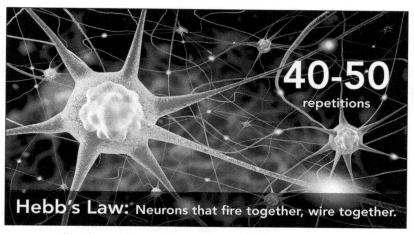

It takes, on average, 40 to 50 repetitions to form a habit

This is where we can do a better job when designing learning events. To build a skill or a habit, we shouldn't just talk about it. Learners need to *do* the behavior, in the correct sequence, to build the right neural pathway. I can't tell you how many workshops or trainings I've attended where the instructor tells us about certain principles, and we might even discuss them, but we never actually DO them. For example, at a mandatory three-day training on becoming a better manager, we were introduced to some models and theories of good management. And we talked about those models in pairs and small groups but we never actually did an activity that replicated managing people. We didn't role-play a one-on-one meeting. We didn't try delegating a task or practice coaching. And since we did not practice a single activity related to managing people, it will not surprise you to learn that, according to answers on the annual employee engagement survey, the program didn't shift people's management skills. While the attendees "liked" the program, it didn't deliver real results.

Experiences like that are one reason I went on to build my own brain science–based training programs. I have people start building the right behaviors and habit loops during the learning event itself. They practice skills several times while they are in the training, to help them transfer that learning back to their regular work environment. If we don't, their existing workplace cues will steer them back to their old way of doing things, so I counter that pull with repetitions in the training. In the process, they also get better at tackling real and difficult issues because they learn to work on them in an environment where it's safe to make mistakes.

This idea of building habits can be applied to any professional learning situation. Let's say you're implementing a new software system in your company and you want people to get comfortable quickly. And let's say that they will be using this software twice a week. How many weeks will it take before the habit is built? At least 20 weeks, right? But if you have them use that software 5 to 10 times in the training session, they are well on their way to forming that habit. That's a much better use of everyone's time than just hearing about the change and then having to muddle through on their own when they are back at their desks.

This is a big part of why 70 percent of all change initiatives fail. Every year, organizations spend billions of dollars implementing change. But they rarely consider the habit implications for that change, and what it means to someone's currently rewarding, well-grooved routine. People will always resist change, in large part because they're likely being asked to not only start a new (and therefore awkward and uncomfortable) habit, but to give up an easy, well-grooved habit. When a company launches a change, leaders can get frustrated with the inevitable resistance and grumbling but the length of time people will resist or complain will be that predictable 40 to 50 repetitions. If it's something that occurs daily, folks will move through it in seven to eight weeks. If it's a behavior that they do weekly or monthly, it means a longer, drawn out adjustment period, unless you build some repetitions into a learning event, or implementation phase, to shorten the time frame and lessen frustration. (Learn more in my book on change titled *Wired to Resist: The Brain Science of Why Change Fails and a New Model for Driving Success*.)

Harness the power of habit for yourself and consider how you might adjust the cue, routine, and reward to build the positive habits that support your success in all areas of your life.

18. The Right Rewards

Habits are a natural part of our biological functioning and they are at the heart of thousands of daily behaviors around the world. If you think about it, all kinds of habit loops run in your life every day. And if you break them down you will be able to identify the cue or trigger, the routine, and the reward. See Table 2.

Table 2. *Examples of common habit loops*

Cue	Routine	Reward
get in car	drive	arrive at destination + sense of freedom
wake up	make coffee	caffeine + taste
order arrives	process the order	make money
bedtime	brush your teeth	refreshing taste + avoiding cavities
8:00 a.m.	start working	be productive + don't get fired
cable bill arrives	pay it	watching favorite shows + surf the web

You can see that rewards can be positive, like that clean taste in your mouth from brushing your teeth, or avoiding something negative, like growing cavities and going to the dentist. While humans can be motivated toward a positive reward or away from a negative punishment, the research shows that positive is more compelling and therefore better for habit-building.

We have all experienced this. I know in my mind that exercising more will improve my health and help me avoid gaining weight but that doesn't feel very compelling when I am comfy in my warm bed. Duhigg's book helped me make a shift: I realized that in the places I felt stuck in my life, none had compelling rewards. To motivate myself to exercise, I now save the podcasts of my favorite shows and only allow myself to listen to them while working out. Exercising with others is another good motivator for me, so I'm more likely to get to that early spin class.

And it turns out I am not alone. The science of habits can be used to shift all sorts of behaviors. Doctors Daphne Bavelier and Shawn Green research the neuroscience of action video games and have found that players experience several gains as a result of hours of playing (repetitions!) and the rewards they get for successful choices. These gains include a heightened ability to focus, faster processing of information and decision-making, and greater flexibility of switching between tasks.

Planners in Stockholm, Sweden, are also harnessing the power of the right rewards. Like most cities, they had a problem with people speeding and, like most cities, they were trying to solve the problem through law enforcement and punishments like tickets and fines. Guess how much that strategy changed behavior? Not much. Because driving faster has its own reward of getting the person to their destination quicker and perhaps even a little thrill from not being caught breaking the rules.

Then the authorities in Stockholm decided to use the research on habit design and try something different. They built a device with a radar gun inside that sits at intersections. When a driver comes through the intersection, the machine reads the speed and displays it. Speeders get shown their speed with a red thumbs down sign and the machine takes a picture of their license plate so they can be fined. While many of us are familiar with similar machines that track and display a driver's speed to catch speeders, Stockholm did something revolutionary: Their machine also rewards drivers who do *not* speed. The machine shows their speed with a green thumbs up and takes a picture of their license plate to enter them in a lottery to win the speeders' fines!

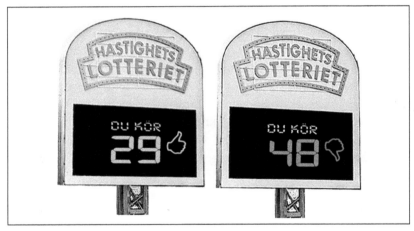

Sweden's speed monitoring and lottery device

Brilliant, huh? And it worked. Speeding went down by 22 percent and stayed down. That's a phenomenal, significant result. This shows that the possibility of punishment is only so motivating, but the possibility of reward, even a remote one like winning that lottery, is enough for us to change our behavior.

As Duhigg shows us, our current habits are not our destiny. We all have the ability to change habits and create the powerful and positive behaviors we want to see in our lives. So when you want to change an old habit or create a new one, be sure to build in meaningful rewards.

Social connection can be a powerful reward because we respond to acknowledgment and encouragement. Getting that "good job!" works because it releases dopamine. When human skin touches human skin—think high five, fist bump, or hug—our brain also releases oxytocin, another feel-good chemical that codes as a reward to the basal ganglia.

And, of course, prizes, points, and chocolate work, too. Duhigg shares one study of a group of people who wanted to exercise more. Split into two groups, both had the same cue (waking up) and routine (going for a run). But Group A was given a small piece of chocolate when they returned and Group B was not. They didn't do this forever, only until the habit was well formed. But the results were clear. Participants in Group A both formed the habit and maintained it for far longer than those in Group B. It is also interesting that Group A maintained the habit long after the chocolate was removed, suggesting that once habits are set, rewards can shift, often becoming built into the activity itself (like the endorphins or sense of accomplishment from running).

Rewards do not need to be big or showy. They just need to mark that the behavior was done correctly. And they need to be meaningful to the person in some way. Duhigg's book is filled with stories and examples of people who have made powerful transformations in their lives by working with their habit loops, from obvious choices around health and wellness to managing people and leading organizations. (Visit Charlesduhigg.com for helpful videos and resources.)

This is what is behind the power of gamification. It feels good to get a reward, so it motivates people to learn and/or perform tasks, in turn building skills and habits. Karl Kapp, author of *The Gamification of Learning and Instruction*, states, "Gamified solutions provide the right mix of engaging elements from games like a sense of progress or immediate feedback and visible signs of improvement over time with content to motivate learners."

Habits are not just for grownups, either. Dr. Alan Kazdin at Yale University has applied habit research and design to children and created a powerful parenting method that can shift even the most difficult and defiant child. Many people try to control children's behavior with punishments, which works against the brain's wiring for habits and rewards. By simply rewarding "good" behaviors, you can create huge shifts in every human, no matter their age. (Parents and teachers, I highly recommend that you look at the resources offered by the Yale Parenting Center.)

19. Harness the Habenula to Learn from Failure

Another powerful brain structure plays a role in how we learn and build new skills and habits: the habenula. Only recently has imaging technology allowed scientists to truly see and study the habenula, which is located deep in the center of our brain, near the thalamus. The habenula is responsible for helping us avoid future failures, so we make better decisions and take better actions, by creating chemical guardrails that moderate our behavior.

Our brain naturally releases dopamine and serotonin, the "feel-good" chemicals, when we do something right. This is part of the brain's reward system. You probably feel it when you accomplish a task or receive praise for a job well done. However, when we make a poor choice that does not lead to a reward, the habenula restricts the flow of those chemicals, cutting off the drip, so to speak, making us feel bad.

The habenula's role is quite important to the survival of our species. In our hunter-gatherer days, it would help us repeat good choices like going back to a trail that led to a food source (reward) and making us uncomfortable about the trail that didn't have food. It's almost like a chemical game of "warmer/colder" guiding us toward and away from good choices.

In our modern world, it still helps us repeat successful behaviors like returning to a restaurant where we had a good meal or approaching a new work project the way you approached your last successful one. Scientists have also discovered that the habenula is hyperactive in people with severe depression, over-restricting their serotonin and dopamine so that they feel bad all the time.

But the habenula does more than help us repeat behaviors that will bring rewards. It also helps us avoid punishment. According to Dr. Okihide Hikosaka, at the National Institutes of Health Laboratory of Sensorimotor Research, "Failing to obtain a reward is disappointing and disheartening, but to be punished may be worse." Studies have shown that the habenula is also very active when we approach a task where we have received a punishment. In fact, it suppresses both our motivation and our physical movements through the sensorimotor cortex of our brain. In other words, it's more difficult to make our body do the behavior. Talk about a double whammy! You can't get excited to do it but even if you managed to psych yourself up, your body won't get on board. If you ever find yourself thinking, *I just can't seem to make myself do it*, you're probably caught in this cycle.

Stress exacerbates this whole process. The body of a person under sustained, uncontrollable stress will produce various immune responses, such as increasing inflammatory chemicals. The body treats the stress as a physical threat and responds like it would to bacteria or virus, such as the flu, including suppressing motivation and motor movements. In other words, you feel tired all the time, with little energy or desire to get things done.

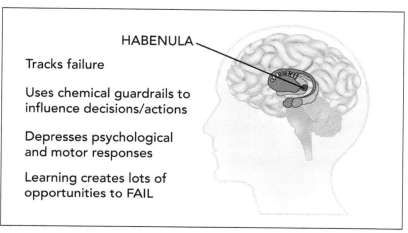

HABENULA

Tracks failure

Uses chemical guardrails to influence decisions/actions

Depresses psychological and motor responses

Learning creates lots of opportunities to FAIL

The habenula tracks our failure to influence future choices

When we're physically sick, this response helps us to get better. It forces us to rest, saving energy so our immune system can overcome the illness and return us to health. But in situations of sustained stress, it creates depression and lethargy that can go on and on.

An unhealthy combination of stress and the habenula's natural function to avoid failure can unintentionally create conditions that lead to "learned helplessness." Psychologist Dr. Martin Seligman, founder of the positive psychology movement, first identified this concept while conducting experiments with dogs that were being classically conditioned by receiving a mild shock, a form of punishment, when they heard a bell. Once that conditioning was in place, he put the dogs in a room where they had freedom to move away from the source of the shock. But what happened? They laid down and gave up.

Seligman's research, and many subsequent studies, have shown that enough negative experiences condition us to expect failure, and we just give up and stop trying. Many psychologists have identified learned helplessness in all kinds of situations: people who cannot leave an abusive relationship, students who no longer try to succeed in a challenging subject, people with health problems who continue to make the same unhealthy choices. In the work setting, learned helplessness can affect people and teams.

If conditions have been bad enough for long enough, change won't necessarily overcome the learned helplessness, either. We reach a point where we just can't motivate ourselves emotionally or physically to try anymore, even when there is a glimmer of hope. Many times, I have seen situations where a good solution has been implemented, like a poor leader is replaced or more resources are provided, but the attitudes of the people involved don't adjust accordingly.

Failure as an adult can also trigger some of our most painful memories of childhood failure and shame. As Dr. Brené Brown, an internationally recognized scholar on the effects of shame, describes in her book *Daring Greatly*, "childhood experiences of shame change who we are, how we think about ourselves, and our sense of self-worth." Most often, children are shamed by parents and teachers when they make mistakes at home and at school.

Sadly, shaming doesn't stop when we grow up. I have seen managers attempt to "motivate" their employees by publicly shaming them. And coworkers may use shaming as a defensive technique when they're feeling vulnerable. Dr. Brown's research goes on to show the profound and negative impacts of shaming in the workplace and how it harms creativity, innovation, collaboration, and productivity. If failure is combined with shame, the negative feelings will completely suppress both the motivation and willingness to try again.

The reality is that failure is part of learning. It's part of how we wire our brains to do new things and how we improve over time. So if it's not okay to fail, then it's not okay to learn. How you treat failure is as much, if not more, important than how you treat learning. I have gone into organizations that claim to have a positive culture that supports learning but whose leaders and managers in reality engage in "shame and blame" techniques whenever an employee makes a mistake. The habenula is going to track that and biologically move people to take few risks and cover up errors. This obviously leads to an organization that it not improving nor innovating. So, what is the antidote to this? It's called psychological safety and we'll cover it next.

20. Create Psychological Safety

Psychological safety was first discovered by Dr. Amy Edmondson, a professor at the Harvard Business School and the author of *Teaming: How Organizations Learn, Innovate, and Compete in the Knowledge Economy*. Dr. Edmondson's research showed that psychological safety is not the mere absence of intimidation or harassment; it's what creates the climate for people to do their best work. She defines it as, "a sense of confidence that the team will not embarrass, reject, or punish someone for speaking up with ideas, questions, concerns, or mistakes. It is a shared belief that the team is safe for interpersonal risk-taking. It describes a team climate characterized by interpersonal trust and mutual respect in which people are comfortable being themselves." You can learn more by watching her TEDx talk or her course on LinkedIn Learning.

The success of any group or organization depends on people's ability to speak up, noting potential roadblocks or threats to their progress. In fact, in Edmondson's study, the highest-performing teams also had the highest reporting rates for errors. This might seem paradoxical but it's the sign of a healthy team. When people feel safe enough to mention their errors it means they are also holding themselves accountable, and the whole group can learn from the experience, which in turn supports their success. In addition, when errors are acknowledged they can be addressed and fixed, rather than ignored so they fester into bigger problems later.

Yet, the reality is that many people stay quiet for fear of being embarrassed, rejected, or punished. One study by VitalSmarts found that 50 percent of employees regularly don't speak their minds at work, to colleagues or managers. And only 1 percent of employees feel "extremely confident" when it comes to voicing their concerns at critical moments. If you review recent headlines, it's likely you will find stories where someone stayed silent with devastating or even fatal consequences. In the investigation following the Columbia Shuttle disaster, it became clear that in NASA's culture employees did not feel comfortable raising concerns to their supervisors (Edmondson features court transcripts in her book *Teaming*). This unhealthy type of environment can be found in workplaces of all kinds, from operating rooms to boardrooms. For this reason, psychological safety is especially important—I would argue crucial—for the success of any organization.

Dr. Edmondson is not the only one touting the critical nature of psychological safety. In a massive global study called Project Aristotle, Google found it to be the key differentiator for high-performing teams. The study explored what distinguishes the best teams from the average and poor, and its results, shared in a *New York Times* article by Charles Duhigg, replicated Edmondson's findings. Psychological safety was more important than any other factor, including the quality or performance level of the individual members. Specifically, they discovered that the best teams did two things: they engaged with each other in a consistent practice of empathy and ensured that every member was heard. This went beyond inviting people to share their thoughts, to actively seeking out every member's contributions. Edmondson calls this behavior "teaming," a different way of engaging, that enables and empowers teams to do their best work.

Signs that indicate a group has psychological safety

Edmondson notes that for successful teaming the leader must actively create psychological safety, because their position of power or status naturally suppresses a group's ability to speak up. Effective leaders take intentional steps to invite opinions, ideas, challenges, and critiques. They do this by publicly acknowledging their own fallibility and emphasizing the need for each person's contributions. They also respond appropriately when people do bring things forward, recognizing the courage it takes to do so. Finally, they celebrate failures as learning, harvesting important lessons to drive future improvements and successes. They embrace the idea that FAIL stands for "First Attempt In Learning."

When training team leaders and managers I emphasize that the ability to create psychological safety is the most important skill they need. Yet most people don't even know what it is, let alone how to create it. And we certainly do not measure or reward teams or their leaders for their efforts in this area. But we should.

It's important to note that psychological safety is not about being universally liked by others or being protected from opinions or beliefs that you find uncomfortable. It's about making sure that people are not penalized for speaking up. Period. People might still disagree, and you or they might find what others say incredibly uncomfortable, but a healthy team welcomes the input and feedback because it might just be the key to success. It's also about respecting and trusting people, which comes from finding value in what they contribute to the group's efforts and feeling able to reliably count on them.

Teaching psychological safety is only the beginning. It's vitally important to then watch for signs that groups are healthy. If you see signs like increased complaints to HR, more sick days and turnover, or decreasing engagement, you must take action quickly. Otherwise, you risk the group becoming paralyzed by learned helplessness, which is difficult to shift once established.

21. Shift from Goals to Problem-Solving

Another way to support behavior change is to shift your focus from goals to problem-solving. According to Dr. Kyra Bobinet, a professor at Stanford University, "Goals are typically outcome-oriented, which means we either succeed in our attempts to achieve them—or we fail. If we 'fail' at something, the habenula kills our incentive to give things another go." Problem-solving works with the reward-seeking part of the brain. As we seek and find a solution, the experience becomes a success, something that works with both the habenula and basal ganglia. Additionally, problem-solving is a type of design thinking, where we tinker and adjust as we experiment, getting better with each iteration.

Consider how most project or change plans are constructed. Most have rigid goals and milestones and rarely, if ever, do they unfold as expected, turning the experience into a series of frustrations and failures. To avoid this, frame each phase as an exercise in problem-solving. This allows people to become active participants and it also helps to shift employees from a fixed mindset to a growth mindset. Stanford psychologist Dr. Carol Dweck's research has examined what differentiates people who succeed from those who don't. She found that people who don't succeed tend to have a fixed mindset, meaning that they believe that their inherent traits or characteristics—such as their IQ (intelligence quotient) or people skills—are set once they reach adulthood. Whereas people with a growth mindset believes that they can always get better, that they can always learn something new, or practice something more, and that studying and effort are the pathways to improvement and even mastery. (We'll learn more about the growth mindset in section IV.)

It's also important to recognize both effort and progress. Recognizing effort is part of fostering a growth mindset, which also creates a culture of learning. The more effort is rewarded, the more likely both the basal ganglia and habenula will respond in ways that assist the person and whatever project they work on. Several studies show that people are the most motivated at work when they feel that they can contribute their strengths and when people acknowledge or value their contributions. The annual performance review is too infrequent and fraught with other issues to be of value; instead I recommend you look for or create other, frequent opportunities to recognize effort.

Marking progress is another part of this process. People do best when they know what is expected of them and can see their progress through the project. This not only helps people stay on track but helps them manage their energy and expectations and feel a sense of accomplishment. By communicating regularly about progress, you empower yourself and others to achieve more.

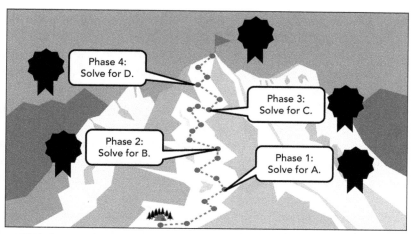

Shift from goals to problem-solving and add rewards for reaching milestones

Also, progress needs to be celebrated! As you and your team cross each milestone, be sure you acknowledge every one. Even if you are behind schedule or over budget, even if it's you alone, you must find ways to mark progress and celebrate or the habenula is likely to code the experience a "failure." This doesn't mean you don't have honest conversations about performance and quality. You must have those too. But too many leaders give too much weight to the constructive and critical feedback and bypass the celebrations because they are busy or behind schedule, leaving the brain with nothing to interpret as reward. Be sure you build in moments that let people know they're making progress even though you're not there yet.

A process from *The Four Disciplines of Execution* by Chris McChesney, Sean Covey, and Jim Huling is one of my favorite ways to ensure that progress is properly measured and recognized. It is very effective for driving all kinds of results. The four disciplines are:

1. **Focus on the wildly important goals.** This is about identifying the goals that will have the most payoff in moving your organization forward and moving them to the top of your priority list.

2. **Act on the lead measures.** Lead measures are the actions that will get the results you're looking for (also known as the lag measure). Losing weight is a lag measure while eating fewer calories and exercising more are lead measures.

3. **Keep a compelling scoreboard.** Use a highly visible scoreboard to constantly track your lead and lag measures, so you can adjust as needed to drive results.

4. **Create a cadence of accountability.** Hold frequent (but short) meetings that focus on assessing progress, identifying new actions to take, and commiting to those actions. The next meeting starts with each person reporting on their commitments.

This highly effective model helps leaders get clear on their metrics of success and "gamifies" them so that employees are both motivated to hit those metrics and take ownership of them. The process includes learning from failures (growth mindset) as well as celebrating successes. Gamification feels good; it rewards and motivates people to learn and/or perform tasks, which can build skills and habits.

Recognition and praise are, of course, rewards but they are not the only ones. Remember, rewards play two vital roles in the neuroscience of change: (1) they help the habenula code an experience as a success, rather than a failure that it will try to avoid, and (2) they help the brain to want to replicate the behavior, because the basal ganglia sees rewards as the third component in the habit loop. All kinds of rewards can work. Rewards do not need to be big or showy, they just need to mark a success and be meaningful to people.

Over the years, I have seen teams create all kinds of rewards. For example, ringing a loud gong when a goal has been hit or earning gold stars or blue chips, which become a symbol of pride. Gift cards are great too (from as little as five dollars to much more). The most successful models seem to have two levels. The first includes small tokens that mark recognition or success, like stars or chips, verbal "shout outs" or electronic kudos. These should be given out abundantly but authentically. The second level includes larger, special prizes that are given to a few who show exemplary performance. The latter requires a nomination and selection process because it's vital that the system feels fair and accurately acknowledge top performers. Again, all of this will be most effective if it reflects what is most meaningful to your people and appropriate for your culture and context.

22. Fire Mirror Neurons with Demonstration

One of the brain's major tools for learning is our mirror neuron system. First discovered in the 1980s by Dr. Giacomo Rizzolatti and other Italian neuroscientists, mirror neurons are a class or type of neuron in the brain that fire or light up when we (1) perform an act that has a specific goal, such as picking up food to feed ourselves or grasping a tool to use it, and (2) feel an emotion. It turns out that the same neurons fire in our brains when we observe someone doing those things, creating an "inner experience" of what we are observing in others.

We can all harness this biological process for observational learning through demonstration. We are a tribal species and we are built to learn by watching others. This is obvious in children—they watch what adults do and then mimic it until they gain the skill themselves. Back in our tribal days, this is how everyone learned critical skills like cooking, hunting, building shelter, and defending attacks from predators. Today, a newly hired employee is a new member of the tribe and they also learn by watching and doing. We used to have industries that leveraged observational learning through an apprentice model. People learned the trade by watching a highly skilled master craftsman, often spending years observing before actually trying and eventually doing. But I have noticed that many organizations, including schools and colleges, don't really use demonstration as a teaching tool. We should. By having top performers demonstrate, train, and teach others, you work with how our body was built to learn.

In addition to observational learning, mirror neurons help us understand each other. UCLA neuroscientist Dr. Marco Iocaboni studies various aspects of social connections and how we communicate our intentions and feelings. He writes, "When I see you smiling, my mirror neurons for smiling fire up, too, initiating a cascade of neural activity that evokes the feeling we typically associate with a smile. I don't need to make any inference on what you are feeling, I experience immediately and effortlessly (in a milder form, of course) what you are experiencing."

This is the basis for empathy: the ability to understand or identify with the perspective, experiences, and motivations of another person and to comprehend and share another person's emotional state. Empathy is different than sympathy, which is caring for the suffering of others but from a separate, more distant place. Sympathy is feeling sorry for you while empathy is feeling your pain with you. You may have experienced this when a colleague has laughed and you found yourself laughing too, or when a friend has cried and you teared up as well. Mirror neurons are also at play when we see someone get hurt or injured and we feel that clench in our belly. Dr. Iocaboni has published groundbreaking work on how reduced mirror neuron activity is observed in people with autism, who often struggle with social interactions and correctly identifying emotions in others. He claims that a deficit in mirror neurons is tied to the regions of the brain affiliated with social engagement, language acquisition, and motor skills, the three major symptoms of autism. You can learn more in his book *Mirroring People: The Science of How We Connect to Others.*

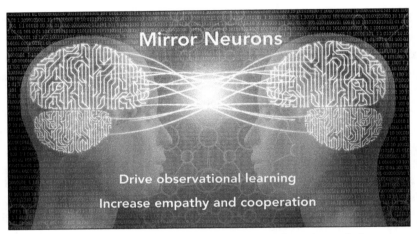

Mirror neurons fire when we watch another person take action or feel emotions

Mirror neurons have profound implications for adult learning. When we work together, we are naturally exposed to each other's feelings, intentions, and actions. Mirror neurons are there, working in the background to help us quickly understand each other. Positive impacts include observational learning and enhanced communication and empathy. Through observation, we can learn from each other, quickening how we gain new skills and competencies. Putting highly skilled members with others could uplevel the group if the right opportunities for observational learning are put in place.

Also importantly, mirror neurons can help teams convey and comprehend emotions, so they experience empathy for each other. Studies have shown that empathy is a core component of creating psychological safety. The downside is that the effect of mirror neurons can also hasten a group's decline. If members are not appropriately skilled, they may learn each other's bad habits. And when members of a group are anxious or disengaged, other members are more likely to join them in those negative states.

Mirror neurons are operating and influencing how we work in pairs and in groups every day. We need to be mindful of the powerful impact of this system and make sure we maximize the benefits and minimize risks. However real their effects may be, researchers are still not exactly sure how the mirror neuron process happens. They are just now discovering what parts of the brain are involved. Different, physically unconnected parts of the brain can be simultaneously involved in complex processes. Perhaps the signals pass via chemicals or electrical pulses; perhaps they transmit invisibly between people, much like radio waves and cell phone signals. There is no doubt that we are only beginning to discover the brain's many mysteries.

And mirror neurons can be effectively combined with repetitions, such as Model Mugging, a self-defense technique taught specifically to women. When the founder, Matt Thomas, learned that women with black belts in karate and other techniques were being attacked and raped, he learned that under the stress of an attack, the women were pulling their punches, like they did in the training room to avoid hurting their partners. What they needed was the opportunity to experience fighting full out, to gain experience managing the adrenaline rush that comes during a real attack. So Model Mugging was born.

I have taken the classes. In a weekend, a group of women can learn techniques that work, especially when attacked by a larger, stronger assailant. The "mugger" wears a full, padded suit and helmet so participants can practice what it feels like to defend themselves in real time and at full, uninhibited strength. They also get to watch other women doing the same. Together, this creates enough repetitions that they can count on the training should they ever need it. It's a life-changing experience and built on the neuroscience principles of behavior change.

23. Empower the Right Kind of Practice

Practice is a vital element in the learning process. Getting better at something takes practice. Period. Sure, you can convey information quickly but the skills that require instruction, the ones that really drive performance and innovation, also require practice. Practice is how we build those neural pathways and turn behaviors into habits because we all gain so much from the *doing* of something.

The challenge is that people are busy. Work is so fast-paced these days, even the most well-meaning learners will struggle to find the time to practice. As a result, it's imperative that we build practice time into our learning events, to both create that safe space for trying and failing and build those desired behaviors and habits so they can be repeated out on the job. And it's really the only way to ensure that things are done correctly, because we can coach and instruct to improve.

Let's explore some practice options:

Have people practice skills as they are learning. Whether using software, giving performance feedback, or managing a project, just trying the behavior a few times is effective and starts creating the repetitions for the habit. It's amazing how much people can accomplish in just a few minutes of focused effort. I've found that as little as 5 or 10 minutes of practice can make a world of difference.

If it's a complex skill or behavior, I break it into segments, have them practice each part separately, and then string them all together. For example, I teach coaching skills to managers and leaders. I have broken a typical coaching session into four separate steps. We spend 2 to 10 minutes on each, talking about how it went after each step. This is a great way to pull out important learning moments and leverage insights across the group. Once we have done all the parts, I give them 30 minutes to do the whole thing as one fluid experience. And of course, have them switch roles so everyone gets a turn being the coach. This strategy can be used for a whole range of behaviors and really helps learners gain both competence and confidence.

You can also pair up learners as practice buddies outside of the learning event. This creates accountability and helps transfer the learning into the real work environment. I have people practice in the room and then assign those partners or groups a couple more sessions that they need to report back on. This also works with people who are geographically dispersed and adds the bonus of helping them build new relationships.

Modelling ideal behavior is powerful. Many of us really benefit from first seeing a behavior done well by an expert; and, of course, this leverages the mirror neuron system and how we learn by observing others. To this end, one of my favorite tools is a video-based peer coaching tool called Practice (go figure), and it's part of the suite of services offered by Bridge. It uses the power of interactive video to demonstrate ideal behaviors as well as create an environment for learners to receive authentic assessment and coaching from both peers and experts. I have seen it create amazing results in several companies like Domino's, Comcast, Bayada Home Health Care, and Cox Automotive.

Another option is to create realistic practice environments. We all have access to low-tech role-plays, which are quite effective. But now technology can create realistic virtual scenarios, also known as immersive training simulators, that replicate the realities of the job in a safe situation. For example, one large hotel chain wanted to help their front desk staff learn to deal with various scenarios. They created virtual lobbies and had various avatar "customers" walk up to the front counter, giving the employees a powerful and realistic experience with handling various requests and attitudes. This is just one type of the new extended reality (XR) options that exist for training.

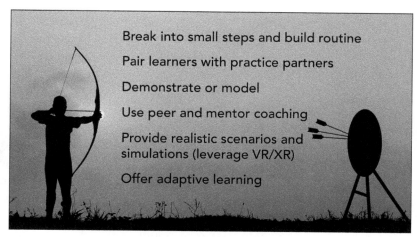

Break into small steps and build routine

Pair learners with practice partners

Demonstrate or model

Use peer and mentor coaching

Provide realistic scenarios and simulations (leverage VR/XR)

Offer adaptive learning

There are many ways to leverage the power of practice

You can also create scenarios that are completely responsive in real time. People can animate the computer avatars, making the interaction spontaneous and authentic. These sessions can be recorded and reviewed, allowing employees and coaches to gain important insights. Check out companies like Mursion, Cubic, Strivr, and Academy925. Since the graphics are so realistic, the brain and body get a very "real" experience of practice that activates the same neural pathways.

Another amazing option is to use adaptive learning. Companies like Amplifire and Area9 Innovation can create learning solutions that are unique to each and every person, meeting their skill level at the starting point and then progressing on pace with that individual. They include features to practice in safe but realistic scenarios. For example, it's vital that health care workers stay up on the latest information and skills. They can practice in realistic hospital room scenarios, analyzing data from machines and charts in the room, observing or interacting with the patient, and offering a diagnosis.

Real simulations are also incredibly powerful and should be used whenever possible. Most medical professions have opportunities for practice on dummy patients before moving to live humans. Car mechanics take apart and fix many real training cars before they are certified to work on a customer's property. One incredible example is the Shell Robert Training and Conference Center in Louisiana. Shell Oil uses this multimillion-dollar facility to train their oil rig workers, fully emulating life off-shore. Learners live onsite for two weeks, working the same schedule, eating the same food, and operating the same machinery. They are taken through full immersion experiences in problems and emergencies. As learning expert Elliott Masie puts it, "Most of the learning is done in experiential lab mode, giving learners rigor, challenges, and the ability to 'fail their way to success' in the simulations. This reinforced my belief that we should add a deeper set of immersive experiences to all of our learning models—both face-to-face and online."

Now, virtual reality is giving us more affordable and scalable options to create lifelike simulations that can be used for a whole host of training applications. Companies like Pixvana and SilVR Thread can film real work environments featuring top performers doing tasks correctly. Then learners can use an affordable VR headset to gain a real, embodied memory of the location and the skill. This is accelerating learning and also creating a psychologically safe environment in which to try, fail, and improve. These are just a few examples of innovative learning solutions that support practice. And more are being developed all the time.

Practice is also the path to mastery. Mastery can take hundreds or thousands of repetitions. In fact, Dr. Anders Ericsson, author of *Peak: Secrets from the New Science of Expertise*, conducted research on what it takes to develop expertise by studying hundreds of peak performers from a variety of fields. He is the one who coined the idea of the "10,000 hours" needed to master tasks that Malcolm Gladwell explored in his book *Outliers*. But Ericsson's research shows that it's not just putting in hours that creates mastery but rather the right kind of practice. He identified three levels:

1. **Naive or mindless practice** has no specific goals or feedback; it is just blindly trying and hoping.
2. **Purposeful practice** has well-defined goals and clear targets, a plan of small steps to accomplish those goals, internal feedback to know when you're off track, and constant and maximum effort outside of current comfort zone.
3. **Deliberate practice** is purposeful practice informed by the guidance of an expert teacher who provides feedback that increasingly leads to the development of internal self-monitoring.

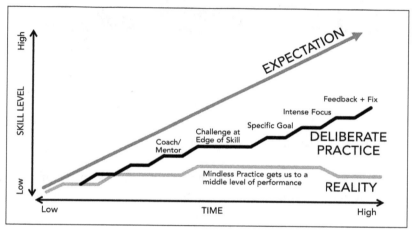

Mindless practice versus deliberate practice

So, the ideal combination to speed up the road to mastery is practice plus coaching, because feedback allows us to benchmark our skill level and make the necessary adjustments to improve. According to Ericsson, "The right sort of practice carried out over a sufficient period of time leads to improvement. Nothing else."

He also found that most of us use purposeful or deliberate practice at the beginning of learning something new but once we hit a sufficient level of skill, we shift into mindless practice, meaning we are repeating the behavior but no longer actually improving. Be cautious of this, however, as we can lull ourselves into a false sense of competence because, in our minds, we are repeating the behavior and therefore "practicing"—but without clear goals, hard/uncomfortable work, and feedback, we have stalled out.

Obviously, we don't all need to achieve expert status with every skill but it's important to understand this model so that you can make an intentional choice about how and when you want to grow by leveraging different kinds of practice.

24. Grow Your Doing Skills

So, the key components of the Do phase are habits, repetitions, rewards, and practice. You'll notice that all three phases now sit within the container of psychological safety.

The Do phase of the Three Phase Model of Learning

Here are tips and strategies you can use to grow your "Do-ing" skills.

1. Explore ways to get into the state of flow for as many of your life commitments as you can. Find that balance of skill to challenge, so you feel like you're growing without being too stressed or bored.

2. Consider your current skills and habits and those you want to develop. Get clear about what you need to build so you can set better goals and proactively support your transition.

3. Identify the cue, routine, and reward already in place and then intentionally design the shift you want to see. Use a compelling reward for the first few weeks, until the habit is established.

4. Pay attention to repetitions, knowing that you need 40 to 50 to groove a habit. Quality matters, so get the right coaching or training to make sure you're practicing the correct actions.

5. Counterbalance the habenula's effects by recognizing progress and celebrating accomplishments. Leverage tools like star charts and smart phone apps to keep you moving forward in positive ways.

6. Find the right kind of support. Look for experts you can observe and/or receive coaching from. And be sure to pay attention to how psychologically safe an environment feels. It's a must-have for great learning.

7. Do the right kind of practice. Intentionally choose purposeful or deliberate practice so that you can maximize your learning and change your behavior. That's the only way to get the results you want to see.

Your Learning Journey

At the end of each section, take the opportunity to apply the concepts to your own life and the thing you want to learn. Use these questions to help you identify possible strategies to support your learning goal.

- How could you design a learning experience that's the right challenge-to-skills balance, so you can find your state of flow?
- Look at the thing you want to learn as a habit. What are a couple potential cues? How can you break your routine into small, doable steps? What are some possible and meaningful rewards you could give yourself each time you complete the routine?
- How will you build up to 40 to 50 repetitions? Try creating a timeline to ensure you fully develop the habit.
- How good do you want to get at this thing you want to learn? Will naive or mindless practice be sufficient or will you need to engage in deliberate practice by setting challenge goals, getting coaching, and responding to feedback?

LEARN:
WHERE IT ALL STARTS

"If you're not learning, you're not reaching your potential."

Jim Rohn, author,
7 Strategies for Wealth & Happiness: Power Ideas from America's Foremost Business Philosopher

25. Learning versus Adult Learning

Now that we have laid the foundation for the Three-Phase Model of Learning, getting clear on the different types of memories (Remember) and how to drive behavior change (Do), we can turn our attention to the first phase of the model: Learn. The focus here will be the senses, breaking learning into segments, leveraging story and demonstration, as well as the power of priming for learning.

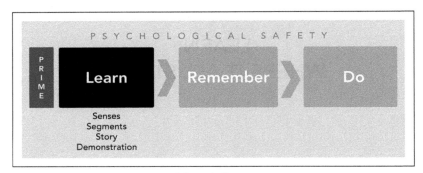

Phase 1: Learn

Learning happens when we acquire information and experiences that shift us in some way. According to Dr. Eric Kandel, Nobel Prize winner and author of *Principles of Neuroscience,* "Learning is the process by which we acquire knowledge about the world while memory is the process by which that knowledge of the world is encoded, stored, and later retrieved." As we learn, the brain converts our sensory perceptions into meaningful representations through a complex system of electrical and chemical reactions.

As we discovered in section II, there are nine types of memory: every aspect of learning starts with sensory and working memory; then, depending on the kind of memory, processes through different parts of the brain. This section mainly focuses on four types of long-term memory: semantic (facts and concepts), episodic (experiential), procedural (skills and habits), and priming

As a species, we learn every day. Our learning ranges from the simple to the complex and from the irrelevant to the deeply impactful. The purpose of learning also varies, from the primal need to survive to fulfilling educational requirements for school. And from following our interests to developing our professional skills in order to be better at our current jobs or more marketable for a new one in this ever-changing world.

We go from one state of knowing or understanding to a different state. Sometimes learning is intentional, like taking a class or reading a book—we knowingly want to shift our understanding or skill and engage in a learning activity to do so. Some learning is accidental, like discovering that you have an allergic reaction when you eat eggplant. And some learning is experiential, like stumbling upon a new coffeeshop when you're out for a walk or figuring out a unique way to do your work more effectively.

Learning actually starts in utero. As mentioned in section II, several studies have shown that fetuses as young as 30 weeks are learning about language and have memories for sounds and sensations. We are born with 100 million neurons and our brains quickly develop neural connections (synapses) as we experience the world. In fact, by age two, we have 50 percent more synapses than we'll have as adults because we are processing massive volumes of information. By the time we enter first grade, synaptic formation levels out and stays relatively stable through young adulthood.

We do an extraordinary amount of learning, both in and out of the classroom. As working adults, we continue to learn, with professional development a vital part of how we improve and grow in our careers. We learn all the way until we take our last breath. Many health care and spiritual workers who support people through the dying process say that some of our most profound learning happens at the very end of our lives.

With the landscape of human learning so broad and deep, for the purpose of this book, this section focuses on adult learning and professional development. But the principles easily apply to a variety of settings and ages. For educators of children and young adults, I'd encourage you to explore the conferences hosted by Learning and the Brain as well as books like *How the Brain Learns* by David Sousa, *Make it Stick* by Peter Brown, *Why We Learn* by Benedict Carey, and *The Whole-Brain Child* by Daniel Siegel.

Adult Learning Defined

Before we jump into the specifics, let's first examine how adults learn. Alexander Kapp, an important theorist of adult learning from Germany, created the concept of *andragogy*, how adults learn, in contrast with *pedagogy*, how children learn. Malcolm Knowles, an American educator, built upon Kapp's work and helped to integrate it into the humanistic learning theory, developed by luminaries such as Abraham Maslow and Carl Rogers, which first described learning as a means to fulfilling potential.

Knowles identified five key assumptions of adult learners that make their learning different from children:

1. As we grow, we become more independent from our families of origin. This allows us to become self-directed in what we learn and gives us our unique self-concept.

2. As we live longer, we accumulate an ever-growing base of knowledge and experience, which becomes a resource for learning. For example, you may have an "aha!" moment today that connects to something you read five years ago or something that happened in your last job.

3. As independent adults we have many responsibilities, and this actually increases our readiness to learn because we are seeking to solve real-life challenges. This makes learning much more salient for us.

4. Our orientation similarly shifts to finding solutions to our day-to-day problems rather than the more abstract learning we did as children. When we seek learning as adults, it's often to solve a current problem.

5. Our motivation to learn becomes internalized. While we are born learners, the structure and pressure of school often casts learning as a duty or responsibility. Being forced to learn every day according to a school district's plans often diminishes our love of learning. As adults we can reclaim that internal motivation and learn something simply because it interests us.

These assumptions led Knowles to identify some key principles for working with adult learners, which guide today's learning designers:

- Learning materials should honor the wide range of backgrounds and experiences that learners bring with them, and be designed to work for different skill levels, learning preferences, modalities, etc.
- Learning should allow learners to discover things for themselves through self-directed experiences. And, making mistakes should be considered an important part of the learning process.
- Learning should be contextualized for how the learner will actually apply the information to their lives, including understanding the "why" behind what is being taught.

Frankly, this list works for children too, but I'm sorry to say it's often not applied in many school systems, at least in the United States. Good teachers seek to create engaging and empowering environments but are challenged by the sheer size of their classes, coupled with rigid and impersonal goals from district, state, and federal agencies. Many alternative school systems for children do seek to empower independent learning, most notably the Montessori and Waldorf systems. In my opinion, if we truly focused on learning in our schools, rather than education, we would better prepare people to become the thoughtful citizens, leaders, and parents that we want them to be.

In the next three chapters, we will focus on some relevant learning theories that work together to create a cohesive approach to adult learning.

26. Levels of Knowledge and Cycle of Learning

Bloom's taxonomy of knowledge is another theory related to the Learn phase. This model has stood the test of time because it tapped into neuroscience principles before we really knew what they were. Dr. Benjamin Bloom discovered that all knowledge is not the same, and that different levels of knowledge mean different levels of learning too.

The most basic level is memorization: rote repetition of what is told to you. For example, a child can recite, "Two plus two equals four" without knowing what it means. The next level up is comprehension or understanding. ("I am doing addition here. I can add three plus five to get eight.") The next level up is application, where you take what you learned into a new context. In this case, you would take math and use it in real life. ("I'm going to use addition and subtraction to calculate whether I have enough money to go to the movies and buy a popcorn.") These first three levels are often the hallmarks of kindergarten through grade 12 education and work with all subjects. For example, you can memorize history, you can truly comprehend the forces that led to different historical events, and you can apply that knowledge to current events. Students can experience all of these levels through assignments like papers or tests.

The next three levels—called higher-order thinking—are the hallmarks of higher education and professional learning. You're taking that base knowledge and doing something new with it. Some people rank these levels, but I believe they are equally complex so I put them on the same plane. Analysis is where you take something apart. For example, using math, in this case statistical calculations, to analyze a host of data. Or looking at your recent months of business to analyze your top-selling products and figure out where your customers live. Evaluation requires you to judge something using some specific criteria. For example, you could evaluate your business using key performance indicators (KPIs) like customer satisfaction, profitability, and environmental impact. Finally, we have creativity, which is taking information and doing something completely new with it. You might take what you learned about production processes and reengineer them. Or you might innovate a new way of leading or providing a service.

The following table shows the six levels of Bloom's taxonomy and how the higher-order thinking skills of analysis, evaluation, and creativity rest upon a bedrock of memorization, comprehension, and application. It also shows common actions affiliated with each level.

Evaluate which explicit levels of Bloom's taxonomy you need for your learning goal. Most working adults need learning experiences that address all six levels to provide them with a robust set of skills. But sometimes it's challenging to work through them quickly, so you may choose to focus on one or two per learning event and then build up over time.

Table 3. *Bloom's taxonomy of knowledge*

CREATION	EVALUATION	ANALYZATION
Produce or imagine new or original work; create something new. *Actions: Design, Invent, Produce, Construct, Compose, Formulate, Develop, Author*	Critically assess or judge the value of something based on specific standards. *Actions: Evaluate, Judge, Test, Assess, Critique, Justify, Rank, Recommend*	Identify the component parts of something and explore relationships. *Actions: Analyze, Compare, Contrast, Organize, Experiment, Examine, Authenticate*
APPLICATION Select, transfer, and use information, ideas, and principles in new situations with a minimum of direction. *Actions: Apply, Use, Demonstrate, Solve, Execute, Operate, Illustrate, Implement*		
COMPREHENSION Understand, explain, or interpret information, ideas, or principles based on prior learning. *Actions: Explain, Summarize, Illustrate, Exemplify, Paraphrase, Discuss, Classify*		
MEMORIZATION Remember or recognize information, ideas, and principles in the approximate form in which they were learned. *Actions: Define, Describe, Recognize, Identify, Write, Label*		

Let's look at an example of how to use Bloom's levels to maximize professional learning. I have designed a six-session manager training based on brain science. It gives managers the ability to leverage human biology to create better employees and teams. When I built it, I made sure that I utilized elements from Bloom's various levels.

I begin each session by giving managers various conceptual models for that specific topic, such as coaching, emotional intelligence, or creating accounability. I then have them apply those models to their employees, so that it fits their current context. They analyze their team using specific assessments, which gives them hard data to track over time. They evaluate their challenges and implement solutions. This is where creativity comes in. Perhaps the model isn't an exact fit for their context. Maybe they need to tweak it or combine two models to make it work better or to make something really unique and effective. The ability to innovate and think creatively are essential here, as are the skills to help others do the same.

The Learning Cycle

Created by Dr. David Kolb in 1984, Kolb's learning cycle maps learning against two continuums. First, you have the axis of perception that ranges from conceptual or abstract on one end to concrete experience on the other. The second axis is the processing continuum, which ranges from observing someone else to doing it yourself.

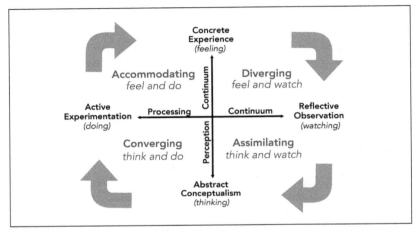

Kolb's cycle of learning

Kolb identified that good learning actually takes the learner through all four quadrants. You can jump in at any point on the model but then mindfully take the learner through the entire cycle and the intersections of the perception and process continuums.

If we revisit my example from the previous section on teaching change management, learning about models of change is on the abstract-conceptual end of the perception continuum, while applying them to a project or team is on the opposite, concrete-experience end. As leaders roll out a change, they might reflect and observe how it's going, perhaps doing some analysis and, if it's not unfolding smoothly, actively experiment with new solutions. Finally, evaluating the ROI or "return on investment" of the change gets back to abstract again, so the learner has had the opportunity to move through all of the quadrants.

Clearly, Bloom and Kolb's models have some overlap between them as well. And when research done at different times by different people lines up, I pay attention. As we continue with the Three-Phase Model of Learning, you will see that both Bloom and Kolb tapped into the neuroscience of learning and how our brains and bodies are wired to learn through doing.

27. Multiple Intelligences and Growth Mindset

A third component of adult learning is the theory of multiple intelligences, proposed by Harvard professor Dr. Howard Gardner in the 1980s. As we explored in chapter 2, one of the new developments in the neuroscience of learning is the neural proof of the eight intelligences: linguistic, logical-mathematical, musical, bodily-kinesthetic, special, intrapersonal, interpersonal, and naturalist.

So how does this relate to adult learning? First, it means that many of your beliefs about your own intelligence, abilities, and limitations are perhaps incorrect and that you have far more potential than you were perhaps led to believe. Second, it can help you now find ways to honor and cultivate your various intelligences. If you embrace that you are smart in a range of ways, it can help you seek out learning experiences and teachers who can best support and guide you. Third, it can help you appreciate and value different strengths that people bring to our professional and personal lives. Every person has unique gifts and talents and yet we are often judged by a narrow and static set of criteria. What if you started to look for and acknowledge these gifts in others? Perhaps you might help them thrive and grow—and they are likely to do the same for you. Fourth, you can create learning experiences for others that honor and support different intelligences. This is especially true for parents, educators and trainers. Consider how you could frame an activity or deliver information in ways that align with different intelligences.

I think it's also important to realize that people may have not had the best experience in school and often come to adult learning events with both skepticism and cynicism. I consider us all a little bit scarred by school and that adult learning has the opportunity to revive our natural curiosity, and our desire to learn and grow.

Growth Mindset

First identified by Dr. Carol Dweck, author of *Mindset: The New Psychology of Success*, mindset is a way we see our abilities. As we learned in chapter 21, Dweck's research at Stanford found that people who don't succeed tend to have a fixed mindset. In essence, they believe that their inherent traits or characteristics—such as their IQ or people skills—are set once they reach adulthood. Whereas successful people have a growth mindset, believing that they can always get better.

The growth mindset yields all kinds of other benefits too. Look at this comparison of how mindset influences everything, from how we view effort, challenges, and feedback to the success of others.

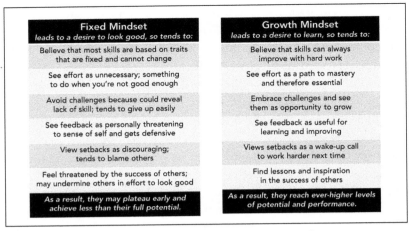

A comparison of the two mindsets at work.

While people with the growth mindset achieve ever-higher levels of potential and performance, the organizations they work for reap those benefits. Keep in mind that the growth mindset is actually the truth of human nature, as the brain naturally exhibits neuroplasticity and neurogenesis. It's a challenge to get folks holding a fixed mindset to shift their worldview and align with their potential, but the good news is that people can. Especially if they are exposed to this information on the different mindsets and the research proving our brains are ever-growing and changing structures.

It also matters how we talk to people about their learning. A study of high school students by Dr. Ruth Butler, a professor of educational psychology, broke participants into two groups and gave them all an exam split into two parts: questions 1 to 5 and questions 6 to 10. Remember the traditional bell-curve test-taking model from school, which compared your performance to the class and assigned rank relative to the highest and lowest scores? In this particular study, the first group was told that their whole test would be compared to the group. When asked to speculate why, students described the purpose of relative grading as, "To show how good you are." See what their speculation revealed there? Comparisons activate the fixed mindset.

The second group was given different information: They were told they would be taking the same exam in two parts but that they would be compared to themselves. In other words, their performance on questions 1 to 5 would be compared to how they individually did on questions 6 to 10. When asked to suggest what the purpose might be, the students said, "To show improvement," which is essentially the growth mindset of getting better.

The results were fascinating. On the first part of the exam, questions 1 to 5, both groups did about the same. Their scores were statistically identical. Then something remarkable happened on the second part: the students who were compared to the others in the group did about the same as the first part. There was no noticeable improvement. But guess what happened to the group that was told that improvement mattered? Their performance improved! And not by a little, by a lot.

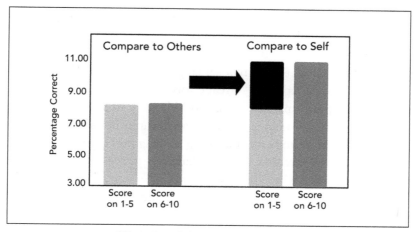

The value of measuring improvement

In this diagram, the dark zone shows the growth mindset. When people are told that growth matters, they step up and they improve. To me, that black box means potential. Those students had unrealized ability in their knowledge of the material. And it wasn't more studying that brought it out, but rather the motivation that comes from knowing that improvement matters.

We know the same dynamic applies to performance evaluations in the workplace. A lot of organizations are rethinking their performance review processes, moving away from ratings, and instead focusing on growth and improvement. When we rate people in any setting as "average," "excellent," or "poor," we essentially replicate the fixed mindset and say, *You are what you are*. But when we move to evaluating growth and improvement, we activate motivation and ultimately potential, saying, *You are what you reach for*.

In my consulting work, I have helped some global companies shift their performance reviews to create a growth mindset. An employee who is struggling to meet goals will receive the message "not yet" rather than being "poor" or "below expectations." For example, "not meeting expectations" becomes "not *yet* meeting expectations." That shift signifies so much: it says that the person has potential and the organization has faith that they can improve. We are finding that this positive, aspirational expectation is far more likely to motivate an employee than being labelled substandard.

We can also do this with children. As a parent, Po Bronson and Ashley Merryman's book *NurtureShock: New Thinking about Children* changed my world, showing me how we can cultivate mindsets in our children by how we parent and teach them. Take the typical example of a child bringing home a good grade. Complimenting them based on traits—"Honey, you are so smart"—instills a fixed mindset, while complimenting them for their improvement and effort—"Honey, you worked really hard on that and look how it paid off"—instills a growth mindset.

Dweck herself warns that one of the biggest mistakes parents and teachers make is to use growth mindset language to reward effort even when learning has not happened, as in "Great effort. You tried your best." Or to use mindset to hide a performance or skill gap, "He has a fixed mindset." Instead, the focus should be on helping students and employees see that they need a range of skill sets to improve, including making an effort, following their curiosity, the ability to try new things, willingness to seek input or help from others, and persistence when things are hard.

Dweck offers some clear examples of using growth mindset language with children. We can make sure that teachers and parents are using the right language, and we can also help children and adults reword how they talk to themselves, switching from fixed mindset to growth. (See Table 4.)

Table 4. *Comparing adult comments and self-talk for both mindsets*

Adult Comments that Cultivate Fixed Mindset	Adult Comments that Cultivate Growth Mindset
Not everybody is good at math. Just do your best.	That feeling of math being hard is the feeling of your brain growing.
That's okay. Maybe math is not one of your strengths.	If you catch yourself saying, "I'm not a math person" just add the word "yet" to the end of the sentence.
Don't worry. You tried your best.	The point isn't to get it all right away. The point is to grow your understanding step by step. What can you try next?

Self-Talk that Cultivates Fixed Mindset	Self-Talk that Cultivates Growth Mindset
This is too hard.	Maybe I can try this another way.
I can't do math.	If I practice, I can grow my math brain.
I made a mistake.	I will learn from my mistakes and do better.
I give up.	Giving up will only make it harder. I'll try again.
I am awesome at this!	Since I am so awesome at this, I should give myself a challenge.

But does it really matter if we activate the growth mindset? Yes, because it's tied to a whole host of other important issues. In 2018, Dweck conducted several more studies exploring the impact that fixed and growth mindset has on our ability to develop our interests and passions. The results showed that people with fixed mindsets were likely to believe that interests and passions are discovered (rather than developed) and also did not anticipate possible difficulties, so their motivation decreased when they hit challenges. Dweck states, "Urging people to find their passion may lead them to put all their eggs in one basket but then to drop that basket when it becomes difficult to carry."

An article in *Harvard Business Review* by Dweck and coauthors Paul O'Keefe and Greg Walton generalizes this finding to today's workplace: "Innovation requires both reaching across fields and, often, acquiring more than a surface-level understanding of those fields. This means that when people reach across fields, they must maintain that interest even when the material becomes complex and challenging. A growth mindset of interest may help promote this kind of resilience."

How do you promote growth mindset when people might have to compete with each other? After all, not everyone can get straight A's in school or be the best employee at work. While it might be true that rewards are limited to top performers and that some organizations need to control access to certain rewards, leaders can also use a process in which rewards are proportionately distributed, and growth and improvement are measured along with performance. These and similar changes are revolutionizing today's work environments.

The evidence on growth mindset is so compelling that Satya Nadella, the CEO of Microsoft, has focused on bringing growth mindset principles to every level of the organization and its products. *Forbes* credits this culture overhaul for tripling the company's value, according to a 2018 feature article. "Nadella made lifelong learning a priority at Microsoft—it's even highlighted on employee badges. The focus shifted from 'Know it all to learn it all.'" To help reinforce the culture, Nadella models growth mindset practices, including sharing his own learning in monthly videos.

As you manage your personal learning goals, remember the mantra of the growth mindset: *yet*. Adding yet is often the simplest way to change from fixed to growth mindset. Some examples would be *I don't know how to do it yet.* Or, *I'm not good at it* yet, *but I can be.* So, let's embrace the power of yet, and figure out where you want to go with the things you want to learn.

28. The Cycle of Renewal

Another aspect of adult learning is the vital role it plays in what Dr. Frederic Hudson calls "the cycle of renewal." In his book, *The Adult Years: Mastering the Art of Self-Renewal*, Hudson says that adults move through a series of life chapters that begin with dreams and plans, move to achievements and accomplishments, and then begin to decline, creating feelings of discord. As a life chapter ends, we move into what he terms a life transition, a time of internal renewal. At first, we focus on healing or recovering from the chapter, but then we start to set new goals and find a renewed sense of purpose. This cycle spans our personal and working lives, our years in retirement, and continues until we die.

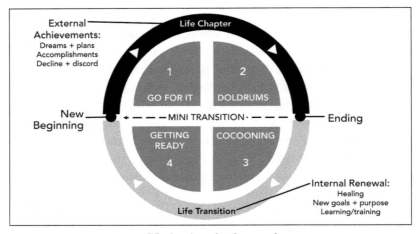

Hudson's cycle of renewal

Life chapters are about "doing" and life transitions are about "being." Each is broken into two phases, making four in total. In the life chapter, Phase 1 is the "go for it" phase where we launch into a new adventure. This is a time of stability, where we feel a sense of purpose, and where we are focused and accomplishing our goals. This is often when we achieve something we have longed for, so it can often feel like we have really arrived. It's generally a very creative time, that feels fearless and even joyful. But at some point, we hit a plateau of some kind and that moves us into Phase 2.

Phase 2 is called "the doldrums" because we feel some level of disenchantment after our major achievement. Perhaps it didn't bring some of the things we thought it would, or now that it has been achieved, it doesn't feel as compelling. It's common to feel disappointment, stress, and even anger depending on the situation. Hudson argues that at this phase, we take one of two paths. We may enter a mini-transition, where we try and retool or restructure our current chapter. Here, people often turn to learning, as they arm themselves with new skills or information to make the mini-transition work. This is all about trying to improve what you have already launched and, for many, it can usher in a new "go for it" phase that brings renewed purpose and joy. Or, we may create an exit strategy so the chapter ends and we can move into the life transition and a state of "being."

Phase 3 of the model is "cocooning," a time of reflection and introspection. This period can feel a little scary as it requires both letting go of the old plan, and patience while you wait for the new vision to emerge. Many people engage learning here for personal growth and development, perhaps going on retreats or taking classes that support their healing, contemplation, and rebirth. Many also turn to spiritual and mindfulness practices in this phase as well.

At some point, the inner work has paid off and people experience a turning point, where they begin to have a new vision. Phase 4 is the "getting ready" phase, as you prepare for the next chapter. It's a time for exploring and experimenting while cultivating new ways of thinking, being, and doing. You experience a new acceptance of self, including strengths and vulnerabilities. This phase can also include a time of learning in order to get ready for the launch of the next chapter.

Another way to look at the model is to think of the left side as phases of construction, where you rebuild yourself and your life, and the right side as phases of deconstruction, where you take apart your life and self-identity in preparation for reforming them again. It's a bit like caterpillar to butterfly, except we get to return to our cocoon state and reemerge in a new flight of transformation.

As creativity and leadership consultant Lisa Slavid puts it, "It's important to respect where you are in the cycle as each phase meets various needs, like reflecting, exploring, producing, etc. Many people can feel stuck in the 'doldrums' phase and it's typically a good time to seek support as you move through the reflecting, talking, and even grieving that are common to this phase."

Hudson founded the Hudson Institute, which offers model-based coaching certifications and courses designed to help people move through the phases. He also coauthored *LifeLaunch: A Passionate Guide to the Rest of Your Life* with Pamela McLean, which is filled with tips and strategies any adult will find helpful.

I find Hudson's model useful because it helps me know that life is not an endless staircase, forever moving upward, only getting better. It's normal to have periods where you're unclear about what you want next, interspersed with periods when you achieve a dream, and then again when you feel disappointment afterward. Understanding this has made me much more comfortable and able to embrace the natural cycles of human growth and development. As someone who supports others in their learning, it helps me better design learning to match a person's current cycle. It's also clear to me that organizations go through similar cycles, regardless of the industry or sector. A big part of organizational development is supporting leaders and employees effectively through the natural rises and slumps that occur over time.

29. Learning and the Brain

The human brain is a fascinating and incredibly complex organ. In fact, sitting on your shoulders is the most complex object in the known universe. Dr. Floyd Bloom, a neuroscientist and psychopharmacologist at the Scripps Institute suggests that its best to not consider the brain as a single organ but rather a complex assembly of neural systems that regulate each other through chemical and electrical signals.

Your brain contains approximately 100 billion neurons, made up of 10,000 different types. Each neuron communicates with 5,000 to 200,000 other neurons, leading to a rough total of 100 trillion neural connections. That is, 300 times more connections in your brain than there are stars in the Milky Way Galaxy.

The big takeaway? Wear a helmet. Seriously. If you take away nothing else, know that your head is where everything starts and ends—your personality, your sense of self, and the ability to control every other aspect of your body. So, do everything you can to protect it from injury.

A key discovery in brain science is that the brain is incredibly flexible, growing over our lifetimes. Studies are showing that this is not only part of the healing process but also occurs during learning. Scientists have seen that when we are actively learning the hippocampus creates new neurons. The authors of *Make it Stick: The Science of Successful Learning* state, "The rise in neurogenesis starts before the new learning activity is undertaken, suggesting the brain's intention to learn, and continues for a period after the learning activity, suggesting that neurogenesis plays a role in the consolidation of memory...."

For example, if you decided or were told that you are bad at math or not good with people, brain scientists would tell you that it's not true. While you may not have well-developed neural pathways in those areas, you can absolutely change them by starting to use them and developing them. And here's a critical component of brain health: We must treat our brain much like we treat our muscular body. We can challenge it to try new things and, as we practice those new things, we will get better and stronger. Scientists can now actually see and measure how these cells thicken with use. The more a neuron or neural pathway is used, the stronger it becomes, much like our bicep muscle does when we work out. And this encompasses all learning, both cognitive and behavioral.

The important implication here is that what we think and do matters. With every choice we make, we are strengthening neural pathways. We can strengthen the pathways of happiness and joy or that of judgment and frustration. We can strengthen healthy actions like exercise, play, and mind-fulness, rather than reinforcing mindless eating, distraction, and overwork.

Positive psychologists have discovered that things we used to assume were personality traits, like happiness and resilience, are actually just neural pathways that any of us can develop. To learn more, check out the research and books by Dr. Rick Hanson (*Hardwiring Happiness*), Dr. Brené Brown (*Rising Strong*), and Shawn Achor (*The Happiness Advantage*) to name a few.

Important Brain Structures and Systems

When we learn, visible changes take place in the brain. In fact, some researchers want to *define* learning as an event that creates a physical change in the brain. But as we know from previous chapters, learning involves several brain structures and systems. Here's a quick review:

- **Hippocampus:** The brain region that plays an important role in memory and spatial navigation. It's located in the center of our skull and has prongs that extend into both the left and right hemispheres, essentially uniting the brain. It has at least 27 different types of neurons and performs several critical functions including moving what we learn into memory. In fact, people with damaged hippocampi cannot form new memories.

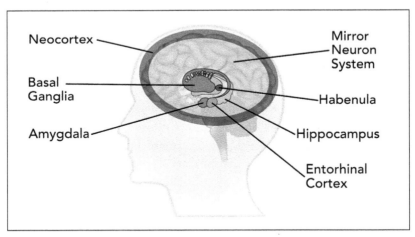

Key brain structures and systems involved in learning

- **Amygdala:** Physically attached to the hippocampus and most recognized for its role in our survival through the fight-flight-freeze response. All of our major sensory nerves—optical, aural, olfactory—feed directly into the amygdala. Associative memories are formed when the amygdala is aroused with strong emotions like fear, and the information is immediately moved to long-term memory to aid in future survival.

- **Entorhinal cortex:** This sits within the hippocampus and works as our internal global positioning system (GPS), helping us place memories in both space and time. It creates 3-D mental maps of places we live and work as we navigate our physical surroundings. In addition, it helps us map social networks by tracking the power levels of the people we interact with along with our affinity for each person. As we covered in section II, (semantic) memory champions activate this structure using the Loci of Memory, which ties memorization of content to physical spaces.

- **Neocortex:** The outer and very intricate layer of the brain. It is the seat of our consciousness, and is also organized into regions that perform very specific functions. For example, decision-making and planning are at the front while motor control is at the sides, by our ears. Visual processing sits at the back of the head, and there are two specific regions that handle language on the left side. The neocortex is involved with taking in learning and also storing the web of detailed long-term memories that we access later through recall.

- **Mirror neurons:** A type of neuron that fires or lights up for emotion and when we perform an act that has a specific goal. When we observe someone else, our own mirror neurons fire, creating an "inner experience" of what we see. Mirror neurons drive observational learning and are also the grounding for empathy and compassion.

- **Basal ganglia:** Responsible for creating procedural memories that involve skills and/or habits. It takes common, routine behaviors and turns them into automatic behaviors that use very little cognitive energy. Anything you do that used to take a lot of effort or focus but is now second nature—for example, driving your car or using a new smart phone—is evidence of the basal ganglia's role. Skills contain many habits and some habits are also skills.

- **Habenula:** Responsible for helping us learn from previous experiences, particularly failures and mistakes. It is located deep in the center of our brain near the thalamus and uses neurotransmitter chemicals to influence our future decisions and behaviors. When activated it can suppress motivation to act as well as sensorimotor actions.

- **Other key players in the learning process:** Neurons (cells that communicate through electrical and chemical signals) and the neural pathways (a series of neurons linked together for a specific activity or thought) they create. These communications occur at the end of their tendril-like extensions throughout our body, called synapses, which are involved with every human function from thinking and feeling to moving and sleeping.

While we know that the brain is highly networked, studies consistently show that these structures do the heavy lifting in how humans learn. At least, that is what we know as of today.

30. To Learn, You Must First Encode

Several brain structures participate in the encoding process. Learning starts with our senses—we take in information and experiences through the five senses. Four of them have nerves in the head that attach directly to the amygdala, which is connected to the hippocampus. As we process what we see, hear, taste, smell, and touch, the neocortex is activated with specific regions assigned to each sense. For example, visual data comes through the retina but is processed at the primary visual cortex on the back of the head. Auditory data is processed on the left side of the brain with regions dedicated to sounds and language.

The quality of the input matters, so if the incoming data (visual, auditory, kinesthetic, etc.) is impaired in some way, the brain has less to work with. Since our five senses are constantly taking in thousands of pieces of data per minute, there has to be a system for determining what qualifies as learning. If you were to look out the window right now, your brain would be processing all of the visual data you see (colors, shapes, objects, etc.) but none of it may be part of a learning process. But as you turn back to reading this paragraph, you are engaging in learning.

This is where our focus or attention comes in. The act of focusing on something starts the process by which sensory data is converted to learning because it activates the hippocampus, the structure responsible for creating memories.

The hippocampus is the first stop on a long and complex journey—and it works in a consistent, predictable way. In fact, many learning challenges start because so often people don't work with how the hippocampus is designed to function. It acts like a camera or video recorder (I call it the "hippocam!") and, like any device, it has an "on" button. Physiologically, when our eyes and ears attune to something—in other words, when we focus—it activates the hippocampus, essentially beginning the recording. Dr. Richard Davidson of the University of Wisconsin calls this "phase locking," and it's the starting point of all learning.

Without focus, we can't capture that important data, so it can't continue the process of being moved to memory or driving behavior change. This is why it's important to design learning environments to help people focus, and to bust the myth that you can multitask while learning. Research has proven that when we divide our attention, our focus actually switches back and forth between the two activities, also known as switch-tasking. I call this "swiss-tasking" because when switching back and forth, the hippocampus loses key pieces of information for each object of attention and we end up with holes in the recording, and therefore irreversible holes in our learning. The hippocampus is physically incapable of recording two complete tracks of data simultaneously, so you must give learning the attention it deserves.

For example, if you have the TV on while you are trying to read this, your brain will go back and forth with your attention. If you focus on the TV for a few seconds, your brain can't really comprehend the words you are reading. And likewise, if you start to really focus on the words on this page and their meaning, the TV will fade in to the background.

Multitasking carries two significant risks: First, we fool ourselves that we can do two things well. This may be true for certain activities—I can absolutely wash the dishes and listen to music—but when trying to learn, you must be able to focus. Second, the hippocampus is affected by those around us. Studies have shown that learners who are trying to focus on something are negatively affected by their neighbor who is multitasking. I've coined the term "second-hand distraction" to describe this phenomenon. And it's almost as dangerous as second-hand smoke in terms of the health of your learning.

So, learning requires our attention. And yet it is hard to maintain for long periods of time. Our minds start to wander and get distracted by the thousands of other things vying for our attention in one moment, even when we are trying to concentrate and learn. Over the years, several researchers have explored attention spans and published consistent findings about how long humans can focus.

Now, if I was in the room with you, I would ask you to pause and guess how many minutes you think that is. If you want to play along, just cover the paragraph below with your hand for a minute. How long do you think we can focus before we start to lose our attention? Another way to think about this is to just remember the last time you sat in a class or listened to a webinar or read a book for learning. How long before you felt kind of saturated or distracted?

When I ask this in a presentation, I hear everything from one hour to 5 minutes. Here is the big shocker. . . you ready? Studies show that the maximum is 20 minutes. Yep, 20 minutes. And that's the maximum. For most people it's more around 15 minutes.

The "Hippocam"

Dependent on focus

More data is better

Attention span =
20 minutes max

20-minute segments are ideal for learning

Once we are distracted and lose focus, the "hippocam" doesn't have clear or clean data to move into short-term memory (the first stop to long-term memory). So, while you may sit there for longer, the learning is paused until you focus in again. Also known as attention restoration theory, a large body of knowledge has found how important it is for learners to notice they are distracted so they can bring their attention back. It also points to changes educators can make in how we design and deliver learning.

Despite being the overwhelmingly pervasive approach to learning, lecture-style sessions have never demonstrated good retention results and now we know why. Sitting for hours and trying to learn works against the brain's natural functioning. We are meant to learn in short bursts of focus, which we can string together to create longer learning events.

And a break from focus doesn't mean you have to get up and leave the room. It just means you have to shift your focus to something else for a brief period of time before you come back. Here's the good news: these minibreaks can also serve learning if you shift the focus to some kind of processing activity. Whether it's a moment of private reflection, a discussion with a partner, or an experiential activity, processing the content that was just learned helps the hippocampus push it into short-term memory. And it can refresh your focus so you are ready to learn more.

I now build all my learning events in 15-minutes chunks of information, followed by a processing activity. I then string these mini-modules together into a longer session, like an hour or two or three—although I rarely go longer than a half-day now because of what I have learned about the brain's need for time away from learning for reflection (the resting neocortex that drives "aha!" moments).

Since adopting this approach, I have seen a real increase in the effectiveness of learning events in terms of comprehension, retention, and, ultimately, behavior change. It has also changed how I approach my own learning. Having gone through both a master's and a doctorate program, I have spent more than my fair share of hours in lectures, half-day seminars, full-day programs and trying to read really dense material that doesn't have the benefit of a leading character or a storyline. I always knew that after a certain point I wasn't retaining information, but I thought it was because I just needed to work harder than other people.

Not so.

All this time, we have been designing education around a business delivery model, ignoring how the brain actually learns. When people start tuning out or getting restless, it's not necessarily because they are bored. It's because they are full. There is a difference.

There is one more thing to know about focus or attention. The amygdala plays a role in helping us learn for the purpose of survival. Sitting between the sensory nerves and the hippocampus, the amygdala serves as a filter. If our senses process information that might be a precursor to danger, such as smelling smoke or hearing a loud bang, the amygdala turns on the hippocampus. It's a form of uber-attention or focus and it's why we can often remember threatening events with crystal clear detail or in slow motion. The amygdala is activating the learning process, like a person with a megaphone yelling, "PAY ATTENTION! THIS IS IMPORTANT!" It's all in service of our survival—a clear memory of this event will help us survive this situation the next time it happens. Studies have shown that mild to strong arousal activates the hippocampus and the learning process. We'll explore this more in the next chapter.

31. The Emotional Sweet Spot

Brain science shows us that our emotions play an important role in most aspects of our lives, including when and how we learn. Before we dive into emotions, let's first look at the layers of the brain that relate to emotions.

First, the brain has three layers of increasing sophistication, known collectively as the triune brain. While this is a simplified description of a complex organ, it's useful for understanding emotions. The base layer is called the reptilian brain and is tied to survival. Through our senses, we constantly scan our environment and if we perceive danger the amygdala kicks off the fight-flight-freeze response and floods our system with adrenalin and cortisol in less than 200 milliseconds. This hormonal rush is not pleasant, but it does prepare the body to literally escape, hide from, or face the danger by quickening the heart to drive blood to the muscles, expanding the lungs to take in more oxygen and fibrinogen, and releasing endorphins to enable blood clotting and reduce pain (if injured).

The middle layer is the limbic brain, also known as our emotional brain. This layer allows for more complex emotions than fear and anger, expanding to emotional categories like happiness, sadness, love, and disgust. This is also where our working memory lives. Our survival is also tied to this portion because we need to connect with others, care for our young, and navigate social groups.

The outer layer is the neocortex or our thinking brain. Also known as the executive center, it's our highest-functioning state, used for logical analysis and effective decision-making. Our emotional palette expands to include more nuances and shades of emotions (such as the difference between calm, pleased, amused, content, and joyous). More importantly, it allows us to have thoughts about emotions and to tune into much subtler indicators than the other brain layers can read.

When our reptilian brain switches on it shuts down other brain functions, including self-awareness and logical analysis. This serves an important purpose: when you are fighting for your life, you probably won't be doing complex calculations, which conserves energy. Additionally, if you are injured, your lack of self-awareness will protect you from perceiving how hurt you really are, reducing risk of shock.

This would be all fine and good if the amygdala only fired when we were truly in danger, like during a car accident or a robbery. However, our own personal history shapes our amygdala and what it sees as "danger." For example, I was attacked by a dog in my twenties after being a dog owner my whole life. During the incident, my amygdala legitimately responded, but it continued past that one event. For several months my amygdala would kick off every time I saw a dog, even dogs I knew. Even photos of dogs!

People can also set off our amygdalas. If your boss reminds you of someone who harmed you, your poor amygdala could be going off in your workplace. And it's generally not good if you lose your self-awareness and logical reasoning at work! This is what is behind good people making bad choices. It's called the "amygdala hijack" and it literally makes us incapable of intelligent action, emotional or otherwise. Every day, headlines are filled with examples of politicians, athletes, celebrities, and even police officers in the throes of an amygdala hijack.

How does this relate to learning? Recall that the amygdala is physically attached to the hippocampus. Data comes in from the sensory nerves and the amygdala sorts it for safety. If right now you smelled a fire or a stranger burst into your room, you would go on alert.

As we learned earlier, when the amygdala is aroused, it automatically switches on the hippocampus and says, "This is important, remember this! Something is going down right now and you need to start recording to help me survive it next time." This, again, is why we often remember stressful events with crystal-clear detail—and happy emotionally charged events as well. (Winning the lottery would also arouse your amygdala and start the hippocampus recording.)

So, emotions matter. The big, powerful emotions like mad and scared and joyful certainly turn on the hippocampus. But others do too. Years ago, psychologist Abraham Maslow identified a hierarchy of five human needs that are tied to motivation. I have found that collapsing them into just three categories aligns with how issues play out in today's workplaces. Namely, we are wired to do three things: Survive. Belong. Become.™

1. **Survive:** Our primary motivation. Any threat to our physical safety arouses the amygdala and turns on the hippocampus. This includes impending physical danger, like a fire, but also happens if we worry we won't make enough for our house payment or if we might get fired, because shelter and food are also part of our physical safety.

2. **Belong:** When we are safe, we focus on our need for meaning-ful connections with others. As social beings, our chances of survival are greater when we are part of a tribe. The amygdala-hippocampus connection turns on when we enter a new social setting, take a risk in front of our peers, or perceive that some-one is unhappy with us or excluding us.

3. **Become:** Once the other two needs are met, our final and perhaps greatest need is to become our best selves—to grow into our potential and make the contribution we are here to make. This "seeking" part of human nature distinguishes us from all other living organisms on the planet. The amygdala and hippocampus turn on when we feel the joyful, excited emotions experienced in moments of realized potential and meaningful purpose, and also when we are in that state of flow that Mihaly Csikszentmihalyi identified.

We can use the power of emotions to enhance learning experiences. But there is a sweet spot: slightly positive creates the best learning environments. Emotions at the most frightening or joyful ends of the spectrum, like the room being on fire or winning the lottery, are going to distract learners. And while you can use the power of mild threats (for example, calling on people to speak and criticizing their work) to activate the amygdala and hippocampus, if you want real learning to take place that isn't nearly as effective as more positive measures like these:

- **Sharing with others** ties into that social connection; pair up for discussions or work in small groups.
- **Light competition and quizzes** can mildly arouse positive responses as long as they are set up to be safe and not activate fears of failure or ridicule.
- **Games and playfulness** are great tools. You just have to be sure that they are the right match for your audience and don't come across as childish or cheesy. Gamification works because it naturally leverages the reward-seeking part of the brain
- **Application and reflection** allow people to personalize the learning to themselves and their work context, which generally creates positive feelings. In addition, they are forms of metacognition (one of the powerful connections that drives long-term memory) so you get that as an added bonus.
- **Virtual reality** can boost learning because it creates deep immersion that the brain codes as a lived experience. Use it to boost your practice of task skills, empathy, and geospatial mastery.
- **Learning generated by the learner's curiosity** always creates a feeling of success when the answer is found because we get that rush of serotonin and dopamine. This is what makes on-demand learning so powerful.

- **The flash of insight or "aha!" moment** also creates positive emotions as the synapses fire and make the connection.
- **Humor** is good too as long as it's appropriate and not offensive. This can be tricky because what may seem funny to you might cause another to feel ridiculed or excluded. Take care that your humor creates inclusion and connection for all, and not just some of your learners.
- **Gratitude and mindfulness** generate slightly positive emotions in learning, and yield all kinds of other good benefits too, like unlocking emotional intelligence, calming an overactive amygdala, and increasing happiness.

Sharing with others   Humor (when used appropriately)

Light competition   Gratitude

Games/playfulness   Mindfulness

Application/reflection

Virtual reality

On-demand learning

Insight/"aha!" moment

The stars of learning

In my presentations, people always ask about gratitude and mindfulness. Several studies have shown that both gratitude and mindfulness make the brain more receptive to learning. Dr. Alex Korb synthesized some of the key findings on gratitude in his *Psychology Today* article titled "The Grateful Brain: The Neuroscience of Giving Thanks." Intentional gratitude practices boost everything from attention, determination, and enthusiasm and reduce things like anxiety, depression, and physical ailments.

Gratitude has an amazing calming effect on the brain and body because it shifts our perspective to what really matters. In my events, if I'm having a leader or manager assess their talent, I might ask them to identify the team members they are most grateful for. Or, if they're leading a change initiative, I might have them identify available resources or tools they are grateful for. And I often close a learning session with appreciative inquiry (the metacognition described in chapter 12), which can help express gratitude as well.

Mindfulness is a form of focus in which you become completely present to the here and now. Evidence strongly suggests that mindfulness also benefits education. Dr. Patricia Broderick, author of *Learning to Breathe: A Mindfulness Curriculum for Adolescents to Cultivate Emotion Regulation, Attention, and Performance*, details the many positive results for teens and young adults. The Association for Mindfulness in Education uses an evidence-based approach to help teachers and schools implement mindfulness training, and they identify at least 14 key benefits including increased executive function, social skills, and caring for others. Similarly, renowned mindfulness researcher Dr. Richard Davidson has been studying the effects of a mindfulness-based kindness curriculum with children and seen higher grades and greater social competence in children who participated in a mindfulness program compared to those in the control group.

Davidson's research has really shifted my view on the importance of mindfulness practices. Using MRIs to explore how the brain changes, he has compared the brains of long-time meditators (like Tibetan monks), people who have never meditated, and first-time meditators, with astounding results. Even meditating one time changes the brain in a measurable way, and more builds stronger neural pathways. Regular meditators are able to focus longer, are less likely to ruminate and worry about future events, and when something stressful does happen, they experience less distress in the moment and quickly return to their normal state. These amazing benefits aid learning with the "side" benefit of boosting resilience and happiness. (Learn more in his book, *Altered Traits: Science Reveals How Meditation Changes Your Mind, Brain, and Body*.)

As a result of Davidson's research, I have become a meditator myself. I use the 20-minute daily meditations from the Chopra Center, led by Dr. Deepak Chopra. He has partnered with neuroscientist Dr. Rudolph Tanzi to write the book *Super Brain: Unleashing the Explosive Power of Your Mind to Maximize Health, Happiness, and Spiritual Well-Being.*

32. The Power of Show-and-Tell

Humans have been learning for over 200,000 years and a large part of our success is due to the power of storytelling and observational learning. As we learned in chapter 22, thanks to our mirror neuron system we naturally learn by watching others, then trying ourselves and fine-tuning as we go. We may enhance observational learning by seeking out opportunities to learn by watching others (particularly those who are highly skilled) and at any age we may also learn through the power of storytelling, which is the focus of this chapter.

Our species has been sitting around the fire listening to stories for generations. We even created visual aids by painting on the cave walls, the early PowerPoint. Today, television and smart devices are versions of the campfire, but instead of the warm glow of flames, we stare at the blue light of the digital world. Our brain is especially built for story because it was critical for our species' survival. We had to be able to listen to and learn from each other. So, our biology developed an interesting pattern—when we hear a story, we get hooked by the intrigue of not knowing what happens next. And when a story is told, we get a neurochemical reward in the form dopamine that keeps us listening for the lesson that will help us. The brain is so wired for story we are far more likely to focus and learn when someone tells a story than when they just share information.

The human brain is uniquely wired for story

Stories have a pattern that the brain recognizes—a dilemma with no clear way forward. We must work through a challenge or a conflict and, when we do, we arrive victorious at the other side.

Stories also have a beginning, a middle, and an end. In fact, the formula for a good story is derived from the patterns that stories around the world all demonstrate. It's no accident that every culture from the past until now has similar stories—that there is not only a consistent pattern but that the themes are ubiquitous. For example, the hero's journey is a pattern repeated in stories from Herman Melville's *Moby Dick* to Disney's *Moana*, with examples in every language and community. Renowned researchers Dr. Carl Jung and Dr. Joseph Campbell believe that this is because stories emerge from something they call the collective unconscious.

Our brain is so committed to story that it can be a detriment. As Benedict Carey, states, "It's more than an interpreter. It's a story maker." He's the author of *How We Learn: The Surprising Truth about When, Where, and Why It Happens* and detailed the amazing research of Dr. Michael Gazzaniga, who studied the effects of split brain surgery.

Back in the 1960s, surgeons conducted experimental split brain surgeries to control or resolve certain medical issues, like seizures, literally cutting the connections between the left and right hemispheres. Several researchers, Gazzaniga included, began studying patients who had split brain surgery (e.g., the aforementioned Henry Molaison) in an attempt to better understand the brain. Over the past five decades and hundreds of studies, it has become clear that the left brain is constantly narrating our lives. It's not merely an interpreter of the data coming in, but also fills in the gaps with assumptions. It's constantly "seeking patterns and inserting judgments based on the material...creating meaning, narrative, cause, and effect."

Obviously, this can help us make sense of what is happening, but it can also spin a tale that is not true and even very far from reality. This is largely what is at play in bias, which is prejudice in favor of or against one thing, person, or group compared with another, usually in a way considered to be unfair. Some of our bias is conscious but most of it is largely unconscious, driving subtle feelings of like or dislike that impact our thoughts, beliefs, and ultimately, behaviors with others.

Just think about what you do when someone says to you, "We need to talk." Personally, I will worry that I have done something wrong and start to replay all of our recent interactions in my mind, trying to figure out what I did. Even when I logically know that it's probably nothing, I cannot stop worrying until I actually speak with the person and get things cleared up.

Stereotypes are further evidence of our brain's desire for story. We take a few experiences, often not even our own, and weave entire narratives around what a group of people is like, giving them either positive or negative attributes.

Our brain's hunger for story impacts us on a personal level every day and these stories can even cause us great anguish. Because the brain's first priority is survival, its protection mechanism is to always plan for the worst-case scenario. On a biological level, we're better off assuming our colleagues are gossiping about us rather than being surprised when the tribe ousts us. So, when we don't know, our brain will likely offer up the more negative interpretation as a way to protect itself and improve chances of survival. But that doesn't necessarily make us happy and can even get us into trouble when engaging with others.

Dr. Brené Brown studies shame, vulnerability, and resilience and has written several national bestselling books. Her two TED talks are the most viewed in history. In her recent Netflix special, she shares a common theme that occurred across decades of research. People who are happiest and have the most resilience share something; they know that their brain loves a good story. And in fact, nearly all of them use the phrase, "The story I am telling myself is...", which allows them to get out of the assumptions to see other possibilities.

Byron Katie, a leader in the self-help movement, had her own experience with this shift when she realized that much of her unhappiness came from believing the stories she was telling herself. She created a process called The Work that focuses on freeing people from this pattern. It focuses on four key questions: Is it true? Can you absolutely know that it's true? How do you react when you believe that thought? Who would you be without the thought? I have personally witnessed her taking several people through an astounding transformation, letting go of long-held sadness and anger in the course of less than an hour.

Story is really the fabric of our lives and is already at the heart of how we learn. But it must be used with awareness and intention. The best educators leverage story to create learning experiences for others. Once I learned this, I became better at designing learning. I now design all my learning events as a story—a journey that the learners and I take together, with a beginning, middle, and end. I also like to use metaphors as a framework for the content, because I know it will activate their schemas and make the learning more likely to stick. I use a lot of imagery and create a visual story arc as well. Most importantly, I make sure that each person gets to apply the content to their own lives. I have people work in pairs and small groups so they can share their thoughts and ideas, creating a proverbial fire in the middle of the room that we all get to sit around. Consider how you can use our brain's predilection for story to enhance the learning of yourself and others.

33. Priming, Notes, and Doodles

One of the new developments in learning is the power of priming. Priming is essentially exposing yourself to information you have not yet learned. Ideally, it's done in the form of questions, even though the likelihood of getting them right is very small. An instructor can prime students by asking questions about content before it is taught. And a learner can prime themselves by skimming the table of contents or major topics and trying to describe what they are, even though it's a blind guess.

Why does this help with learning? Priming is a type of implicit memory that involves the neocortex. Scientists believe that the brain essentially creates a placeholder so that when you do learn that information, it becomes more memorable. Something clicks into place—a special kind of "aha!" moment.

Plus, priming activates your schemas. As Henry Roediger and Jeffrey Karpicke, authors of *The Power of Testing Memory: Basic Research and Implications for Educational Practice*, say, "It may seem counterintuitive to answer questions about topics you have not studied yet, but research suggests that... answering questions beforehand activates any related knowledge you have about the topic and makes it easier to connect new information to what you already know."

Priming also helps with what scientists call "the illusion of knowledge." Sometimes, we think we know more than we actually do, and that confidence can get us in trouble. By doing some priming, learners are reminded how much they don't know and it makes them more receptive to the new information.

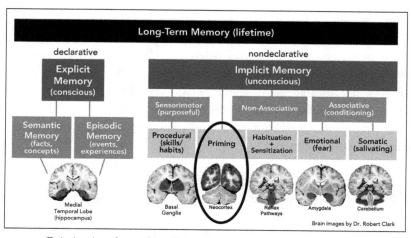

Priming is a form of implicit memory and involves the neocortex

Handwrite your notes

During the encoding process, it turns out that effort matters. The more effort we spend on learning, the more likely it is to stick because it helps the hippocampus push learning into short-term memory. One way to do this is to handwrite your notes. Taking notes actually helps with learning because it adds another sensory element beyond our eyes and ears. It makes it more kinesthetic. Even more fascinating, hand writing notes is measurably better than typing them. With the advent of laptop computers, it's increasingly common for people to use their computers for taking notes in class. But, it turns out, while we can type faster than we write we actually retain more of what we learn when we handwrite notes.

A series of interesting studies by researchers at Princeton University and UCLA compared students who took handwritten notes to those who used a laptop. The laptops only contained word processing software and were not connected to the Internet, to minimize distraction. The results consistently showed that the students who handwrote their notes had better short-term *and* long-term retention of the material. They discovered that when people type, because it is so much faster, they end up transcribing the lecture verbatim. Since handwriting is slower, students had to do some mental heavy lifting by summarizing key points and organizing the material.

After this discovery, researchers ran more studies where they explicitly told the computer notetakers to focus on summarizing rather than typing verbatim. But despite these instructions, the students were seemingly unable to stop themselves from transcribing the speakers' words. And in reality, laptops do come with endless opportunities for distraction, and many of these, like the Internet, photos, and music, can easily create a switch-tasking experience that splits focus and hampers the hippocampus's ability to record the learning data.

These findings have been replicated by other researchers and map to the experiences of myself and others. A client of mine, a writer who interviews people for her work, has found that when she takes notes on her laptop, she doesn't retain what a person says. But when she takes notes by hand, she remembers details, and retains more information longer than when she types. Put the effort into handwriting notes and it will boost your learning and your memory.

Do Your Doodles

Doodling (yes, doodling) is another surprisingly powerful type of notetaking that supports learning. Sunni Brown, author of *The Doodle Revolution: Unlock the Power to Think Differently*, calls doodling "applied visual thinking." Several studies back up her position, showing that visual note-taking boosts both retention (by up to 29 percent over non-doodlers) and also drives enhanced creative thinking.

Doodling is not just goofing off—it's actually "making spontaneous marks to help yourself think." This is because our brains are designed to be visual. Our species existed thousands of years before we even created written language and cave drawings show that our earliest forms of written communication were through images—the ancient doodle or modern emoji.

Consider how a sighted child learns. A baby can learn what a cat is and point to a picture of one months before she can say the word *cat*. And she can say or sign the word *cat* years before she knows her letters and learns that C-A-T is the written representation of her furry friend. When we consider the complexity of different languages and discover that there is also *gato* (Spanish), *chat* (French), *kitte* (Arabic), and *neko* (Japanese)—well, it's no wonder our ancestors drew pictures and why emojis are so popular.

The human brain often grasps understanding of visual information much more quickly than the same concept explained in words because it doesn't have to be translated through our language center. Just imagine putting together your IKEA furniture if they wrote out the instructions in paragraphs instead of those cool pictographs? Mind maps are another visual way to organize concepts and ideas, but they don't traditionally have the images that are the hallmark of doodles.

The Animate video series by RSA (the Royal Society for the Encouragement of Arts, Manufactures and Commerce) are popular because they are doodle murals of important talks. They animate meaningful voice recordings of thought leaders to visually emphasize the main points. We don't just hear the information but also see the concepts brought to life before our eyes. As a learning designer, I sometimes leverage the power of doodling by showing the RSA versions of my favorite TED talks rather than the talks themselves, such as Dan Pink's "Drive," Brené Brown's "Empathy," and Jeremy Rifkin's "The Empathic Civilization" (see links in References).

I've also noticed that many events and conferences use professional doodlers to capture the main messages from keynote speakers. For example, the Elliott Masie Learning conference (one of my favorite events for learning professionals) uses this technique for every one of their keynote addresses. Here is an example from Learning 2018, used with permission, for Dan Pink, who spoke on themes from his recent book titled *When: The Scientific Secrets of Perfect Timing.*

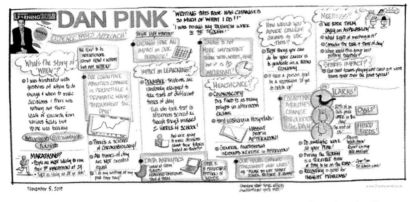

Graphic recording of Dan Pink's keynote, created by Crowley & Co.

Now, Sunni Brown would argue that watching someone else doodle does not have the same kinesthetic power of doing our own, and she is right. But I have found that adding visual elements still augments learning in powerful and entertaining ways. In fact, as Nitya Wahklu, an associate at Crowley & Co. has found, "Three days after a typical meeting most people remember just 10 percent of what happened. When a graphic recorder creates visuals to reinforce the auditory content this percent of recall actually goes up to 65 percent. This giant leap is called the 'picture superiority effect.'"

Brown states that doodling is a form of mental processing, so it not only aids in focus, it can help the hippocampus move information into short-term memory. By taking notes that are a combination of doodles (visual) and key words or phrases (linguistic), we actually leverage more neural pathways as we tap into those regions of our brain. So, the next time you are learning, think twice before grabbing your laptop, unless you happen to have a drawing tablet attached to it. Grab your markers and see what happens when you handwrite notes and doodles.

34. Grow Your Learning Skills

As we wrap this section on the Learn phase of the Three-Phase Model of Learning, the key components are priming, senses, segments, story, and demonstration.

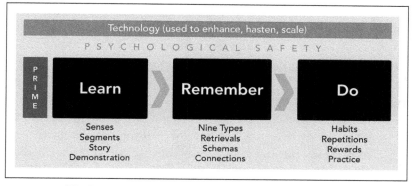

The Learn phase of the Three Phase Model of Learning

Here are tips and strategies you can start using today for growing your learning skills.

1. **Leverage adult learning:** Be proactive in setting up your own learning. When you can, use concepts from the various adult learning theories to design your own learning experiences or to evaluate the effectiveness of ones you attend.

2. **Do some priming:** Whenever you can, skim the topics and try to answer comprehensive questions about the content you have not yet learned. Sure, you will likely get it all wrong, but in the process you will leverage the neuroscience of priming, setting you up for better and more memorable learning later.

3. **Get the best input data you can:** Learning starts with your senses and the more information your brain has, the better. When you want to learn, make sure nothing is impairing your senses to take in as much as possible. Get an unobstructed view so you can see all the information. Turn up the volume so you can hear all there is to hear. Access materials in your language or ask for them to be translated. If you can, take in data in more than one sensory channel. If you have the option of seeing and hearing something, it's twice as much data for your

brain to work with. If you can add touch, smell, or taste to a learning experience, even better.

4. **Focus and refocus your attention:** Part of being a good learner is giving your full attention. Your hippocam won't activate without your focus, so be intentional about it. Give up the notion that you can multitask. No, you cannot learn while simultaneously watching a TV show, or reading emails, or texting someone. Some people argue that they focus better when there is ambient noise in the background like TV or music. As long as it's in the background and not pulling your focus away from the learning, it is likely not a problem. But only you will know if it's distracting you.

    - For better learning, eliminate distractions so that it's easier to keep your focus where you want it to be. For me, that means that I need to not only put my phone away, but I have to put it on silent or airplane mode because the minute it makes a sound, it's going to tempt me.
    - For those of us who work in open-concept offices, it means investing in noise-cancelling headphones and finding those quiet spaces to get away from potential distractions.
    - Finally, you have to notice when you have drifted and bring your attention back. Remember, our attention naturally drifts every 15 to 20 minutes, so it's normal. But when you're trying to learn, you have to know how to refocus and how to fill in the gaps for what you missed while you zoned out.
    - Learning is not the only activity that benefits from focus. Daniel Goleman's book *Focus: The Hidden Driver in Excellence* details the positive impact focusing has on leadership, decision-making, and creativity. And it makes sense. If focus is what kicks off key parts of our nervous system, it's the gateway to all kinds of important skills and abilities.

5. **Break learning into segments:** When you can, learn in short, 15 to 20-minute bursts of content and then do a quick processing activity or take a short break. The research on the brain science of learning is shifting the learning industry, so you will likely find many learning resources that are set up this way. For example, at Lynda.com (now LinkedIn Learning) we have always made the videos less than 10 minutes and, as a general rule, less than 5. That was by design and helped launch the micro-learning movement. TED Talks are

another example, with the maximum time set at 18 minutes. But if learning is not already broken into segments, do it for yourself. For any online learning or reading experience, you can control your own learning and set a timer, so you work with your brain's natural function. If your materials do not have any processing activities, create your own. Spending even as little as one minute reflecting on how the content relates to your experiences can be impactful. And, certainly, use this information to make better choices about your learning sources. Ask how the presenters segment the content and what kind of activities they include. If they don't seem to be aware of the neuroscience of learning, then move on to another source.

6. **Leverage show-and-tell:** When possible, harness the power of your mirror neuron system and learn by first watching others. Seek out learning experiences that offer demonstrations by peak performers. If these are not provided by your organization, look for other sources like professional associations, online videos, and augmented or virtual reality with the right components. Also seek out learning experiences that utilize the impact of story. This can come in a variety of forms, such as a visual story told with images around a metaphor, storytelling by the facilitators or participants, or the use of a literal story or fable as a way to drive learning.

7. **Write notes and doodles:** While learning, spend the extra energy on handwriting your notes and/or creating visual doodles of the content. Both will boost your learning capacity and the memorability of the content. One of these may be better for you than another so experiment to explore which helps you learn the best.

Your Learning Journey

Take a moment now to apply the concepts from this section to the thing you want to learn. Use these questions to help you identify possible strategies to support your leaning goal.

- When you think about your learning goal, which of the adult learning theories would be useful? Consider which levels of Bloom's taxonomy are relevant, what would be the right order to move through Kolb's learning cycle, and how to leverage your natural intelligences.

- Which phase of Hudson's cycle of renewal are you currently in or moving through? How could you be intentional about maximizing your journey?

- How can you set up your learning goal so you can focus? What distractions typically get in your way and how can you neutralize them?

- How can you break your learning into short segments of 20 minutes or less with a short activity or break? How many of these could you string together before you would need a substantial break?

- Which of the stars of learning lend themselves to your learning goal? Identify three that you could use.

- As a final step, look over your notes from the previous sections and create your cohesive learning plan. What are your key action items in the coming days, weeks, and months?

DESIGNING + DELIVERING LEARNING

"Tell me and I forget. Teach me and I remember. Involve me and I learn."

Benjamin Franklin, journalist, inventor, diplomat, and founding father of the United States of America

35. Using Information, Instruction, and Inspiration

We are all familiar with some types of learning professionals, most of whom specialize in supporting a range of learners, from complete beginner up to the most advanced. This includes academic and music instructors, sports coaches, fitness class leaders, and anyone who designs training and learning events for a range of employees and work environments. But, whether we realize it or not, most of us are designing learning experiences for others: If we manage employees, we probably do some teaching, training, and mentoring. If we work in health care, much of our work may be about educating people on healthful behaviors. As parents, we design learning experiences every day to teach children information, skills, and behaviors. And, of course, we teach our romantic partners some stuff too.

This section is a mini-handbook of ideas to help you guide others in their learning journeys. I focus on professional learning for adults, as this best matches my expertise as a former chief learning officer and a consultant, but the tips and strategies I offer for learning professionals are easily applied to the other settings mentioned above. Now, we'll dive into designing and delivering great learning experiences to your learners. (And in the last section focus on creating a culture of learning across your organization.)

For instruction to happen, you need an instructor and a learner. But they don't need to be physically together because instruction can come in so many forms. If you think about it, following a recipe is a form of instruction. The chef writes down all the ingredients and steps to make the dish. While they are not there to provide coaching or give feedback, a hungry learner (pun intended) will use trial and error to get it right. Watching an online video is another form of instruction, as is taking an in-person class. No matter where it is sourced, all professional learning draws from three main forms, which I call "The 3 I's":

The first is information. This is learning about something and includes facts and knowledge. It might be a piece of data, the wording of a policy, or the location of a resource, but once the learner has the information, she or he can take action. An example might be the amount of money left in the budget, or that salt enhances the flavor of foods. The source of the information can be many things—a book, a manual, a person, a website, an app. We are living in a world that has been transformed by immediate access to information. Within seconds, you can look up virtually anything, any time of day, using a device you carry in your pocket.

Next is instruction. This is learning how to do something and includes gaining or improving a skill. Instruction always includes a person who has experience or expertise of the skill (an instructor), who then takes the learner through a process to learn that same skill. For example, a manager could teach an employee how to balance a budget and a chef could teach a learner how to make a delicious meal.

The third form, inspiration, is learning why something matters and often includes things like values, vision, purpose, and passion. Inspiration helps learners understand the *why* of the learning, motivating them to replicate and even improve on it in the future. For example, balancing a budget is important because it helps an organization stay in business and even grow, enabling its vision and mission. And any good chef will tell you that getting the right flavor profile is crucial to creating a joyful eating experience for the diner; one who will come back again and bring their friends. When learners know the why behind something, they can actively participate in innovating better ways to achieve the same goal. This can drive both continuous improvement and adaptability.

In fact, of the many reasons for professional learning, perhaps adapting to our rapidly changing world is the most powerful. Other reasons include addressing a specific challenge or problem, improving skills, complying with laws and regulations, imparting information, cultivating high-potential employees, developing good managers and leaders, and empowering career growth at all levels, to name a few.

Three Types of Instruction

While instruction may occur through any number of vehicles—books, videos, apps, and classes—instruction itself happens via three key (and overlapping) activities:

- **Communication (Tell):** Whether through spoken or written word—delivered real-time, in person, or through a static mode— the instructor *tells* the learner what to do and when.

- **Demonstration (Show):** The instructor *shows* the learner what the behavior or skill should look like, whether live, in person, or via technology like video and virtual reality. This activates the visual cortex and the mirror neuron system, so seeing a behavior done correctly is neurologically far more impactful than reading or hearing the same thing described. Images simply convey thousands of more pieces of information that the brain can use.

- **Experimentation (Try/Do):** The learner starts to *do* the new behavior and skill. This is where the real transformation takes place because, until learners actually try the behavior, they have yet to form a neural pathway in their own body. As we fire the neurons of doing the skill, we start to build that neural pathway—hopefully, correctly. Without someone to provide feedback and coaching, a learner can develop the skill incorrectly, and by the time we get to 40 to 50 repetitions, our brain has formed a habit. (Also, hopefully, it's a good habit but, if it's a bad one, it will now take just as many, if not more, repetitions to rewire correctly.)

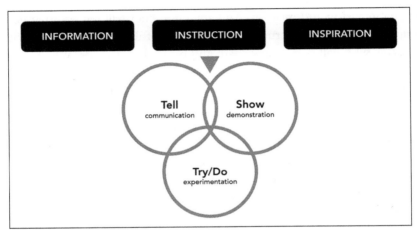

Three types of instruction

Instruction is a powerful tool for people to gain new skills, from the most basic level of introductory skill to the deepest expertise and mastery. An employee might be fine knowing the basics of budget management while the chief financial officer will need deep skills. Do you want a surgeon operating who knows the basics of tying a surgical knot or who has mastery? What about the engineer who designs an airplane? Is novice level acceptable or is expert status required? One of the biggest mistakes I see in organizations is that their learning strategy does not clearly identify the level of skill that different roles need to achieve. As a result, learning programs may not create a clear path to mastery, or resources may not be appropriately assigned to get people to the right level at the right time.

Another common problem I see is a lack of practice time in learning programs, so people don't get a chance to actually change behavior. As Dr. Anders Ericsson, author of *Peak: Secrets from the New Science of Expertise*, discovered, the only way to get from beginner to expert is through hours and hours of deliberate practice. He defines an expert as someone who can consistently perform at a very high level and he found that experts regularly engage in deliberate practice, seeking feedback and coaching; they set goals, focus on improvements, and commit to honing their craft, whatever it takes.

Consider who needs to develop high levels of performance in your organization. Are you offering well-constructed learning paths that get them there? With access to coaching and time to dedicate to practice? Taking the time to tighten up your organization's learning procedures will ensure that people at all levels are ready to perform at their best.

36. Meeting the Needs of Adult Learners

I have taught or facilitated all age groups, and adults are often the most challenging audience because they usually have a clear idea of what they want to achieve when they walk in the door. They can also be resistant to handing over the reins to a new authority because they are used to controlling their daily experiences.

Every learning professional can benefit from learning something about adult learning theory. Typically, as we mature out of school, we gain more freedom for self-directed learning and shift to finding solutions for our real-life challenges. As adults, we have some internal motivation to learn something simply because it interests us. And as we live longer we accumulate more knowledge and experience, which becomes a resource for more learning and those flashes of insight or "aha!" moments that happen when we connect things. (Review chapters 25 through 28 for the specific theories.)

Since adult learners are trying to solve real world problems, the best learning is what's available right when they need it most. After all, if I am stuck on something today, whether it's how to use some software or how to have a difficult conversation with a coworker, I need it *now*. I don't want to have to sign up for a class that starts in three weeks. That's why on-demand learning is so powerful: It usually has an online component, so it's available and accessible just when it's needed. It may take the form of PDF files, video courses, books, or even self-paced, online classes, but the key is that the learner can get answers easily and immediately so they can move on with their work. On-demand learning, in all its forms, should be a key part of your offerings.

Adult learners are also individuals. We are each pursuing different careers and at different levels of experience and expertise in our respective fields. The "one size" approach really fits no one. So, the most effective learning solutions are flexible enough to meet a range of needs. If each of your learners cannot immediately connect to what you are offering and find it relevant, they're likely to move onto something else. It is *your* responsibility to engage your learners, not the other way around. Consider how you can design solutions for different levels of experience and different categories of workers.

I have two big critiques of the learning industry. The first is that a lot of learning is just misaligned to the needs of the organization and the people it is supposed to be serving. If it's not solving real problems, then it's not a good use of anyone's time. My second is that a lot of learning is just not sophisticated enough for adult learners. In our attempt to create the one-size solution, we can oversimplify things or gloss over the sticky issues—but that is exactly where we need to focus. And don't get me started on facilitators who think that being perky and high-energy is how you create engagement.

Transformative Learning

One way to solve these challenges is to offer transformative learning. As mentioned in the introduction, transformative learning has three dimensions, which I have found aligns well with the needs of adult learners:

1. **Psychological:** This is a change in understanding. The tools you can use to create this shift include providing knowledge, information, models, or theories to explain the "why" of something, and giving people first-hand experiences.

2. **Convictional:** Where a person's belief system changes. This usually comes from epiphanies, flashes of insight and "aha!" moments, which means you need to set your audience up to have them. It is interesting to note that insight causes a permanent shift in the brain and is largely unforgettable, unlike information.

3. **Behavioral:** Where people change their actions in a way that sustains over time. Tools you can use here are observation, application, experimentation, and practice.

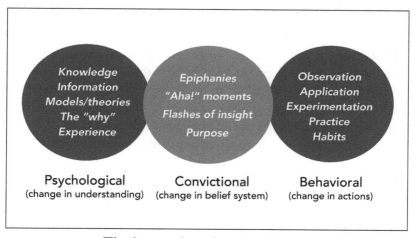

The elements of transformational learning

Each of these helps generate and groove the neural pathways and habits of the behaviors you're trying to create. Think about how you can incorporate psychological, convictional, and behavioral elements into any learning you're creating for others.

The secret to delivering great learning and development lives in your ability to assess your audiences and meet their needs. You have at least two different audiences: The first is your stakeholders, the leaders in your organization who have business issues that need to be solved. The second audience is the learners who will use or attend the learning solution and whose behavior you're trying to shift. You might have others too. It's vitally important that you spend time understanding your audiences. This becomes the data that will help you build an impactful and effective solution. I'll walk you through my process using a real example.

Recently, I was asked by several organizations to help them with change—specifically to help their managers and leaders become better equipped to lead people through change. For me to deliver the right solution, I need to know a few things. First, I need to understand current state of their skills and abilities and where they need to get to. I can get this information through asking great consulting questions (see next chapter for my list). I first get the view of the leaders who are requesting my assistance. In this case, the newly hired chief technology officer for a large organization was in the process of completely overhauling the structure and services of the group. He wanted his managers to get their direct reports on board for these changes and then execute them over a 36-month period. We identified that the key skills would be communicating the change plan, keeping people motivated over the long haul, and executing the plan.

Second, I need to understand the perspective of the learners, in this case, the managers. As part of my design process, I spoke to a few of them, and I cannot emphasize enough how helpful this was. It's almost always the case that the leader's view differs from the experience of folks on the ground. The learners' view is crucial for giving me the complete picture. Neither is right or wrong, but my solution *must* close the gap.

In this case, I discovered that their employees were already overwhelmed with their current workload and not sure how to fit in more. Plus, the teams had a lot of cross-dependencies and were not necessarily collaborating well across the groups. Finally, many were concerned that they don't have enough staff to pull off the leaders' expectations. Some staff are new, and others are burned out or overwhelmed.

After gathering the info, I spent some time mapping both perspectives because I needed to solve for all of it. The participants needed to find value in the training, or they would just tune out; and if I didn't solve their real pain points, I could not accomplish what the leader needed.

This may seem like a tall order, and it was. Yet, it's the truth of the situation. In fact, it's the truth of every professional development learning situation, yours included. If we really want to solve for the organization's needs, we must address the *real* stuff—the issues, the context, and the people—or else it will ultimately be unsuccessful.

Based on these conversations, I knew I needed to create something that promoted awareness and dialogue across the groups and gave them tools they could immediately use. Because all change is an emotional process, I needed to give them some emotional intelligence skills, and some strategies for mapping how the team was doing and executing the plan. I proposed that I offer six hours of training, spread out as three sessions of two hours each. That way, they could practice and tinker in between, as they applied the learning to their day-to-day work. Since they all worked at one location, we scheduled it as an in-person training.

As you can see, taking the time to thoroughly assess audiences will help you build the most effective solutions.

37. Asking the Right Questions

To gather the information you need to create great learning, you must ask the *right* questions.

Maybe this has happened to you: Someone calls with a training request and they are really clear on what they need. You, of course, rise to the occasion and do a great job of delivering the training they asked for. But it ultimately doesn't solve their problem. This is likely because the real problem was more complex. As learning professionals, we need to stop playing the role of "service provider" and work more like consultants; partnering with leaders to help identify and address the root causes, thus driving the long-term health and success of an organization.

In my experience, great learning professionals do a few things that can make them very effective. First, they establish a two-way relationship. They make it clear that the partnership is vital and that both they and the group they are helping have invaluable insight and information that will shape the success of the outcome. Second, good consultants ask lots of questions to learn everything they can about the challenges that need to be addressed. They identify not only the current state, but focus on what the ideal state looks like. This includes getting clear on measurable metrics as well as specific words and actions that employees should do. Finally, great consultants design and deliver a solution that creates the needed results. This requires using agile design principles, which includes piloting first drafts, seeking critical feedback from both partners and participants, and iterating until the data shows that the results are achieved.

So, let's apply this to a real situation. Most requests for training start with some kind of problem. Perhaps there has been a rise in attrition of top talent or a dip in product quality, or a key metric has gone up or down and someone decides that it can be fixed with training. The call is likely to come from either a leader in that department or perhaps someone in Human Resources who works directly with that team. If you have not yet established yourself as a trusted consultant and business partner, they will likely call you with a developed plan that they just want you to execute.

Let's see what this looks like. John and Maria both work at a global hospitality company. (Size and industry are truly irrelevant here.) John is the director of the marketing department and Maria works in learning and development (L&D). John contacts Maria and says, "We really need a workshop or training on communication. We want to put 30 people through it before the quarter ends." If Maria is not thinking like a consultant, she might say something like, "Yes, we have a 90-minute workshop on communication, and I have a facilitator that can deliver it on these dates." She and John will set it up and deliver it, both feeling pretty good about how they worked together to address a problem. And you know what is likely to happen? It probably won't solve the real problem and later the training will be deemed a waste of time or the L&D department will be seen as ineffective.

But if Maria steps into her role as a consultant, the interaction with John will go more like this.

John: "The team is missing key deadlines and some things have gone out with errors that someone should have caught."

Maria: "Is everyone on the marketing team involved?"

John: "No, it's really the coordination between the content team and the social media group. Ten people total. Right now, they either miss the deadline and get it right or we get it out the door on time but then we find errors."

Maria: "What would it look like if everyone was performing optimally?"

John: "People would follow the project plan to the letter. We would make release deadlines and what we release would be high-quality and error-free."

Maria: "When you think about these 10 people, do they have the skills they need to make the shift? And is anyone doing an outstanding job at this?"

John: "Yes, I think they need to have better time management and error-checking skills. Kelly and Abdi are my top performers and they're doing the best."

Maria: "Do you know what they're doing differently than the rest of the group?"

John: "No, but they've been here the longest. I wonder if they've come up with some helpful strategies?"

John: "That sounds like it will help turn things around. Thanks for helping me sort that out."

Maria: "That's a great question. Let's connect with them to see what insights they can provide. Using what they share, let's do a focused training for these 10 people around executing the project plan, adding some elements of time management and quality control."

As you can see, Maria's questions were vital for getting to the heart of the matter on John's team. And they are now going to leverage their internal experts, Kelly and Abdi, to create something that it much more focused on solving the real problem.

Below, see my list of consulting questions—as you use them, the process will get smoother. In fact, as your client gets familiar with the process they will likely come to you earlier and ready to engage in the exchange.

Consulting Questions

Remember to step fully into the consultant role, so you can focus on listening for the real problem that needs to be solved. Often clients come to us having already engaged in a diagnostic process and they have likely made assumptions about what they think is a good solution without necessarily breaking the problem down enough to know.

To establish rapport, you'll want them to feel that you are truly listening. You may need to artfully validate the work they have already done and gently invite yourself to explore further with them, so that you can design the best solution possible.

Kick it off by asking for their help: *Is it okay if I ask you a few questions? This will help me design the best solution for you.* Then ask these types of questions to unpack the problem:

1. What

Envision that the client is painting you a picture and if a portion of the image is fuzzy or missing details, ask them about it. You should feel that you are seeing exactly what they are seeing.

I want to make sure I fully understand the problem. You said....

[Summarize what you heard.]

Is that correct?

[Listen for new details.]

What is currently happening that is not working? or *Tell me more about what is happening now.*

[Listen for natural follow-up questions.]

2. Who
These questions can be really powerful for homing in on important insights.

Is the whole group involved? or *Who, specifically, is involved with this issue?*

[Listen for natural follow-up questions.]

Do you see any differences between...?

[Based on what you have heard, choose some of the relevant pairings below that might tease out important issues.]
*   *new hires and experienced employees*
*   *on-site and remote employees*
*   *job levels/titles*
*   *team A and team B*
*   *groupings that might indicate unconscious bias or a diversity/inclusion challenge (gender, race, ethnicity, age, assertiveness, size, etc.)*

3. The Ideal versus the Gap
Now turn to the desired outcome. Focus on what ideal state or optimal performance looks like.

What would it look like if everyone was performing optimally?

How would you measure this? What metrics could you use?

What are the words you would hear and the actions you would see if people were performing optimally?

What is in the way of them performing this way now?

Is anyone already performing optimally/doing an outstanding job at this?

What are they doing differently than the rest of the group? Do they have different...?
*   *knowledge*
*   *skills*
*   *motivation*
*   *resources*
*   *skills*
*   *experience*
*   *capacity*
*   *environment*

How can we leverage their knowledge/experience to help shift this situation?

4. Solutions

Before you offer your own solutions, see what solutions the client has in mind. This will give you concrete information to consider and respond to.

Based on what we have discussed so far, do you have any new perspectives or ideas about the situation and how to solve it?

What do we still need to learn to design the best solution possible?

Are there any assumptions we need to test or data to gather to gain more clarity?

Based on how your team works, what length of training would be best?

Is there a time of day or week that will be most effective?

What learning format would be most accessible?

[Offer relevant options like self-paced, instructor-led, remote access, etc.]

If our success was completely guaranteed, what bold steps might we choose?

5. Action

Wrap up the consultation by summarizing the highlights of what you have heard so far.

So, what I have noted is ABC. Is that correct? Would you add anything?

What needs our immediate attention going forward?

What are our next steps? What contribution will we each make and by when?

What possible challenges/roadblocks might arise and how might we meet them?

Once you conclude the meeting, I recommend sending a quick email summarizing the highlights and action plan.

38. Building the Learning Plan and Story Arc

It can't be overstated: to create any kind of learning program, you have to be clear about the issue it aims to solve. This is the finish line—the end point and promised results. Well-designed learning programs have a clear set of outcomes, often framed as learning objectives. They should answer the question, "At the end of the program, what new knowledge and skills will the participants have?" Once you have the end point, you need the starting point, which is "What knowledge and skills are participants walking in the door with?"

A learning program should be based on a plan to move the attendees from point A to point B through a series of content presentations and activities. This also becomes your agenda or timeline.

It also needs a story arc, with three parts: a beginning that meets the learners in their current state; a middle, that serves as a bridge; and an end or final state, which is the desired behaviors and results. Thinking of learning in a story arc will both help you organize your content and make the learner's journey more powerful because, as mentioned, the human brain responds to story. (Another aspect of the neuroscience of learning.) I don't mean starting presentations with "Once upon a time..." but rather to keep in mind that your learners are going on a journey. The scene opens with their current state and they need to traverse to a new and better state of skills and knowledge.

As you build your learning plan and agenda, here are some good things to remember. First, figure out the right order of content. I have found that there seems to be a "right" or "best" order for moving your audience from point A to point B. I do this by asking myself what "aha!" moments or insights do they need to create shifts in understanding and belief that will drive behavior change? I put the various topics on index cards or sticky notes and start moving them around until the order works. Whenever possible, I also build in some options that I can use depending on how things are going in the room on the day of the facilitation. Every group is different, and some groups will need more or less information at different points, so I always build in a few extra slides of relevant content that I can hide or show as needed.

Next, brainstorm activities to highlight the learning moments. Once I have the content order, I start to think about different processing activities that might work. I try to be as expansive as possible during this part because options give me more flexibility and will make it easier for subsequent facilitators to lead as well. Sometimes presenting content comes first, with an activity that anchors the concepts in the participants' experience. Sometimes the activity comes first, setting up the "aha!" moments the content needs. Sometimes a 5-minute discussion is all you need, and sometimes it's important to have a 30- to 90-minute hands-on experience.

Third, sketch out the timing for the agenda. Once you have a learning plan and possible activities, start figuring out timing. This part will take a few attempts so don't worry if it doesn't come together right away. But it is really important to be realistic about how long things actually take so you are not always feeling stressed and behind.

Additionally, keep these important considerations in mind: People need to use the restroom about every 90 to 120 minutes, so plan for that. Remember that the brain processes best when content presentations are kept to 15 to 20 minutes followed by a processing activity. Among the options for activities, pick the ones that will best move your group along to achieving their goals. And add the time you need to open and close the training, as well as answer questions.

Inevitably, it's not all going to fit. So now you have to go back and tinker. But do *not* start cutting breaks and processing activities, which is everyone's first reaction. If you do, then you'll end up with a day filled with talking *at* them, which will undermine your goals and their engagement. Sometimes you can swap activities, sometimes you can shorten a section of content, and sometimes you can combine things. For example, I often merge introductions with the first processing activity or assign some content as a pre- or post-event activity. You might also rethink your learning objectives and narrow the scope to match your timing or ask for more time and lead a longer workshop. Or perhaps you can consider a series with multiple parts.

The bottom line: you want an agenda that moves your participants from point A to point B so that they leave with the new levels of information or skill that you promised.

In our working example, the CTO needed his managers to lead a lot of big change initiatives effectively over the next three years. The current state was an overwhelmed team that was not communicating or collaborating effectively and there were a lot of emotions at play. Because I had three sessions with them, the overall story arc unfolded over those six hours. In the opening session, I gave them the big picture of how different types of change affect people and why humans are biologically wired to resist change.

During the middle session, I wanted to give them lots of time to try the assessment tools, to build that habit and also give them crucial data for what their team needed from them as leaders and managers. All this group work also provided opportunities for them to communicate and share information, improving collaboration. The last session focused on building their action plan and some shared strategies for how they will lead and manage change. In addition, I gave them some tools for aligning priorities and driving execution in the midst of being overwhelmed. In between, they used the materials and came back with questions and insights. I chose not to assign any pre-work because it was likely that people would be too busy to complete it, but I did assign my book, *Wired to Resist: The Brain Science of Why Change Fails and a New Model for Driving Success*, to extend the learning after the training.

Within each two-hour session, I also had a story arc. After I assess my audiences, I think about how I can set the learners up to have their own moments of insight. This occurs through working with the concepts in their own context. This aligns with adult learning theory and studies on habits. It also creates engaging learning experiences.

To do this, I play with these three core elements: the why, the how, and the try.

The *why* is the big picture of the topic or issue. It might be a conceptual model or data, but the goal is to get the high-level view of what is happening and why. This information often shifts their knowledge.

The *how* is what the learners can do to influence the topic or issue. It's the instructional aspect of the learning, and it's the skills that need to be developed. It can also include a model or method.

The *try* is the hands-on work and habit-building part of the learning. It can be assessments, practice sessions, case studies, you name it. But it's where we roll up our sleeves and give it a go so that they can replicate it when they get back to their work areas.

My secret sauce is using these three elements in different orders, depending on what will take my learners to their insights. Sometimes, I start with the try element because it sets them up to naturally see the why or how. Sometimes, the why needs to come first so that the try connects the dots. For example, when I am setting them up for an insight about how emotional change can be, I can teach them the change curve, or have them map the emotions of change, or I can ask them to reflect on a change they have experienced and capture what they were thinking or feeling at that time.

There may be no hard and fast rule but, I promise you, for every learning you design, there is an optimal path to take *your* group of learners to insight. When you find it, the results will speak for themselves.

39. Blended Learning and Creating Engaging Activities

Knowing the ins and outs of what you are going to teach is critical but it's only one part of the equation. In order to help your learners fully digest and process the lessons you must pay equal attention to both the format and the delivery of your learning solution. You have lots of options to choose from, and an infinite number of combinations. The key is to make choices that both accomplish your learning goals *and* work for your intended audience.

This is what blended learning is all about: blending various elements to make a cohesive whole. Let's first look at all our options for format and delivery. Some of these are either/or choices and others are more on a continuum with hybrids in the middle.

1. **Static or adaptive:** Static learning is delivered the exact same way every time to every learner, such as an instructional video. Compare that to adaptive, which shifts or changes depending on the needs or abilities of each individual learner.

2. **Structured or unstructured:** Structured learning unfolds as a designed or created experience, like a workshop or course. Whereas unstructured learning happens in the moment and is an interplay of the learner's curiosity and experience through exploration.

3. **Synchronous or asynchronous:** This is about whether a group of learners is sharing the experience at the same exact moment (like a live workshop or webinar) or at different times (like a self-paced course).

4. **Online or offline:** Online learning involves an electronic device like a phone, tablet, or computer to access or experience the learning. So, accessing company policies through a portal or even a PDF stored on a shared drive is online learning, while reading it in a printed binder is not. The amazing online learning options these days include video training, webinars, e-courses, virtual or augmented reality, and mobile apps for smart devices.

5. **Off-the-shelf or bespoke:** Off-the-shelf solutions are usually created by a provider and you use them "as is," while bespoke solutions are customized to an organization or group with specific elements like culture, language, and branding. When I work with organizations, I often blend these by assigning some of my online training program as

the pre-learning and then come in to deliver an in-person element that is customized for their culture and context.

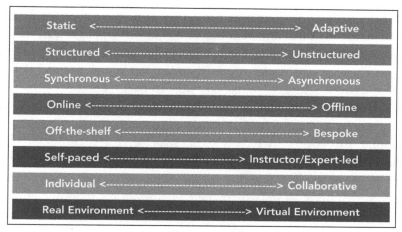

Types of learning formats

6. **Self-paced or instructor-led:** If it's something the learner chooses to speed up, slow down, or repeat as they need, then it's self-paced learning. By comparison, instructor-led learning has a set agenda, timing, and structure.

7. **Individual or collaborative, with individual learning happening one person at a time:** Collaborative means that several learners are experiencing the learning together and influencing each other. Collaborative learning harnesses the collective wisdom and experience of the group.

8. **Real or virtual environment:** This is the extended reality (XR) continuum covered in chapter 5. You can set up your learners to be in the real, tangible environment, a computer-generated reality (VR), or a combination with augmented (AR) or mixed reality (MR).

As you see, you can design learning programs using an infinite number of possibilities. And what you choose depends on your learning strategy and the needs of your audience and organization. Most learning events are combinations of these methods. When I build management and leadership development programs, I map various methods together to create a holistic learning journey that accomplishes several goals. I also like to use what is known as "the flipped classroom" because it allows you to get the most learning possible out of limited contact time. The truth is that in-person training time is very expensive so it should be saved for the real hands-on work. That's why I love using the flipped classroom, which consists of (1) pre-event learning that gets your audience on the same page about information or content; (2) then meeting to focus on hands-on application to their real culture and context, building the habit through practice; and (3) assigning post-event resources or actions to further develop knowledge and skills.

For example, in the "Coaching for Impact" session of my brain science–based manager training, I give managers a pre-learning task: They watch portions of Lisa Gates's LinkedIn Learning course "Coaching and Developing Employees," which is static, structured, asynchronous, online, off-the-shelf, both self-paced and instructor-led, and an individual activity. Then I bring the learners together for an in-person session where I present more information, customized to their organization's unique culture and context. We also do several practice coaching discussions in the room, building that neural pathway and habit. This element is adaptive, structured, synchronous, offline, bespoke, instructor-led, and collaborative. Afterward, I encourage them to further their learning through reading a great book on coaching (Beverly Kaye and Julie Winkle Giulioni's *Help Them Grow or Watch Them Go: Career Conversations Organizations Need and Employees Want*) and doing several more practice coaching sessions either in person and/or mediated through a virtual or augmented reality.

For example, I am VR-ifying some of my current trainings on emotional intelligence and inclusion. I'm using the power of the medium to give people embodied experiences to drive insight and empathy.

VR offers a variety of new ways to enhance learning and connection

As you build your next learning solution, consider and play with these choices to create a powerful experience for your learners. We have so many new and wonderful learning methods to choose from. Today's technology has made it easy to create and share both information and instruction with people all around the world. Designing the right activities is vitally important to the success of your learning program. When you get it right, the group's understanding, beliefs, and behaviors shift in ways that are sustained long after your time together. And when you get it wrong, people may disengage, get bored, and even get up and leave. (No pressure or anything.) I hope, as you outline the content and design the learning plan and agenda, that you brainstorm a lot of possibilities. Let's look at some key characteristics.

First, you want activities that make the learning "sticky," so people will remember it and use it. One way to do this is to hook learning to something the participants already know (such as schemas). When you connect learning to knowledge, skills, or experiences they already have, you greatly enhance their ability to understand and remember it. You won't typically know what their knowledge, skills, or experiences are—and the good news is that you don't have to. But you *do* have to set up your activities in a way that brings that to the surface. One of the easiest ways to make learning sticky is to ask questions that elicit learners' previous or current experiences because this naturally connects with their own schemas. This also creates more inclusion than trying to find an example that works for every type of person or background.

For example, in my Change Quest™ model workshops, I teach people how to lead and manage change. I have built flexibility into the activities so that facilitators can adjust course content based on their audience's needs. We can ask the participants to think back on changes they've previously experienced, or assess current changes while right in the middle of them, or look to the future and prepare for an upcoming change. This approach can apply to almost any topic and your choice depends on what is best for your audience and the goals of your workshop.

Metaphors and analogies activate schemas by connecting the new content to something they already know. For example, demystify project management by drawing connections to buying groceries. Most people have bought groceries so it can help them understand something they might find intimidating and complex. Be sure you pick a common experience for the audience and not just something from your own sphere. For example, while project management can also be compared to planning a vacation, I would not use it because lots of people have never flown on a plane or travelled outside their state let alone their country.

Second, use activities that work for a wide range of styles and preferences. Some people love to talk things through while others really prefer to think deeply about something on their own. Some people love to engage and interact while others want to roll up their sleeves and create something. While no one activity accounts for all that variety, you can cover a range over the course of your workshop. You can also give choices within your activities. For example, I often create worksheets with key questions. But I give participants a choice whether they want to work on it on their own or talk it through with another person. For group activities, I give them choices to brainstorm on posters or build a prototype using provided supplies. You get the idea.

Third, make sure activities bring out what people are really thinking, feeling, and have questions about. All of that unspoken stuff is often where the real transformation happens so bring it to the surface. But since people don't always feel safe enough to be vulnerable—especially if their boss is in the room—use activities that allow for anonymous or confidential comments. For better privacy, you might give people larger post-it notes and have them write answers to key questions you asked, or you can have them voice their worries, concerns, or questions. Then you collect them from everyone and post them on the wall. Then do what's called a "gallery walk" so that everyone can read them (see more information in the next chapter). This can lead to a great discussion about the issues or themes that need to be worked on.

Finally, if the workshop is about producing some outcome, I love using a form of design sprinting that Jake Knapp created for Google Ventures Sprint. Read more in his book titled *Sprint: How to Solve Big Problems and Test New Ideas in Just Five Days* or from his videos on YouTube. It's a fast and fun way to take a group through a process of designing and prototyping something new. It's built on a series of quick exercises that bring out all kinds of new thinking, and it moves people past their over-focus on perfection. I always find that it drives amazing collaboration, creative thinking, and is highly engaging with lots of laughter and bonding. I have applied it to all kinds of topics and forms of workshop.

40. Creating Safety for Group Interaction

In addition to delivering great content, the most important thing you can do for your participants is to make it safe for them to take risks and make mistakes. This is the only way people really learn so creating a safe environment should be your top priority. Here are some ways to do that.

First, create ground rules. Ground rules are the way that participants agree to engage and interact with each other during the workshop. By starting with ground rules, you signal that you care about making the workshop conducive for their learning. I usually ask the participants to come up with their own ground rules by asking something like "In order to fully participate, and even to take risks and make mistakes, what ground rules would you need in place during this workshop?" Then I capture their suggestions on a poster, asking clarifying questions when needed. I ask "what else?" until the group is satisfied with the list. This takes 15 to 20 minutes and we can always add to it later if needed.

I also let them know that, as the facilitator, it's my job to keep us all accountable for the ground rules, myself included. As a result, have some practiced phrases handy to gently remind the group if they start to violate anything on the list. And think ahead about how you'll handle repeat offenders and big violations. That way, you'll be prepared for anything.

You'll also want to help people connect with each other. Human biology is a powerful thing and behind our need to survive, we have a strong need to belong. This is true for all groups, even ones that are together only for a short time. The truth is that people will be much more willing to take risks and make mistakes if they feel like they know the others in the group. So be intentional with your introductions and activities, making choices that enhance connection. For example, you could ask people to introduce themselves with typical information, but your group will feel more connected if you ask them to share something more personal, like their favorite meal or the superpower they wish they had.

I usually start a workshop with low-risk questions, but I'll get deeper the more time we spend together. I might ask, "Tell us about a cherished memory from childhood" or "Share a time you struggled. What did you do to move through it?" Obviously, knowing your group will help you pick the right kinds of questions to ask—some people enjoy sillier questions while others strongly dislike them. Choose what will help your group connect and move forward.

Then, give participants several opportunities to work together. Nothing helps people connect like interacting. And what's great is that these can simultaneously be the processing activities that break your learning into those 20-minute chunks. I often have people do a quick 5-minute discussion in pairs, trios, or quads. That means that every person gets a chance to be heard even if they don't speak in front of the large group. I switch back and forth between pairs or trios and then combine them into larger groups of six or eight people, extending time to 10 to 15 minutes.

And if you are teaching a skill, have learners practice together. They can provide each other with valuable opportunities to practice, and offer suggestions, coaching, and encouragement. It can be helpful to set up practice sessions as just that: practice. I usually say something like, "All right, let's give this new skill a try. Embrace making mistakes because that's how we learn. Let's jump in and see what happens."

Finally, as you consider your options to create connection, be sure you think about what will make your participants feel most included. Inclusion is a powerful feeling—in fact, brain science shows that being excluded registers in the brain the same way as physical pain. So be sensitive to creating moments of inclusion. For example, I say "get in pairs or trios" so that no one feels left out if there is not an even number of people. I also make sure that my activities work for people of different physical abilities; if someone is in a wheelchair, for example, they can easily and seamlessly participate. If you have not yet immersed yourself in training on diversity and inclusion, I encourage you to do so because it will help you be more effective with a wide range of people. Learn more by reading *Wired to Connect: The Brain Science of Teams and a New Model for Creating Collaboration and Inclusion*.

Being a great learning facilitator is an ongoing journey because the more you expand your experience and toolkit, the better you get. I am always picking up new ideas for how to increase participation and collaboration. Here are some of my favorite activities and exercises that can work for almost any type of content or topic.

1. **The interview:** Interviewing another person is a great way to increase listening skills and empathy. Give participants a list of questions and have them interview each other, taking a certain amount of time before they switch. This can be especially helpful if you have people who are overly talkative or competitive.

2. **Freewrite:** Many people prefer to process internally and/or are uncomfortable sharing in front of a large group. I have found that a 1- to 2-minute freewrite allows people time to gather and organize their thoughts. Participation always goes way up after I do this quick activity.

3. **Anonymous questions or comments:** Anonymity is a really great tool for getting the unspoken issues on the table where they can be addressed. There are several ways to do this, but the most important aspect is that you truly protect people's identity. One option is to use electronic polling with a smart phone; several companies offer easy and effective solutions for asking questions and displaying real time feedback in the form of graphs or even word clouds. Good old-fashioned pen and paper work too. Just make sure you think through how you keep people from seeing what others write. One option is called "popcorn" where everyone balls up their paper and throws it to the front of the room. Then you can pick up several to answer and it adds a lighter, playful tone to the experience.

4. **Gallery walk:** Another option is to collect all the papers, tape them around the room, and do a "gallery walk." This always leads to a great discussion because people inevitably learn what all the other participants are thinking and feeling. I set this up so that people read in silence, which helps eliminate unnecessary or insensitive commentary. This method makes it easy to see common themes, which can be helpful for making decisions about what actions to take.

Doing a gallery walk allows new and more perspectives to come to light

5. **Heat map:** After a gallery walk, you might try "heat mapping" to create focus around what the group feels is most important, and where you and the group feel the energy. Give everyone small stickers and let participants place them on the comments or ideas that resonate most. I usually give each person three to five stickers to start. Then I cull the

ideas with the most stickers and do a second or even third round, giving people fewer stickers to place each time. It only takes a few minutes but provides a strikingly clear and visible representation that helps the group coalesce around the top issues or priorities.

6. **The magic wand:** This is my favorite way to move a group into a super creative space or help get them unstuck. You basically remove all limitations. I will often say something like "You've been given a magic wand, so time is no longer a factor. Neither is money or staffing or _____ [fill in the blank with whatever seems to be holding them back]. Use this magic wand to dream big and imagine the seemingly impossible." It's amazing how this frees people up.

7. **Take a break:** For me, one of the biggest revelations of my brain science research was that our best moments of insight come when we *stop* thinking about something. That's because we do our big thinking in the prefrontal cortex and we often need to let that go for connections to be made in other parts of our brain. I have come to really value the power of a break—one that's longer than just using the restroom. While it might feel like "wasted" time, give it a try and see what new insights people have when they reconvene.

Taking the time to carefully design the most effective activities will enhance the participants' engagement and experiences. And creating an environment where your participants feel like it's okay to take risks and make mistakes will greatly enhance their ability to learn and build the right skills, which only improves the effectiveness of your learning program.

41. Keeping on Track and Solving Challenges

All right, it's the day of your learning event and you're ready to go. Let's talk about how you keep things on track as the event unfolds. A large part of being a great facilitator is keeping things on time. You should already have a well-thought-out learning plan with accurate time estimates for each section. I always keep the agenda in front of me with timing clearly marked so I can easily see where we are. I also put notes about timing in my slide deck, so I know if I am on track, ahead, or behind at any given moment.

At the same time, there needs to be some flexibility so you can let a valuable conversation continue or rein in an unproductive activity. Your participants will be very appreciative if you start and end on time, and if you can adapt to their needs while achieving the goals of the learning program. So, your agenda needs to be a flexible plan that you can adjust as needed. Here are some strategies you can use:

- **Explain a bit about your role.** I find it helpful to tell my audience that I am both the timekeeper and goal tender. I'll be making sure we stay on track while simultaneously meeting the needs of the group. This means that our agenda is approximate, as we may adjust 10 minutes here or there. I always promise that we will end on time since many people have made plans based on the stated end time.

- **Build signposts into your slide deck.** Even though your audience has the agenda in front of them, I find it helpful to align the presentation to the agenda with clearly marked segues from one topic to the next. This helps participants feel oriented to where we are and what is still coming.

- **Be a talking clock.** Saying things like "We have 10 minutes for this discussion" or "This activity will take about 30 minutes" can really help your audience gauge their participation. If people seem antsy, I might also say, "We're about 20 minutes away from lunch or a break" to help them settle down. I used to dislike trying to call people back together once they were actively engaged in an activity or discussion. Starting to shush people or yell never feels good to me, so I had some little timer movies made that I drop into my slide deck. These movies count down on screen so that the audience can see exactly how much time is left and can wrap up accordingly.

- **Trim or expand at the breaks.** You should have built-in flexibility to your content and activities. So, at the break, pop into your slide deck and hide or show slides accordingly. For example, I might have a section that I can do either a quick summary of in 5 minutes or present in more depth for 15 minutes. Both versions sit in my deck and I use the break to adjust based on what we need.

- **Give participants choices.** Instead of making all the decisions for the group, I will sometimes let them choose between how they want to use the next chunk of time. For example, I can say "Let me check in with you about what you want to do. We could allot 10 more minutes to the discussion you are having, and then doing a quicker run through of the next segment on X. Or we can wrap up here and have more time for X. Which do you prefer?" This can be especially helpful for intact groups, for example, doing strategic planning, because they have a better sense of the best use of their time. But it works with all kinds of learning programs.

Keeping sessions on track is one of the things that distinguishes the best facilitators from the mediocre ones. Knowing how to read your audience and adjusting the workshop to meet their needs is an advanced skill but one that will pay off many times over.

Dealing with Challenging Dynamics

Working with a group of people can be both incredibly rewarding and sometimes challenging. The dynamics among a group can be unpredictable, which may require you to respond in the moment to keep everything flowing smoothly. When I train facilitators, I always have a session where I ask them to write down their worst-case scenarios. Then we tackle each one, so they are prepared to deal with them. Here are the most common ones:

1. **You have a group that is very quiet.** This has happened to me and it can be uncomfortable if they aren't engaging, or worse, not laughing at your awesome jokes. Sometimes, they just need time to warm up. One strategy is just to wait. That silence seems longer to you than it really is, so I encourage you to just breathe and count to 20 in your head. Someone usually speaks up. Sometimes, you truly do have a quiet group. In that case, the best thing to do is make participating easier, which means doing lots of work in pairs and small groups.

Be prepared to handle a variety of challenges

2. **Someone is doing all the talking** or taking up a lot of time on his or her individual needs. At first, I just focus on making it easy for others to participate. I might ask folks to chat in groups and then ask for a volunteer from each group to share some highlights. Or I might go around the room and hear from everyone. If the person persists, move up to saying something more direct like "I really appreciate your participation—and I'd like to open it up to folks who have not yet had a chance to say something." And if I need to, I will speak to the person privately during a break, asking them in a kind manner to hold back so we can create space for others.

3. **Someone violates the ground rules.** This is bound to happen so be prepared with ways to gently remind the group about the ground rules because they are counting on you to hold everyone accountable. If the behavior persists, I will then speak to it more directly, getting more firm as needed.

4. **Someone is overly aggressive, making others uncomfortable.** Start with the strategies I just mentioned but be prepared to interrupt someone as needed. If the person seems triggered or upset, I will call a break and connect with them directly to see if we can get them settled. But if the person is truly disruptive and not able to shift, you may need to ask them to leave or get other facilitators or hosts involved.

5. **The existing conflict is hijacking the experience of the whole group.** With a conflict that seems to involve many members of the

group, I have found it helpful to give them a choice. I'll ask if they feel they can set aside their differences long enough to complete the learning program, or if they want to use our time together to resolve the conflict. At this point, I essentially flip the session to be on having difficult conversations and conflict resolution. (This is a topic that you should be prepared to lead if necessary. This is why the more work-shops you facilitate, the more adept you get, because you have all this content at your fingertips, and you can be super responsive to your group's needs.) You can also "freeze" the moment so that people can get a new perspective. I'll ask people to stop all conversation and say something like, "Let's stop for a minute. What's happening here in the room? What different views or opinions are being debated?" This can also be a great way to bring in others, who are not in the conflict, and it also gives people time to breathe and calm down.

6. **A participant openly challenges you in front of the room**, questioning your content or your credentials. Obviously, the more you know your content, the more confident you will be and can calmly address their questions. But if they truly disagree, have some elegant language ready to essentially say that you regret that they feel this way *and* you need to continue delivering what you were engaged to do.

7. **You make a mistake,** like giving out wrong information or saying something spontaneous that comes out in a way you didn't intend. If I misspeak, as soon as I notice, I take responsibility for my error and try to fix it. If it's something I realize later, I will send a follow-up email to the group.

Like anything, facing your worst fears can be really empowering because you know you can handle it if it happens. That doesn't mean that it's enjoyable, but the best facilitators can navigate almost any sticky situation while remaining calm and professional.

42. Creating Closure and Extending Learning

People don't realize, but how you close out your learning program is almost more important than how you start it. It is the last thing that people will remember, and you have an opportunity to send them off feeling motivated and inspired, no matter what the topic is. The end is also where things can get chaotic because you might be feeling rushed if you got behind in your agenda. And there are also tactical issues to take care of like evaluations. But take the time to design the ending of your event so that you create the appropriate emotional closure for your group.

Here are some things to consider when wrapping up your learning experience. There will probably be an ideal order for the topic and group you are leading, so move them around accordingly.

1. **Be sure you review the key points.** I find it helpful to put a second copy of the agenda or learning objectives slide at the end and use it as a way to do a quick review of the material we covered.

2. **Give people time to synthesize their own key takeaways.** After I review the agenda, I give people 5 minutes to work on this and it really helps them focus in on what they learned.

3. **Have your participants create an action plan.** If you're asking them to do any post-event work or extended learning, give people a handout where they can write down their action plan. Depending on the content, I sometimes I frame this as a 30-60-90-day plan.

4. **Have learners schedule some initial items on their calendar.** This can be a powerful way to make sure they keep the momentum going after they leave the event. You could have them take out their smart phones right then and put some time on their calendar to work on an action item, review the workshop materials, or schedule a coffee with another participant. But be careful. It can also take people away from being present if they start reading their email or thinking about how busy they are. So, make a judgment call about what is best for your group.

5. **Take care of important logistics.** This can include a range of things like evaluations, post-event work, exchanging contact information, and leaving the building or assigned parking lot.

6. **Finally, leave the group on a high note of inspiration.** I will save an activity, fun video, or great quote to share at the end, to bring the group back from the tactical stuff to the event's positive tone. And if it feels right, I will ask people to close by sharing something they are feeling or that they learned. If you have time, it's nice to go around the room and hear from everyone (ask them to keep it brief; just a few words). If you don't have time, take at least one minute to have them share in pairs or trios. That way, every person gets to say something.

Closing your program is an important part of the facilitator's role. You want to set your participants up for success as they leave the special environment you created and integrate what they learned back into their regular lives. By making it positive and memorable, you will send them off with a last touch of your valuable guidance.

If you have done a good job, your participants are excited about what they learned in your program and are eager to do more. Take advantage of that energy by setting them up with clear next steps for extending their learning. This keeps their momentum going, but it's also great practice for learning design based on what we know about how the brain works. Extending learning helps move the content into long-term memory and adds more repetitions to the neural pathways, building the right habits.

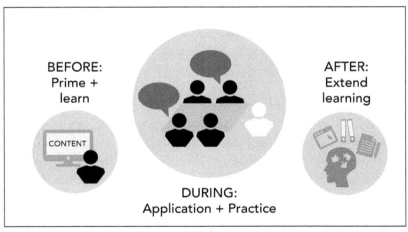

The flipped classrom extends learning after the event

There are lots of ways to extend the learning. The right choice will depend on what kind of workshop you led and what change you are trying to create in the participants. Here are some good examples.

First, provide a list of relevant or related materials. This can include articles, books, chapters, videos, websites, online courses, etc. Ask people to pick something from the list that interests them and commit to doing it in the next two weeks. It is fairly easy to make the list. I often share the source material I used when creating the workshop in case people want to do a deeper dive into something specific we covered. If you are trying to elicit more critical or creative thinking, also include materials that diverge from or openly challenge what you taught. And even ask for participants to contribute to the list if they find articles, videos, and other resources that inspired them. In fact, if you have some for this book, please email me at Info@BrittAndreatta.com.

Next, set up opportunities to practice. Practice is the only way we get better at things. But it can be challenging for learners to find the time to practice or even know how to set up the right kind. Help them by giving them specific activities to do when they return to their regular environments. Whether it's a set of worksheets to complete, online assessments to submit, or a certain number of repetitions of a behavior to finish, help your learners get that valuable practice that will set them up for success.

Third, empower shared learning in pairs or groups. When people learn together, it can amplify their progress because they build on each other's insights and experiences. In addition, the content gets anchored to the relationship, which reinforces it when they see each other later. You can continue this outside of the workshop by requesting or requiring people to meet in pairs or groups for discussions or practice work. This can include online interactions as well as face-to-face meetings. Shared learning also creates accountability since they are more likely to keep a commitment to their partner even when their schedule gets busy.

Finally, hold your learners accountable to finish their work. The more your learners are supported in completing the work and the practice, the more likely you are to see the real behavior change you are seeking. Many learning platforms have features that enable different kinds of activities and engagements. Set these up with clear deadlines and scheduling reminders.

I love the results I get with extended learning. It gives the eager and motivated learners something to work with, and it allows me to see who the eager and motivated learners are. In addition, it helps me think more clearly about which level of depth is enough for the goals of the workshop while allowing for more to unfold outside the formal bounds of the event. Give it a try and see how it works for you. I think you'll be pleased with the results.

43. Evaluating Learning

One of things you'll likely be asked to demonstrate is the impact of your learning. After all, a learning program needs to drive results, but it's important to get clear about what those results are. Did you know that there are actually five levels of evaluation? The success of your program depends on your ability to demonstrate all five. These were initially identified by Donald Kirkpatrick but were updated by Jack Phillips, who runs the ROI Institute.

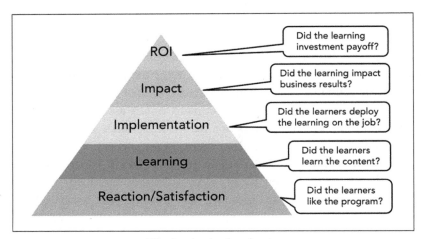

The five levels of evaluation

As we go through them, let's apply them to our example with John and Maria at the hospitality company. John has contacted Maria because his marketing team isn't delivering the right level of quality on time. Maria runs L&D and builds a learning solution to address his needs.

Let's look at the first, most basic level of evaluation: participant satisfaction. Did they like it or not? After the training, Maria asks participants how much they liked or were satisfied with the program. Some people use Net Promoter Score or NPS, which is an example of this base level of evaluation. (I also like to ask learners to comment on how valuable the learning was to them and whether they improved their knowledge and skill.)

The second level measures comprehension and whether people learned the content. This can only be truly measured through an assessment, since self-reports can be inaccurate. But it is easy to use tools like Survey Monkey or interactive videos like HapYak to assess understanding. Maria assesses their comprehension on executing the project plan, time management, and quality control. Because the results show low comprehension on an element, Maria rolls out post-event booster material to close the gap.

The third level is implementation and measures if people are able to deploy that learning on the job. I'm sad to say that this is where a lot of learning programs fall short. Which is why thinking like a consultant is so important. It allows you and your stakeholders to get clear about what behaviors you need to see on the job and by when. You can track this by observing their behaviors or by looking for changes in the metrics you identified. John should be able to observe and track change in his team's behaviors.

The fourth level is about impact and whether that behavior change has moved the needle on the metrics that matter. In our example, we should see the percentage of on-time delivery of marketing materials increase at the same time we see percentage of errors decrease. If that's not happening, then Maria works with John to adjust the learning solution or add more elements until the results are achieved. If your organization is investing time and money in learning, it needs to demonstrate the necessary results. Period.

Finally, the last level is to calculate ROI (return on investment). It's a measure of the costs spent on the learning solution as it relates to the savings created by the behavior change. There are three different things you can measure here, and they can be calculated with any currency:

1. **You can measure the benefit-cost ratio**, which is the program benefits divided by the costs. Expressed as a ratio, the benefit (return) of an investment is compared to the cost. Let's say Maria's learning solution costs $20,000 to rollout, but over time it saves $35,000; that would be a cost-benefit ratio of 1.75 to 1. Meaning for every $1 she spent, the organization received $1.75 in benefit. That's a good return.

2. **You can also calculate ROI**, which is expressed as a percentage: You take the program benefits minus the program costs, then divide that by the program costs. Using this same example, the ROI was 75 percent, meaning that every dollar gave back 75 percent more in benefit.

3. **Finally, there is time-to-payoff**, a measure of how long it takes for the investment to pay for itself. To calculate this, take the program costs and divide them by the program benefits, and then multiply that number by a unit of time (e.g., months, weeks, etc.). In this case, we'll use 12 months, so this learning solution paid for itself in just over 6 months. Every month after that is all benefit.

BCR = $\dfrac{\text{Program Benefits}}{\text{Program Costs}}$ (x:y)	Example	$\dfrac{\$35,000}{\$20,000}$	**BCR = 1.75:1** Every $1 spent, yielded $1.75 in *total* benefit.
ROI % = $\dfrac{\text{Program Benefits} - \text{Program Costs}}{\text{Program Costs}}$ X100	Example	$\dfrac{¥35,000 - ¥20,000}{¥\,20,000}$	**ROI = 75%** Every ¥1 spent, yielded ¥.75 in *net* benefit.
Time to Payoff = $\dfrac{\text{Program Costs}}{\text{Program Benefits}}$ X Unit of Time	Example	$\dfrac{₹20,000}{₹35,000}$ X 12 months	**Time to payoff = 6.84 mos** The program will pay for itself in 6.84 months.

Three ways to calculate the benefits of learning programs

In these examples, we were tracking actual financial costs of money spent and saved. But all kinds of costs and benefits can be explored. You can look at hard data like cost, output, time, quality, and energy, all of which translates to financial data. And there are other people-based indicators that have a crucial impact on your business too, including customer service, creativity or innovation, the development of your talent, and the culture of your organization. Table 5 gives you examples of each.

Be thorough when you explore the metrics that matter in your organization. Draw from different data sources to create a thorough and accurate picture. If you want a deeper dive, I encourage you to read books by Jack Philips as he has several that feature detailed case studies and examples. Or you might want to attend trainings through his ROI Institute.

As learning professionals, we must design learning to deliver on all five levels of evaluation and track the results. This both helps us show real ROI on learning and allows us to course correct as needed so that we're always delivering the metrics that matter to our organization.

Table 5. *Examples of different financial and people-based costs*

	Types of Financial and People-Based Costs
Cost	Unit Costs, Overhead Costs, Operating Costs, Variances, Insurance, Legal Penalties/Fines, Accident Costs, Sales Expenses
Output	Units Produced, Tons Manufactured, Items Assembled, Students Graduated, Tasks Completed, Accounts Signed, Packages Shipped
Time	Response Time, Downtime, Overtime, Cycle Time, Time to Market, Supervisory Time, Work Stoppages
Quality	Errors, Waste, Rework, Rejects, Defects, Shortages, Failures, Accidents
Energy	Water, Fossil Fuels, Food, Pollution, Water, Electricity, Minerals, Land, Trees
Customer Service	Service, Loyalty, Impression, Retention, Complaints, Returns, Employee Brand
Creativity	Innovation, Risk Taking, Collaboration, New Ideas, Alliances, Partnerships
Development	Job Effectiveness, Capability, Performance, Promotions, Requests for Transfer, Employee Brand, Potential
Culture	Turnover, Complaints, Grievances, Absenteeism, Tardiness, Engagement, Job Satisfaction, Loyalty

Your Learning Journey

For this section, think about a learning program or event you need to create for others. Use these questions to help you identify possible strategies to support your goals.

- Apply the three I's: Information, Instruction, Inspiration. What could you offer in each category? Are all three needed?
- Outline how you would balance communication, demonstration, and experimentation. What content and activities can you use?
- What issue or problem is this learning attempting to solve? What needs do your learners have?
- Try using the consulting questions in chapter 37. What new insights did you gain?
- Identify the starting and ending point for this program. What's the story arc?
- What are some ways you can create safety for your group? Are there any special dynamics or individuals you should account for?
- What is your biggest worry or potential challenge for this learning program? Create a plan, so you are prepared should it happen.
- How can you measure the impact of this learning program? If you can, identify options for each of the five levels of evaluation.

CREATE A GROWTH CULTURE OF LEARNING

"There are 10 seeds in an apple. But how many apples are in a seed? You must help your employees learn and grow so they become the talented workforce you need tomorrow."

Martha Soehren, Chief Talent Development
Officer, Comcast

44. Your Culture of Learning

In this section, we are going to explore the final element in the Three Phase Model of Learning: a growth culture of learning.

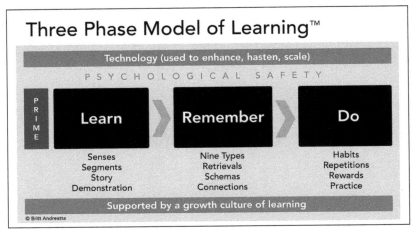

All the elements are supported by a growth culture of learning

Whether you know it or not, your organization *already* has a culture of learning. Every organization does, because humans are biologically wired to learn and we do so every day. Sometimes this learning occurs in formal experiences, like a training event, but most of our learning happens through constant small and informal interactions with peers and leaders.

While employees report that they spend 40 percent of their time at work learning, 80 percent of that learning occurs outside of formal learning programs. They might be learning new information or skills that they can apply to their work. Or they might be learning that the stated values and mission of the organization are honored differently than the learner assumed before joining. And they are definitely learning if it's okay to take risks and make mistakes at the organization.

Is your organization empowering a positive culture of learning? As we've seen, the research shows it enhances an organization's chances of success. Organizations with poor learning cultures breed conformity and stagnation, experience turnover of their top talent, struggle to keep their customers, and ultimately fall behind their competitors on a number of fronts. They may seem profitable on paper for a bit but ultimately the costs of the human factor catch up and they fail in the end. The organizations that do not just succeed but flourish and thrive empower positive cultures of learning.

A study by the Association for Talent Development found that top-performing organizations are five times more likely to have a culture of learning than lower-performing ones. In addition, they are twice as apt to say that their learning department helps meet organizational business goals. And a report by Deloitte found that learning culture accounts for nearly half (46 percent) of overall improved business outcomes including innovation, time to market, and market share.

Culture of learning is a hot topic and you'll find a lot of publications out there talking about how to define it. Let's look at a couple of examples. According to Josh Bersin, it is the "collective set of organizational values, conventions, processes, and practices that influence and encourage both individuals and the collective organization to continuously increase knowledge, competence, and performance." The Corporate Executive Board defines it as a "culture that supports an open mindset, an independent quest for knowledge, and shared learning directed toward the mission and goals of the organization."

The through line seems to be that learning culture goes far beyond the workshops and training programs hosted by the learning team. Those offerings are certainly a big part of the picture but the *real* culture of learning lives in the beliefs and attitudes of its people—specifically around two key questions: How do we help people learn, grow, and improve? And, perhaps more importantly, what do we do when people make a mistake or fail?

As we've seen, the truth is that learning and failing are inextricably linked. You cannot have a positive and vibrant learning culture if you do not also have a culture that is safe for taking risks and making mistakes. Period. Again, this has been verified by a range of research, including Harvard professor Dr. Amy Edmondson's research on psychological safety, a global company culture study conducted by Google, and Dr. Carol Dweck's work on the growth mindset. I combine all of these critical concepts in what I call Growth Culture™.

To illustrate the crucial importance of both learning and failing, I find a tree is a useful metaphor to demonstrate a healthy Growth Culture. For a tree to thrive and grow into its fullest potential, it needs to be rooted in soil, and the quality of that soil determines what we see above the surface.

The soil represents how people are treated when they take risks and make mistakes. It is the very foundation in which the success of your organization is rooted. To grow a healthy tree, you must start with good soil. If it's sitting in toxic soil, it will never reach its full potential, no matter how much sunlight and water it receives. In this metaphor, water and sunlight represent the opportunities to learn and grow.

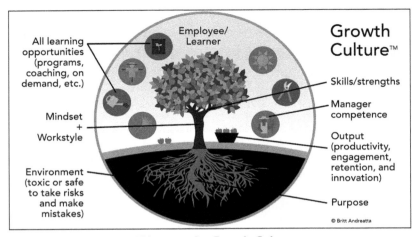

Elements of a Growth Culture

Add to that things that nurture and accelerate growth like fertilizer, deep root watering, and pest control. All of these things happen "above ground" and are the elements that most people think of when they talk about a culture of learning—things like training events, leadership development programs, online learning resources, etc.

In the middle, you have the tree itself: an individual employee. Think of the trunk as mindset and workstyle. The central taproot of the tree represents the individual's sense of purpose. This taproot provides an anchor that creates stability throughout an employee's life and can also help them withstand work stressors like a difficult change, ineffective manager, or challenging colleagues. The branches represent the employee's current skills, which become more developed with age and experience. The overall health of the tree tells you the quality of the soil and whether they are planted in an area that support or hinders their growth. Finally, we can look at the productivity of the employee in terms of quality, performance, efficiency, and other ways we measure output. Humans are just like trees in that when they are thriving, they grow and are highly productive.

If you want to create a great culture of learning, you must first look at your soil and explore how people in your organization really treat each other when they take risks and make mistakes. Some soil or "below ground" questions to consider:

- Do people admit when they don't know something or ask for help when they need it?
- What happens when someone makes a mistake or fails?
- Are they teased or shamed or are they encouraged to look at what happened and try again?

- Do they ultimately get shamed, sidelined, demoted, or fired?
- Do people admit their mistakes and take responsibility for fixing them or do they blame others?
- Do managers and leaders share stories of how they took risks or recovered from a failure?

As you can see, this is a crucial aspect of your culture. The most amazing training programs in the world won't help if people don't feel safe enough to stretch and grow. The soil represents your environment's psychological safety. Employees will endure toxic soil for a while but, unlike trees, employees won't just sit in poor soil and allow themselves to wither and die. Instead, they uproot and transplant themselves in another organization. If you have disengagement and/or high turnover, you likely have a problem with your soil. Turnover is rarely evenly dispersed across an entire organization but rather tends to focus within a couple departments or under certain managers.

Now let's look above ground. There are lots of things an organization can do to cultivate their employees. This includes the breadth, depth, and accessibility of opportunities to learn as well as the quality of those programs. Organizations with positive cultures of learning place learning at the top of their values. Leaders believe in it, invest in it, and model it. They also consistently recognize and reward learning. Consider these questions:

- Do managers and leaders act as role models, showing a commitment to their own learning and improvement?
- Are learning programs available for every level of employee, from new hire to top executive?
- Is time for learning encouraged, supported, and seen as part of the "real" work?
- Is progress or improvement recognized and rewarded through informal and formal performance review processes?

The combination of all these pieces together represents an organization's *real* learning culture. So if you want to reap all the benefits the research has found, then make creating a growth culture of learning your top priority. Your short-term investment over the coming weeks and months will more than payoff in the long term.

45. Benefits of a Growth Culture

As we now know, study after study has shown that a positive culture of learning offers many impressive benefits, such as driving all kinds of business metrics that matter. Let's look at some examples.

1. **Increased employee performance and productivity in achieving business outcomes.** A study by Bersin by Deloitte found a direct, positive correlation between learning culture and performance. Learning culture accounts for 46 percent of overall improved business outcomes, such as higher levels of innovation, faster time to market, and greater market share. They found that organizations with designed growth—defined as "the degree to which the organization intentionally creates the culture, conditions, and learning experiences that foster enduring and continuous employee learning and development"—were 5 times more likely to have strong business outcomes and 10 times more likely to have strong learner experience outcomes. According to the Association for Talent Development, "Organizations that commit to helping employees grow will see the value in their bottom line."

2. **Higher levels of employee engagement.** According to Gallup research, approximately 16 percent of US employees—and 19 percent of global employees—are actively disengaged. And their disengagement costs their organizations approximately 34 percent of their annual salary. McLean & Company did a study and found that one of the primary drivers of engagement is opportunities to learn. In addition, they discovered that for every 10 percent improvement in learning effectiveness, employee engagement increased by nearly 4 percent.

3. **Ability to more competitively attract and retain top talent.** The ability to grow and develop your current employees is a distinct advantage in the strong competition for the best workplace talent. ATD found that high-performing organizations are three times more likely to use their learning culture in recruiting new talent. Data from Glassdoor indicates that "the ability to learn and progress" is one of the biggest differentiators for Millennials when they are choosing a place to work. And 42 percent of Millennials say they will likely leave their organization because they are not learning fast enough. And it's not just Millennials. As mentioned in the introduction, Deloitte's *2019 Human Capital Trends* report found that the "opportunity to learn" is

now among the top reasons for most people taking a job, and that their "inability to learn and grow" is the primary reason given for quitting. Given the power of learning, it's no surprise that it tops the 10 trends that organizations around the world are prioritizing.

4. **More readily able to effectively adapt to change.** Adaptability to change is a key differentiator for successful organizations. Yet, 90 percent of all CEOs believe their company is facing disruptive change. And 70 percent say their organization does not currently have the skills to adapt. Yikes! That same study found that executives see learning as the primary driver of employee development. And 84 percent view learning as important or very important. A recent report by the World Economic Forum shows that more than half of all employees will require significant reskilling: "By 2022, no less than 54 percent of all employees will require significant re- and upskilling. Of these, about 35 percent are expected to require additional training of up to six months, 9 percent will require reskilling lasting 6 to 12 months, while 10 percent will require additional skills training of more than a year."

5. **Better customer satisfaction and responsiveness to customer needs.** Bersin by Deloitte found that organizations with high-impact learning cultures had a distinct customer advantage because of their 30 percent higher ratings in both customer satisfaction and customer responsiveness, placing them in the 90th percentile compared to the 60th.

Given all this, it's surprising that only about 30 percent of organizations have a culture of learning, but developing one is quickly becoming a top priority for leaders across all sectors and around the world. According to LinkedIn Learning's *2019 Workplace Learning Report*, 82 percent of learning professionals have active executive support for learning and development.

As you consider how to develop your own culture of learning, focus on developing these top five characteristics, which studies show are essential to success:

*   The organization's learning strategies are closely aligned with its strategic goals and outcomes.
*   The organization's values specifically refer to the importance of learning and development (L&D).
*   The learning function is staffed by qualified learning professionals who know how to create real behavior change.

- Learning is an integral component of the organization's talent management ecosystem.
- Learning is delivered where and when it is needed, creating a cohesive landscape of accessible opportunities.

Of course, none of these can really happen if people are afraid to take risks or make mistakes. When we look at all the potential benefits, it's clear that every dollar invested in creating a positive culture of learning will pay for itself many times over.

The first step is to honor the ever-present nature of learning. Learning is not an event to be scheduled nor something that is owned by one department. However, L&D should be the group driving the conversation and creating the culture and environment where learning is celebrated and supported.

Remember, learning is happening every day in your organization. People learn on their own, through experience and exploration. They learn by watching others, discovering which behaviors are rewarded and ignored. And people help each other learn through those small moments of advising, guiding, and coaching. While this happens naturally and largely unconsciously, it is important for us to value learning as a path to mastery. The process of learning involves curiosity, exploration, taking risks, and most importantly, making mistakes. No one ever really develops mastery without those ever-important stumbles. This means that you need to create a culture where it is safe to take risks and make mistakes, in *every* department, not just your learning events. This also means that people celebrate "aha!" moments as much as they do the results or successes. Let's look at a few key ways to cultivate growth cultures.

First, ensure that your managers are effective coaches. Coaching is a powerful tool in the learning process. When managers apply the right blend of skills coaching and clarity it helps build employees' competence and confidence. I'm also a big fan of strengths-based models or processes, like appreciative inquiry, because it helps employees know how to harness their peak performances to make them daily occurrences.

Second, value growth and improvement in your performance system. Most performance rating systems are based on outcomes, not effort. But if you only assess how people perform you miss an opportunity to empower a positive learning culture. Several studies have shown that when people are measured on growth and improvement they step up and improve. We all know top performers who never grow or improve—they have managed to find a job that is a nice match to their current skills. And while they may do good work, they are not reaching for their fullest potential. I also recommend that you assess every employee's growth, which you can measure through effort put into learning, measurable improvement in a skill, and passion for growing. This should comprise a quarter to a third of your overall assessment, so that in addition to rewarding your top performers, you reward your top learners too.

Third, make learning easily accessible. This is critical. A positive learning culture recognizes and rewards all growth and improvement. On-demand learning empowers employees to seek and find their own answers when they need them most. Neuroscientists have found that people retain this type of learning far longer than just being told what to do. It also aligns with best practices in adult learning theory. I personally love online learning courses. When I am stuck, I need the answer quickly. It doesn't help me much to sign up for a course scheduled three weeks from now, that will force me to sit through a four-hour class to get the answer I need. In those situations I prefer watching a short video that I can access 24/7 from any smart device.

All kinds of valuable learning can be made accessible to employees and you'll find that technology must be a vital part of your learning strategy. And remember, not every type of learning works for every person or situation. This is why you need to use blended learning to maximize your options. In-person learning can contextualize learning for your organization and provide opportunities for hands-on application as well as collaboration. Online instruction is perfect for self-paced learning or as pre-learning for an in-person event.

Listen, you are sitting on a *gold mine* that is just waiting to be harnessed. Your employees possess the potential to drive your organization to new heights. If you create a positive culture of learning, you will naturally reap the many benefits learning provides and set up your organization for success.

46. Mapping Learning to Organizational Development

Organizations grow and change in predictable ways, moving through various stages of development. Each shift requires new skills for the organization's leaders and employees. As a talent development professional, you are in the business of cultivating the potential of your organization and its people. Knowing how to assess your organization's stage of development and, more importantly, the next phase it's growing into will help you anticipate business needs and be ready with the right learning solutions.

I use the Greiner Curve to assess any organization I'm working with. Dr. Larry Greiner is a professor at USC's Marshall School of Business, and his research identified six distinct phases organizations move through as a function of their age and size. There can be profound differences in how quickly an organization moves through the phases, ranging from months to decades. For example, a large, traditional financial institution will have a much slower, gentler progression than a fast-growing tech start-up.

According to the Greiner Curve, every phase of growth ultimately leads to a crisis point, when the current structure can no longer support the organization's needs, and these crisis points push change, transforming the organization to the next phase. The organization may then experience a period of relative stability until it hits the next crisis point. See if you can identify your organization's current phase:

1. **Growth through creativity.** In this phase, the founders build the organization. It starts small, so people wear many hats and communication is spontaneous and informal. But as the organization gets bigger, it leads to the crisis point of leadership, where professional management needs to be brought in to help run the various functions like marketing and human resources (HR).

2. **Growth through direction.** Additional leaders are brought in to manage various functions and the organization continues to develop new products and services. At some point (again, months to decades later), the scale of the offerings gets too big for the leaders to monitor, which creates the crisis point of autonomy where work and authority need to be delegated to others.

3. **Growth through delegation.** Top management adds layers of hierarchy so they can become less involved in the day-to-day details and focus on the organization's long-term strategy. But this transition is

often messy as new leaders may not yet be ready to take the reins or the top leaders struggle to let go, often micromanaging their team. In addition, the sheer size of the organization starts to stress the current policies and channels of communication, creating the crisis point of control, where the different parts of the organization need to work together better. Phase 3 is where problematic inconsistency arises in everything from budget processes to performance reviews.

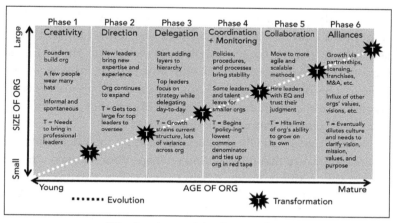

The six phases of the Greiner Curve

4. **Growth through coordination and monitoring.** New policies and procedures are introduced to establish structure. At first, this effort is quite helpful for a period of time, bringing stability and consistency to the broader scope of the organization. Inevitably the organization cannot seem to stop itself from policy-ing (policing?) the bad behavior of a few individuals or the lowest common denomenator. This leads to the crisis point of red tape, where bureaucracy gets burdensome. This phase often sees an exodus of longer-term employees and leaders who prefer the unstructured and informal freedom of the first three phases, but it's also an opportunity to bring in new people who have experience with the remaining stages of growth.

5. **Growth through collaboration.** To unwind the red tape, the organization pivots to replace bureaucracy with a range of scalable and agile systems that support more flexibility. Instead of a rigid system for making decisions, emotionally intelligent leaders are empowered and trusted to use good judgment. Greiner found that the next crisis point is internal growth, where the organization must look outside for new opportunities.

6. **Growth through alliances.** In this final stage, the organization can only solve its challenges by partnering with other organizations through actions like outsourcing, mergers, etc. This expansion ultimately brings in lots of other people and organizational cultures, which creates the crisis point of identity, where the organization must refocus on its vision, mission, and strategy.

It's not uncommon to be on the edge between two phases. It is also common that the core part of the business is more developed and in a different phase than newer/younger functions. When I consult with leaders, I ask them to identify the overall phase as well as the phases for each of the functions, as this can provide valuable information for designing effective learning solutions. I want to ask you the same thing—can you identify your organization's spot on the model? More importantly, can you tell what crisis point and transformation is coming?

Once you've assessed where your organization (or a department) is on the Greiner Curve, use that information to shape your learning strategy and solutions. This is a critical aspect of being a strategic partner to the business.

I've discovered that learning needs to shift with each stage. All kinds of key skills, like communication, collaboration, productivity, and innovation look different at the various phases. For example, someone who is phenomenal at innovation in phase 2 may completely stumble in phase 5 because the process and scope of innovation changes.

What constitutes "good" management and leadership shifts with the phases as well. Someone who is an outstanding leader in phase 3 may or may not be able to lead effectively in phase 4.

That is why I recommend that you map your learning strategy to the Greiner Curve. You really do need to develop and deliver different kinds of programs over time, and a lot of organizations mistakenly develop *The* Management Training or *The* Workshop on Communication—as if one size fits all, forever. They might implement these programs and may even be initially successful, but they will ultimately hold back your organization because they'll remain static while your organization shifts and changes.

In order to have a robust learning strategy, map to your current *and* upcoming phases so that you can stay ahead of the curve (so to speak) delivering what is needed at just the right time. Also identify different programs for managers, leaders, and employees or individual contributors.

If your organization is in phase one or two, you will have just a few offerings, but which are infinitely valuable in helping your talent succeed at the challenges and opportunities that arise.

And as your organization grows into phases three and four, you should develop new and more programs to serve the needs of the business. In other words, shelve what was working great and redirect those resources to meeting the organization's *new* challenges and opportunities. The timing all depends on how fast your organization is growing through the phases. Fast-growth companies need to pivot quickly and often.

This is what it means to be a strategic partner to your organization, and it's vital to be effective in this role. Learning professionals do not often have a seat at the executive table but you should. If you are not initially given access, make it a goal to earn it by helping the organization succeed in its current phase of growth and, more importantly, to start preparing for the next one.

In my experience, when leaders see that I can accurately predict what ends up happening, they realize that the learning and development department or function is more than just "training." It's a vital and competitive advantage that they want to tap into. For example, we all know that identifying, recruiting, and retaining the talent that helps organizations thrive is expensive and time-consuming. But if you apply the Greiner Curve, we can see that employees are inevitably drawn to certain phases of organizational growth. Some love the startup phase and others thrive in the alliances phase.

Gone are the days where employees stayed with an organization until retirement. Now, employees seek their fit and stay with an organization through a couple of phases. If you know this, you can actually predict when you're likely to see some attrition. For example, employees who love phases 1 and 2 often find the transition to phases 3 and 4 uncomfortable as they feel that things are getting too big or bureaucratic. And while it may be disconcerting to see them leave, you can pivot to hiring experienced talent from other, bigger organizations, perhaps people ready to be a bigger fish in a smaller pond, and who have the skills to help your organization succeed.

Additionally, your learning strategy should identify high-potential talent (also called HiPos) and start preparing them for your organization's next crisis point and phase early on, so they are ready to step into the new roles and responsibilities. This will help you avoid having to hire too many folks from outside, which can dilute your culture and discourage employees who have been working toward career opportunities.

Organizational Consciousness

While the Greiner Curve is a great model for organizational growth, another driver of change in organizations is the evolution of consciousness. Frederic Laloux's research on this topic reveals some very interesting developments in his book *Reinventing Organizations: A Guide to Creating Organizations Inspired by the Next Stage of Human Consciousness*. Tony Hsieh, the CEO of Zappos, is a fan of Laloux's work and has used it to intentionally shift the consciousness of his company.

Neuroscientists, biologists, psychologists, sociologists, and anthropologists studying human consciousness have found it develops through stages, which they identify with colors. Laloux discovered that organizational development maps to these stages of human consciousness, and as humans evolve, so do the organizations they build.

Like Greiner's model, human consciousness evolves in sudden transformations. Consciousness is currently evolving more quickly, with five levels of consciousness actively shaping organizations over the past 200 years. Laloux says, "Every transition to a new stage of consciousness has ushered in a whole new era in human history. At every juncture, everything changed: society, the economy, the power structures…and organizational models." He describes each organizational stage with a corresponding color, starting with infrared and magenta, and ending with teal—the latest level that is becoming visible now.

	RED Impulsive	AMBER Conformist	ORANGE Achievement	GREEN Pluralistic	TEAL Evolutionary
Description	Thrives in chaos. Constant exercise of power by leader. Control through fear. Highly reactive and short-term.	Highly formal hierarchical roles. Command and control from top. Stability through rigorous process.	Focus is on profit, competition, and growth. Innovation is key. Management by objectives.	Within classic pyramid, focus is on culture, values, and employee engagement.	Organization is living system. Focus is on moving to integrated wholeness and authenticity.
Key Breakthroughs	Division of labor Command authority	Formal roles Rigorous processes	Innovation Accountability Meritocracy	Empowerment Values culture Stakeholders	Self-management Wholeness Evolutionary purpose
Guiding Metaphor	Wolf pack	Army	Machine	Family	Living organism
Current Examples	Mafia Tribal militias Street gangs	Military Most government agencies Public schools Catholic Church	Multinational companies Charter schools	Culture-driven organizations (e.g., Southwest, Ben & Jerry's, Google)	Consciousness-driven orgs (e.g., Patagonia, Favi, Morning Star, AES, Sounds True)
"Good" decisions judged by…	Achieving leader's desires	Conforming to social norms	Effectiveness and success Rational and logical	Belonging and harmony People/feeling process	Inner rightness Being of service Rational and intuitive

The evolution of consciousness in organizations

Teal organizations are just starting to emerge but by no means are they all young start-ups. Laloux features 11 teal organizations in his book ranging in size from 600 to 40,000 employees across a wide range of industries including apparel, manufacturing, technology, and healthcare. He depicts organizations as living systems with a direction of their own that need to be listened to. This shifts the organizational structure from one of hierarchy to more localized and collaborative teams. This shift ushers in new models of decision-making, job responsibilities, and performance management. Known as holacracy, key breakthroughs include self-management, wholeness, and authenticity. Current examples include Patagonia, Morning Star, and AES (a global energy company).

And Laloux is only one of several people talking about the intersection of consciousness and business—it's not as far in left field as you might think. I have seen clear evidence of this conscious evolution in organizations and it is at the heart of many change initiatives as well as shifts in what employees want and what drives engagement.

It's important to note that while this is an evolutionary process, some organizations align with a certain stage because it best suits their mission and work. For example, the military will likely always align with the Amber/Conformist stage because it must succeed in often chaotic and dangerous environments where adherence to strict processes is paramount. That doesn't mean that it won't adopt some elements of other stages but its core structure and way of working will stay amber.

In most of today's organizations, I see a blend of orange and green consciousness. Many organizations still set strategic and tactical goals using management by objectives (MBO) or key performance indicators (KPI) terminology and productivity/success is measured in goal achievement. At the same time, organizations are exhibiting quite a few green components as they compete for talent, especially among Millennial and technically trained employees. They create values-driven cultures and focus on employee engagement. In addition, there is a feeling of "family" within the organization and leaders seek the input of employees and strive to create an environment of employee empowerment.

Whether as employee or consultant, I have seen evidence supporting Laloux's model in every place I have ever worked. So I consider it an essential tool when assessing organizations. I strongly recommend you read his book and view some of the videos and resources he has posted on his website at ReinventingOrganizations.com. His rich research and detailed descriptions really helped me use his model in my work.

Clearly, the conscious evolution of organizations drives many change initiatives as the different stages come online. These changes are sourced in the consciousness of the employees, the leaders, or the customers, and all will need the right learning programs and events to ensure success.

47. Developing a Cohesive Learning Landscape

Research shows that learning and development is absolutely critical to the success of every organization. Study after study shows that learning is a key factor in increasing employee engagement as well as attracting and retaining top talent. In addition, the act of learning is the *only* way an organization grows and improves. Organizations that succeed have cultures that encourage and empower every individual to learn from their experiences and grow in their mastery of skills.

But the vital role of L&D can be diluted if it is not set up correctly at the beginning. In organizational evolution the HR function is commonly brought in first. After all, once the founders hire a few employees, there is a real and pressing need to address compensation, and benefits, payroll, and adhere to the ever-growing complexity of employment law. And because one of HR's top priorities is risk mitigation, learning often first arrives in the form of compliance training, followed shortly by management training to address problems arising from the actions of some inept managers.

If you are not intentional about shifting the role of learning and development to be a strategic business partner, it can remain in the service of risk mitigation, which is important, but ultimately not in the interest of the organization's long-term success.

It's your job to make sure the learning function takes the lead on maximizing potential of your talent. Initiate your partnership with leaders and HR professionals. Set up the meetings and ask great consulting questions. Take a deep dive into what the various functions need, and the current state of the employees' skills, abilities, and attitudes.

Explore what the top performers are doing that sets them apart from the rest. Get crisp on what peak performance looks like, both for your current phase in the Greiner Curve and the next. As you have these meetings, be sure you spend time identifying what the ideal state looks like and map your findings in a shared document.

This will give you a real picture of what is needed and help you prioritize learning initiatives. It will also help you engage in meaningful conversations about talent acquisition, management, and development. This becomes the roadmap for programs for your "HiPos," as well as every employee group and function. It also helps with succession planning, making sure that every vital employee is backed up by a viable successor who is being prepared to step in when needed.

This learning strategy is something to share widely with key stakeholders, to help you gain support and resources. You will want to drive the execution of your learning strategy over time, holding yourself accountable for delivering the results that matter for your organization.

As you intentionally build a positive culture of learning, one of your goals should be creating a cohesive landscape in which all types and forms of learning can live. If you don't, learning can quickly get dispersed and diluted rather than serving the strategic goals of the organization. I'm not talking about a learning management system or catalog of offerings—although those will certainly play a role—but rather a learning strategy that has a place for all kinds of learning to be recognized and organized.

Let me walk you through how to do that. First, assess your current learning landscape, preferably with a group of people so that you can get as much input as possible. Create a master list of where and how learning happens in your organization—not just the ones the L&D team creates or pays for, but all kinds of learning that happen across the organization and also outside of it.

I recommend that you do two rounds of assessment. This allows you to matrix different learning forms or formats into categories: information, instruction, and inspiration. Within instruction, call out which have elements of communication, demonstration, and experimentation. Ultimately, do this as a spreadsheet so that you can sort the data different ways as well as edit and add as needed.

Second, look at it from the learners' perspective. How do they identify and pursue learning? Sometimes they search by job title and role level, and often they search by skill or topic. Either way, mapping capabilities or competencies organized or coded by level, from beginner to expert or master is a method that works well.

Once you have a thorough understanding of the learning opportunities that do (or should) exist, design a learning landscape that has a place for everything. This will be a visible learning document or webpage that acts as a roadmap where your employees can navigate all the available resources. Your goal is twofold here: make it easy for your learners to find meaningful learning opportunities, and for them to view those opportunities as part of your organization's employee experience. For example, if your company sends an employee to attend an industry conference, what's a better takeaway for that investment? Your employee thinking, "Wow, I learned such great, new information at that conference," or "Wow, I learned such great, new information at that conference because my company made it a priority for me. What a great place to work." Obviously, it's the latter but to make that connection they need to see these things as *part of your organization's* learning landscape.

Do this by branding and marketing your learning strategy so that it is consistently visible to all members of your community and it becomes their go-to place for learning. Frame it in a way that honors your organization's vision, mission, and values.

Most traditional learning management systems are not flexible enough to accurately reflect all existing learning options and can only host limited content. So, many organizations create their own learning site or portal as the gateway to the various options and experiences, allowing them an intuitive learning roadmap where all types of learning have a place. Some products operate more as a platform that host all kinds of learning and diverse content, creating intuitive pathways that allow learners to track and measure their own progress and improvement. Check out current options like Degreed and Pathgather but remember that the industry is constantly evolving, so stay on top of new developments and trends. I find eLearningIndustry.com and TrainingIndustry.com to be great sources of information, along with the Association for Talent Development's annual conference and international exposition, and Elliott Masie's programs.

Finally, in your new learning landscape, you will inevitably need to differentiate those learning experiences that are officially vetted, approved, or aligned with your organization from all the other kinds. This curated list will be a service to your learners; when they are choosing among the over-whelming number of options, it will help them to know which you have given a stamp of approval. Consider how you might use a symbol, color, or some other indicator to distinguish them. Having a cohesive learning land-scape will directly support creating a positive culture of learning and, more importantly, help your learners navigate the many wonderful opportunities that await them.

A cohesive landscape unifies many pieces to support learning

48. Curating Content and Sharing Knowledge

Have you ever done an online search for something you need for your job? Isn't it crazy how much information pops up and how many solutions there are to choose from on a simple search like "online learning"? Technology has made searching for answers as easy as the click of a button—but that one click can send you into total overwhelm. After first sorting out which results are ads and which ones look trustworthy, you're still left with a seemingly endless amount of options. Which ones should you explore? In what order?

Your learners experiences this in the same way. They start with a need but can quickly get overwhelmed with choices, many of them unhelpful. This is one way curating content helps you guide your learners, by enabling them to cut through the noise. Curating just means that you have selected the best and most relevant options and made them easily available. I do this all the time. For example, while I may design a great learning solution on leading change, I love to give my learners the ability to extend their learning. I pull together a small smorgasbord of options that align with the primary material I created but may provide a deeper dive or alternate method that better fits diverse learners. Here are some ideas that have worked for me:

- **Share articles:** I like to link to current articles on a topic, seeking fresh and recent content. I vet the articles to make sure they come from reliable sources like *Harvard Business Review*, *Fast Company*, *Forbes*, etc. I also prefer content that is based in research or best practices and only use "opinion" pieces if they come from an industry expert or thought leader, like a chief executive from a well-known company and/or have a counterpoint article to create balance.

- **Share books and book chapters:** Some learners really like the depth and breadth that a book provides on a topic. I'll create links to books that I've vetted and recommend, listing both print and audio versions. You can also buy subscriptions to digital libraries if you want to make those books accessible to your employees. Sometimes, you may want to recommend one chapter from a book or even assign one as part of the learning solution. (In such cases, you will need to contact the publisher to learn how you can license that one chapter for your learners.)

- **Share videos:** I really love TED talks, which present cutting-edge ideas by thought leaders in less than 20 minutes. Many thought leaders and authors have videos on their own websites, which you can link to as well. I have authored several courses for LinkedIn Learning, so I always create a playlist of either entire courses or of videos from a range of courses (mine and other authors). I encourage you to explore their playlist and learning path features.

- **Don't forget podcasts and websites:** There are lots of great options these days and by offering a range you can honor the diverse needs of adult learners.

- **Give credit:** I always make a point of sharing the source material used in building my solutions. As you've seen in this book, for example, I highly value Dan Pink's work on motivation and Brené Brown's work on vulnerability. Their research is woven into some of my own learning solutions—given proper credit, of course—so I naturally encourage learners to further explore their work.

- **Remember logistics:** You will need to figure out how and where you house your curated materials. In small organizations, things can live on a shared drive. As you grow, you will want to make your materials accessible and searchable through a website or other online portal. This can be a great way to partner with your colleagues in the technology and communications functions of your organization.

Some learners will dig in, devouring everything recommended. Others won't now but may down the road when something arises that prompts the need for more information.

So, get in the habit of curating additional content for your learning solutions, to build a culture of learning and empower your learners to accelerate their own growth. Just be sure that you vet everything first—it's important to make sure the content aligns with your organization's context and culture, and that the quality matches your learning program's brand.

Empower Knowledge Sharing

What amazing learning is happening in your organization today? In one department, an employee might find a great online resource that helps solve a stubborn challenge and allows their work to move forward. In another, a manager provides some great coaching that improves a team's outcomes. Somewhere else, two colleagues might work together to innovate a solution to a cross-functional problem—they give each other a high five and keep on going. Make such learning moments more visible and easier to share with others in your organization.

By empowering knowledge sharing, you leverage those special moments of insight, improvement, and innovation so they can be used by everyone. And you demonstrate that your organization values and promotes learning of all types. In fact, studies have shown that knowledge-sharing is a big differentiator for high-performing organizations, with their employees sharing knowledge at four times the rate of those in lower-performing organizations.

Here are a few ways to empower knowledge sharing. First, create a way for people to share stories of those learning moments. This will depend on what technology you have available and may include sending an email to the L&D team, or posting to a shared portal or social media. On Twitter, people are using the hashtag #AlwaysBeLearning, so if you combine something like this with your organization's Twitter handle, you can create a fun campaign for your current employees that also builds your employer brand. Marriott Hotels uses an app so employees can share learning moments as well as crowdsource how to offer great customer service. Employees upload pictures of real or potential situations and then share what they do at their property to solve it.

Second, talk about the learning that's happening in your organization. You can't do this enough. It should be an ongoing campaign that includes the informal learning you're getting from submissions as well as the formal programs and events you're hosting.

Next, shine a light on great learning and knowledge sharing. When you see interesting examples or stories, feature them. Pick ones that exemplify best practices, amazing results, or influential people. By featuring the best, you both reward good work and you set it up as a model for others.

Fourth, make the knowledge sharing accessible to others. A note of warning here: knowledge sharing can get large quickly. If you let it be a free-for-all, you might soon have hundreds of submissions and no way for folks to find what they need. So, like with your curated learning materials, think through a system or process that will work for cataloguing and displaying them. You might want to consider cross-listing the same piece of learning in these ways: (1) by function or department, since it's likely that sales things will be of most interest for folks in sales, etc.; (2) by form, so that all videos or PDFs can be found together; and, of course, (3) by topic or competency, like communication, coding, time management, or customer service.

Fifth, consider how you'll address issues of quality control. When you empower knowledge sharing, you are going to get a range of submissions, some of which you might not want to "recommend" or put a stamp of approval on because they don't align with your L&D brand or the organization's brand. This is a conversation to have with your team and other stakeholders. I think it's great to separate them so that *all* knowledge sharing gets put up in its own section of your portal or website, and with the formal, approved, vetted materials living together. That allows you to shine the light on the best ones, and being moved to the "approved" category becomes a bit of an honor for the submitters.

Knowledge sharing empowers and uplevels all members of an organization

Sixth, educate your teams on how to create good materials. Hosting an event on how to create good materials is another way to call attention to the launch of your knowledge-sharing efforts. And you will get much better-quality sharing if you teach folks some aspects of good instructional design, how to create an interactive PDF, or edit a video. In addition to learning events, you might make a playlist of good instructional videos for your learners. For example, LinkedIn Learning has several great courses on this topic. There are also a lot of knowledge-sharing tools available.

Finally, leverage brain science with built-in rewards. We know from neuroscience research that if you want to increase something you need to recognize and reward it. So, make sure that you always acknowledge submissions. You might even want to track submissions by department and create some awards or even friendly competitions so that you make it fun and rewarding to share. All these knowledge-sharing strategies will help you amplify the great learning that is already happening and positively reinforce your developing culture of learning.

49. Leveraging Opportunities to Overcome Challenges

As you launch your culture of learning, you will likely hit some of these common challenges. Let's explore some things you can do to address them.

Challenge: The learning program's purpose is not clearly communicated or understood. People often don't really understand the value of building a culture of learning, or they perceive it all as just more training.

Opportunity: To educate your company, use this book and look for other helpful materials (such as my LinkedIn Learning courses on this topic) to build a comprehensive proposal that clearly demonstrates the value to the organization, including their return on investment or ROI. When it's time to roll it out to the company, plan a sustained campaign to get learners of all levels on board.

Challenge: The existing company culture has some negative baggage. Perhaps your current learning programs are missing the mark and your brand or trust in your team has been harmed in the process. A study by the Corporate Executive Board found that only 23 percent of organization leaders were satisfied with the overall effectiveness of L&D. And only 12 percent of CFOs felt that HR/L&D were spending the right amount in the right places. While shocking, this may not be news to learning professionals. In a recent study, LinkedIn Learning discovered that only 25 percent of learning professionals would recommend their own programs to peers. Only 25 percent! This means the majority of learning professionals know that their programs could be better but they may not know how to fix them—yet.

Opportunity: Here are three immediate steps you can take to help people get over any negative associations with your learning programs:

1. Be open to the feedback and take an honest look at what it's telling you. You cannot improve if the issues aren't clear. Are the comments about the skills of specific instructors or facilitators? Then focus on better sourcing, preparation, or practice. Are people dissatisfied with the content or design of certain programs or events? Address this with better learning design, using the principles from this book. Or perhaps there is a mismatch between the identified problem and the solution, which can be fixed with better consulting questions and mapping to the Greiner Curve.

2. Shift your perspective from training to learning, as training is built from the organization's perspective and done *to* employees with a "one size fits all" approach. While learning is designed from the learner's perspective, enabling them to succeed by addressing their real needs and pain points. Learning honors varied backgrounds and experience and the goal is to meaningfully enhance potential and performance.
3. Check out the programs and certifications offered by the Association for Talent Development. There are lots of opportunities to improve across a wide range of skills and topics.
4. Read Jack Phillips's material on demonstrating ROI to understand how to align behavior change with business outcomes and design better learning programs.

Challenge: Learning is not currently recognized or rewarded.

Opportunity: This is a common problem. Research by Deloitte found that there was no link at all between the acquisition of news skills and workforce incentives in 55 percent of surveyed organizations. And only 35 percent were linked through the annual compensation/evaluation process. I have already covered many ways you can uplevel the value and visibility of learning. But in addition to those, let's tackle the big issue: the performance evaluation process. If it's not already, base your rewards system on a *combination* of both outcomes and growth/learning. By focusing only on outcomes, you may reward people for doing a great job but not really encourage them to stretch themselves. When you reward growth and learning, you'll get more of it, from every level of performer, and that will fuel your organization's success.

Challenge: Insufficient resources and support.

Opportunity: It is certainly true that you can do more with more but instead of blindly purchasing more bells and whistles, first focus your energy on making the best use of the resources you have now. Align your programs and events to teach people how to create psychological safety and empower more knowledge sharing and better instruction. When you build your learning strategy around organizational growth and business outcomes, it will be easier for leaders to see your proposal's value, especially if you calculate the real costs of attrition and disengagement. You can make the case that investing in a learning culture will quickly pay for itself.

You might also develop learning advocates within your organization. Approach open and influential leaders to talk about enhancing the learning culture of their team, project, or department. Frame it as a pilot program, so it doesn't sound like a big commitment. Use the techniques I've shared and track metrics so that you'll have great data to demonstrate your success story. Once you have a win, it'll be easier to expand to other groups until you hit the tipping point.

Creative Ways to Maximize Your Resources

Leverage any or all of the many opportunities to build your positive culture of learning. You can also stretch your learning dollars by partnering with groups both inside and outside of your organization. Consider these options:

Internally

- **Repurpose the wheels you have instead of reinventing them.** You already have some great learning materials, so get more uses out of them. Start a repository of presentation decks, exercises, articles, etc., to make it easier to use elements in other ways, like creating a mini-video, an interactive PDF, or another workshop.

- **Pump up your knowledge sharing.** Look for great learning already happening in your organization, and when you find it make it available to a wider audience. This can save your budget by helping you avoid wasting resources developing similar programs.

- **Tap into your people's gifts and passions.** Most organizations do not fully utilize the talents and passions of their people. Yours might just have an expert on communication, marketing, or emotional intelligence, who'd be honored to help. Put out a call and see what happens.

- **Share costs across the organization.** If you see a product or service you want to invest in, but don't quite have the budget, see if you can partner with other departments who might benefit. This can be a great way to stretch your budget while also collaborating with other leaders.

Externally

Possibilities range from regional to state, from federal to international.

- **Partner with local academic institutions.** From elementary schools to universities, your local schools are filled with experts who know how to teach others. I have seen some amazing partnerships develop that are cost effective and mutually beneficial, with expertise shared both ways. Some local classes and workshops might fill your needs and free up some of your budget. Faculty experts might be available to teach on topics you need. Their students might benefit from internships or mentoring. And, of course, employees might uplevel their skills by earning an appropriate certificate or degree, especially if your company offers tuition reimbursement.

- **Explore options with local government and nonprofit organizations.** Look for shared interests and goals with those in your area. Even promoting some of their educational programs might boost your own catalog of offerings in meaningful ways.

- **Make connections with your sister cities.** Most cities have sister cities in other parts of the world. Ask your local chamber of commerce and see what options might exist to share resources and experts as well as offer unique travel opportunities.

- **Ask vendors about flexibility and creative options.** Instead of deciding that you cannot afford something, talk to the vendor first. Some have different price points and others offer discounts for members of national associations like SHRM or ATD. Also, some vendors are looking for opportunities to study the impact of their product or pilot a new version. These can become elements of your negotiation.

- **Utilize professional associations.** Every industry has professional associations that offer ongoing training and professional development. Paying for employee memberships might just open up whole new levels of content while saving you lots of money. They also offer free webinars that might be worthy of advertising to your employees.

Once you get started, ideas start popping. I encourage you to form a cross-organizational committee to explore and build on these ideas. That way you harness their collective wisdom and they're also likely to have connections that open doors to unique possibilities.

The bottom line: building a positive culture of learning is a collective effort, cocreated by members of your community. So, don't feel like it all rests on your shoulders. Instead of doing it all, focus on bringing the right people together and enjoy exploring and building something amazing.

50. Keepers of the Culture

A positive learning culture is not owned nor created by one department or program. It lives in the collective efforts of all members of the community. You might have an amazing offering of learning opportunities with all the state-of-the-art technology money can buy; however, if people feel that it's not safe to take risks and make mistakes, you will never create a positive culture of learning.

In this chapter, we'll look at the roles different groups play. Let's start with the talent professionals like HR and L&D. Obviously, they are intimately involved in creating a positive culture of learning, because they typically develop or sponsor an organization's learning strategy and related offerings. I focus on these four essential components of a talent professional's work.

1. **Attend to both halves of the learning ecosystem.** This means both how we support people improving and growing and also creating an environment where it's okay to take risks and make mistakes. If you are not addressing both halves, you won't succeed. Remember the Growth Culture's tree metaphor: all the sunlight in the world cannot fix toxic soil. So continually track metrics that matter—things like employee engagement, psychological safety, improvement/progress, and attrition of your best people—and when you identify an area or team that is not thriving, proactively intervene until things shift. If you do not, the whole thing is undermined.

2. **Build the critical components of learning culture into your offerings so that people are equipped to play their role in the collective effort.** For example, ensure your management and leadership programs teach leaders how to cultivate growth mindset, create psychological safety, provide effective coaching, give and receive constructive feedback, and demonstrate empathy and other qualities of emotional intelligence. Employee programs need these elements plus information on how to empower their own development, through their supervisor or team and, if necessary, around them. Onboarding practices should help new employees easily integrate into a positive culture of learning by introducing them to the values of continuous improvement and the support and resources available to them.

3. **Be an authentic example and model of an ideal learning culture.** HR and L&D are often called the "keepers of the culture" and it is very true. The organization always reflects the health of the talent professional teams. Always. When HR and L&D are not thriving, the rest of the organization is held back. I have seen this in every single organization I have ever worked with. And I'm not the only one. Globally recognized experts Dr. Brené Brown and Dr. Cherie Carter-Scott have made similar observations. If executive management teams don't have a positive culture of learning, you will see that cascade across the organization because they produce so many aspects that drive the employee experience.

   This is a version of Conway's law, a concept that originated in computer programming or coding, namely that the quality of a product reflects the quality of the team that builds it. *Harvard Business Review* conducted a study of Conway's law that proved this mirror effect in all kinds of organizations. For our purposes in this book, the HR and L&D teams need to be places where it's safe to take risks and make mistakes. Managers need to be great at coaching and people need to frequently engage in learning. If these teams don't model a positive culture of learning, it's difficult to create it across the organization. If HR and L&D are not in good shape, this needs to be your first priority. They also need to work together, trusting each other, and leveraging their unique perspectives and strengths to serve the rest of the organization.

   Remember, you are also a member of the culture, so model lifelong learning by continuing to grow and develop, seeking feedback, and putting in the practice to develop mastery. Make sure you invest in your own learning. Your ability to lead and help others depends on your own growth and development. Attend national talent conferences to stay up on the latest developments and products.

4. **Align your systems and processes with a positive culture of learning.** This is especially true for your performance management process. Remember, if you only measure performance by outcomes, you are missing something vital. Cultivate a growth mindset by measuring and valuing growth and improvement: at least 30 percent of your evaluation reflect efforts spent on learning and improving, and factoring it into how you give rewards like raises and bonuses. If you truly want to create a positive culture of learning, "walking your talk" has to be valued in consistent and visible ways like reviews and rewards. Use your

completed assessment to develop an action plan to address issues and improve your organization.

Now let's look at your top leaders and executives. In my experience, the healthiest and most vibrant organizations have leaders who themselves have a growth mindset and believe in the power of learning. They talk about their own mistakes, insights they've gained, and their own quest for improvement. They also advocate for learning. They empower a leader, and give that person the same status as HR, creating a team of talent equals. They not only promote learning but participate in it. This might include kicking off a new program and authentically attending some events as an eager learner. The key here is humility—the best leaders never assume that because they sit at the top of the organization they have nothing left to learn. In fact, the best leaders are the hungriest learners.

As mentioned, a leader's beliefs, attitudes, and actions cascade through a whole organization, making it much easier for the talent teams to get traction. Finally, and perhaps most importantly, leaders hold managers accountable for the health of their teams. This one is a biggie. All of the above efforts fall flat if managers are not evaluated and rewarded based on the health of their teams. High-performing organizations do not turn a blind eye to the damage being done by poor managers. Let me be clear: When there is high turnover on a team, something is wrong. When teams stumble and underperform, something needs attention. When there are high levels of absenteeism, illness, and complaints to HR, you have a crisis.

Just like with trees, employees will show you the quality of the soil they sit in. And if you ignore them, and allow poor managers to stay in those roles, you will undermine all attempts to create a positive culture of learning. I believe this is the number one problem that needs to be addressed in organizations today. Those that do reap amazing rewards in the form of competitive advantage, employee engagement, and customer loyalty.

Creating a positive culture of learning in your organization is critical to its ongoing success. Sure, expansion is good and new products are important, but nothing is more crucial than creating a culture of learning. A positive culture of learning helps you not only develop your talent to meet *today's* challenges but starts preparing them *now* for what is coming. Everything else will arise from that—and soon you will have an orchard of thriving trees. Martha Soehren, chief talent development officer at Comcast sums it up in quote I used to open this section (a favorite of mine), "There are 10 seeds in an apple. But how many apples are in a seed? You must help your employees learn and grow so they become the talented workforce you need tomorrow."

Conclusion: Final Thoughts on Learning

It's clear that learning is at the heart of how we reach our fullest potential—as individuals, as organizations, and as societies. The good news is that our biology is set up to help us learn every day.

My hope is that the Three Phase Model of Learning gives you a better understanding of how to harness the power of your brain to intentionally maximize the learning process, both for yourself and others in your life.

In your hands, you also hold the key to building a great culture of learning, both in your home and workplace. We all have the opportunity to support learning, so begin today by implementing the model and its corresponding strategies. Even better, convene a team that will help you expand these best practices across the organizations of which you are a part.

This model is also the backbone of training programs I have built on topics like change management, peak-performing teams, coaching skills, emotional intelligence, innovation, strategic vision, and manager excellence. If you'd like to get certified in my programs so you can bring them to your organization, please visit BrittAndreatta.com/Training.

I'll close by saying that we all have the ability to fulfill our potential and to help those around us do the same. Continue to tend to your own growth and development. You have a lot of unrealized ability within you—we all do. And the more we do it together, the more we can change the world. Thank you for taking this learning journey with me. Here's to the power of yet!

Warmly,

Britt Andreatta

Synthesize Your Learning Journey into Action

For this section, think about how you can enhance or develop a growth culture of learning. Use these questions to help you identify possible strategies to support your goals.

- Using the questions in chapter 44 to assess your organization, what can you learn about your current culture of learning?
- What are your organization's current issues or problems? Identify the metrics that matter so you can use them to measure your priorities and progress over the coming months.
- Where does your organization fall in the Greiner Curve? According to the model, what pain points can you predict are coming? How can you best prepare for them?
- Take time to map your current learning offerings. From your analysis, what are your top action items in the coming months?
- What content curation and knowledge sharing currently exist in your organization? What are some short- and long-term improvements you can make?
- Are there any obstacles to creating a growth culture of learning? Identify possible solutions. How can you mobilize others in your organization to cocreate the culture you desire?

As we conclude, look over your notes from the various learning journeys in this book. You should now have a robust understanding of learning. Take a moment to finalize your notes and create an action plan that will unfold over the next few weeks and months.

- What are your three biggest takeaways from this book?
- What are some actions you can take in the next 30, 60, and 90 days that will help you thrive as a lifelong learner?
- If you are in a leadership role, what are some actions you can take in the next 30, 60, and 90 days that will uplevel your team or organization?
- Consider how you might share some of what you have learned with colleagues and leaders in your organization. For additional resources and training materials to help you, visit BrittAndreatta. com or BrittAndreatta.com/Training.

REFERENCES + RESOURCES

INTRODUCTION

Angelou, M. (1996). *I know why the caged bird sings.* New York, NY: Random House.

Deloitte (2019, May). *2019 Global human capital trends: Leading the social enterprise* [PDF]. Retrieved from https://www2.deloitte.com/insights/us/en/focus/human-capital-trends.html

Merriam, S.B., & Bierema, L.L. (2014). *Adult learning: Linking theory and practice.* San Francisco, CA: Jossey-Bass.

Clark, R. E., & Martin, S. J. (Eds.). (2018). *Behavioral neuroscience of learning and memory.* New York, NY: Springer International Publishing.

I. NEW DEVELOPMENTS IN THE NEUROSCIENCE OF LEARNING

Krishnamurti, J. (1977). *Krishnamurti on education.* New York, NY: HarperCollins.

Chapter 1

Demitri, M. (2018). Types of brain imaging techniques [Webpage]. Retrieved from https://psychcentral.com

Baars, B.B., Gage, N.M. (Eds.). (2013). Brain imaging. *Fundamentals of cognitive neuroscience: A beginner's guide.* Cambridge, MA: Academic Press.

Waltz, E. (2018, March 21). A new wearable brain scanner [Blog]. Retrieved from https://spectrum.ieee.org

Gazzaley, A., Anguera, R., Ziegler, D., Jain, R., Mullen, T., Kothe, C., . . . Fesenko, J. (2015). *Glassbrain flythrough 2015* [Video]. Available from https://neuroscape.ucsf.edu

Saul, D. (Producer), & Fleischer, R. (Director). (1966). *Fantastic voyage* [Motion picture]. United States: 20th Century Fox.

Bennett, C.M., Baird, A.A., Miller, M.B., & Wolford, G.L. (2010). Neural correlates of interspecies perspective taking in the post-mortem Atlantic salmon: An argument for proper multiple comparisons correction. *Journal of Serendipitous and Unexpected Results, 1*(1), 1-5.

Scicurious. (2012, September 25). IgNobel Prize in neuroscience: The dead salmon study [Blog]. *Scientific American.* Retrieved from https://blogs.scientificamerican.com

Chapter 2

Gardner, H. (2006). *Multiple intelligences: New horizons in theory and practice.* New York, NY: Basic Books.

Gardner, H. (2011). *Frames of mind: The theory of multiple intelligences.* New York, NY: Basic Books.

Shearer, C.B., & Karanian, J.M. (2017). The neuroscience of intelligence: Empirical support for the theory of multiple intelligences? *Trends in Neuroscience and Education, 6,* 211-223.

Shearer, B. (2018). Multiple intelligences in teaching and education: Lessons learned from neuroscience. *Journal of Intelligence, 6*(3), 38.

Armstrong, T. (2017). *Multiple intelligences in the classroom* (4th ed). Alexandria, VA: ASCD.

Calaprice, A. (2010). *The ultimate quotable Einstein.* Princeton, NY: Princeton University Press.

Chapter 3

Kaufman, S.B. (2017, December 6). The real neuroscience of creativity. *HuffPost.* Retrieved from https://www.huffpost.com/entry/the-real-neuroscience-of_b_3870582/

Kaufman, S.B., & Gregoire, C. (2015). *Wired to create.* New York, NY: Penguin Random House.

Vartanian, O., Bristol, A.S., & Kaufman, J.C. (Eds.). (2013). *Neuroscience of creativity.* Cambridge, MA: MIT Press.

Kounios, J., & Beeman, M. (2014, January). The cognitive neuroscience of insight. *Annual Review of Psychology, 65,* 71-93.

Kounios, J., & Beeman, M. (2015). *The eureka factor: Aha moments, creative insight, and the brain.* New York, NY: Random House.

Erickson, B., Truelove-Hill, M., Oh, Y., Anderson, J., Zhang, F., & Kounios, J. (2018, November). Resting-state brain oscillations predict trait-like cognitive styles. *Neuropsychologia, 120,* 1-8.

MacKenzie, G. (1998). *Orbiting the giant hairball: A corporate fool's guide to surviving with grace.* New York, NY: Viking.

Gilbert, E. (Producer). (2016, July 25). Brené Brown on "big strong magic" [Audio podcast]. *Magic Lessons.* Podcast retrieved from https://www.elizabethgilbert.com/magic-lessons/

Gregoire, C. (2016, March 18). The new science of the creative brain on nature. *Outside.* Retrieved from https://www.outsideonline.com

Merrett, R. (2015, July 27). A neuroscience approach to innovative thinking and problem solving [Webpage]. Retrieved from https://www.cio.com.au

Andreatta, B. (2018, November). The neuroscience of innovation [Keynote address]. *Technology Affinity Group Conference.* Tucson, AZ.

Pollan, M. (2018). *How to change your mind: What the new science of psychedelics teaches us about consciousness, dying, addiction, depression, and transcendence.* New York, NY: Penguin Press.

Carhart-Harris, R., Kaelen, M., & Nutt, D. (2014, September). How do hallucinogens work on the brain? *The Psychologist, 27,* 662-665.

Petri, G., Expert, P., Turkheimer, F., Carhart-Harris, R., Nutt, D., Hellyer, P.J., & Vaccarino, F. (2014, December 6). Homological scaffolds of brain functional networks. *Journal of the Royal Society Interface, 11.*

Chapter 4

Doidge, N. (2007). *The brain that changes itself: Stories of personal triumph from the frontiers of brain science.* New York, NY: Penguin Books.

Doidge, N. (2015). *The brain's way of healing: Remarkable discoveries and recoveries from the frontiers of neuroplasticity.* New York, NY: Penguin Books.

Bolte Taylor, J. (2009). *My stroke of insight: A brain scientist's personal journey.* New York, NY: Penguin Books.

Taylor, J.B. (2008). *My stroke of insight* [Video]. TED. Retrieved from https://www.ted.com

Bhattacharya, A. (2016, August 15). Paraplegics are learning to walk again with virtual reality [Video & Webpage]. Retrieved from https://qz.com

Donati, A., Shokur, S., Morya, E., Campos, D., Moioli, R., Gitti, C., . . . Nicolelis, M. (2016, August 11). Long-term training with a brain-machine interface-based gait protocol induces partial neurological recovery in paraplegic patients. *Scientific Reports, 6.*

Samsung (Producer). (2018). *Human nature: Samsung brand philosophy–Do what you can't* [Video]. Retrieved from https://www.youtube.com/watch?v=m3-8HC1lUTo/

Bionik. (n.d.). *Published research: Neuorecovery within reach* [Webpage]. Retrieved from https://www.bioniklabs.com

Kwon, D. (2018, February 8). DBS with nanoparticle-based optogenetics modifies behavior in mice. Retrieved from https://www.the-scientist.com

Ren, J., Li, H., Palaniyappan, L., Liu, H., Wang, J., Li, C., & Rossini, P.M. (2014, June 3). Repetitive transcranial magnetic stimulation versus electroconvulsive therapy for major depression: A systematic review and meta-analysis. *Progress in Neuro-Psychopharmacology and Biological Psychiatry, 51,* 181-189.

Poston, B. (2014, June). *Transcranial direct current stimulation for the treatment of Parkinson's disease* [Webpage]. Retrieved from https://www.michaeljfox.org/grant/transcranial-direct-current-stimulation-treatment-parkinsons-disease?grant_id=1144/

The Brain Stimulator (n.d.). *Brain stimulation comparison* [Webpage]. Retrieved from https://the-brainstimulator.net

Donati, A., Shokur, S., Morya, E., Campos, D., Moioli, R., Gitti, C., . . . Nicolelis, M. (2016, August 11). Long-term training with a brain-machine interface-based gait protocol induces partial neurological recovery in paraplegic patients. *Scientific Reports, 6.*

Courtine, G., & Bloch, J. (Producers). (2018). *Walking again after spinal cord injury* [Video]. Lausanne, Switzerland: EPFL + CHUV. Retrieved from https://www.youtube.com/watch?v=XFXWR4b9iVA/

Bréchet, L., Mange, R., Herbelin, B., Theillaud, Q., Gauthier, B., Serino, A., & Blanke, O. (2019). First-person view of one's body in immersive virtual reality: Influence on episodic memory. *PLOS ONE, 14*(3).

Chapter 5

Segovia, K.Y., & Bailenson, J.N. (2019, March 5). Memory versus media: Creating false memories with virtual reality. Retrieved from https://brainworldmagazine.com

SilVRthread (n.d.). Virtual reality use cases [Webpage]. Retrieved from https://www.silvrthread.com/usecases

Pixvana (Producer). (2019). *Virtual reality and enterprise training: Seabourn case study* [Video]. Retrieved from https://vimeo.com/310438727/

Herrera, F., Bailenson, J., Weisz, E., Ogle, E., & Zaki, J. (2018, October 17). Building long-term empathy: A large-scale comparison of traditional and virtual reality perspective-taking. *PLOS ONE, 13*(10).

Bailenson, J., & Amway (Producers). (2018, May 22). *How experiencing discrimination in VR can make you less biased* [Video]. Retrieved from https://bigthink.com/videos

Markowitz, D.M., Laha, R., Perone, B.P., Pea, R.D., & Bailenson, J.N. (2018). Immersive virtual reality field trips facilitate learning about climate change. *Frontiers in Psychology, 9.*

Technologies with potential to transform business and business education: Virtual and augmented reality. (n.d.). *AACSB*. Retrieved from https://www.aacsb.edu/publications

Pixvana. (2019, July 17). *XR, VR, AR, MR: What do they all mean?* [Webpage]. Retrieved from https://pixvana.com

Portico Studios (Producer). (2017). *Introducing Portico Studios* [Video]. Retrieved from https://www.youtube.com/watch?v=PttFfsGS3hM&feature=youtu.be/

Kwon, D. (2018, March 1). Intelligent machines that learn like children. *Scientific American, 218*(3), 26-31.

Teach Thought Staff. (2018, September 16). 10 roles for artificial intelligence in education [Webpage]. Retrieved from https://www.teachthought.com

Chapter 6

Silva, A. (2017, July). Memory's intricate web. *Scientific American, 317*(1), 30-37.

Mohs, R. (2007, May 8). How human memory works [Webpage]. Retrieved from https://science.howstuffworks.com

Mohs, R. (2005, November). Commentary on "diagnosis of Alzheimer's disease: Two decades of progress." *Alzheimer's & Dementia: The Journal of the Alzheimer's Association, 1*(2), 116-117.

Suchan, B. (2018, November 15). Why don't we forget how to ride a bike? *Scientific American.* Retrieved from https://www.scientificamerican.com

Clark, R. E., & Martin, S. J. (Eds.). (2018). *Behavioral neuroscience of learning and memory.* New York, NY: Springer International Publishing.

II. REMEMBER: THE MEMORY MATRIX

Williams, T. (1963). *The milk train doesn't stop here anymore.* New York, NY: Dramatists Play Service, Inc.

Chapter 7

Silva, A. (2017, July). Memory's intricate web. *Scientific American, 317*(1), 30-37.

Shen, H. (2018, January 10). How to see a memory. *Nature.* Retrieved from https://www.nature.com/articles

Clark, R.E., & Martin, S. J. (Eds.). (2018). *Behavioral neuroscience of learning and memory.* New York, NY: Springer International Publishing.

MacKay, D.G. (2014, May/June). The engine of memory. *Scientific American, 25*(3), 30-38.

Miller, G.A. (1956) The magical number seven, plus or minus two: Some limits on our capacity for processing information. *Psychological Review, 63*(2), 81-97.

Nee, D., & D'Esposito, M. (2018). The representational basis of working memory. In Clark, R. E., & Martin, S. J. (Eds.). *Behavioral neuroscience of learning and memory* (pp. 213-230). New York, NY: Springer International Publishing.

Giofre, D., Donolato, E., & Mammarella, I.C. (2018, July). The differential role of verbal and visuospatial working memory in mathematics and reading. *Trends in Neuroscience and Education, 12*, 1-6.

Pink, D. (2018). *When: The scientific secrets of perfect timing*. New York, NY: Riverhead Books.

Greenwood, V. (2016, September/October). You smell sick. *Scientific American, 27*(5), 15.

Noonan, D. (2017, September/October). Smell test may sniff out oncoming Parkinson's and Alzheimer's. *Scientific American, 28*(5), 4-7.

Wikipedia/Olfactory nerve. (n.d.). Retrieved July 19, 2019, from Wikipedia: https://en.wikipedia.org/wiki/Olfactory_nerve

Physicians' Review Network. (2016, June 21). Fun facts about your tongue and taste buds [Webpage]. Retrieved from https://www.onhealth.com/content/1/tongue_facts

Skin fun facts [Webpage]. (2017, October 23). Retrieved from https://forefrontdermatology.com/skin-fun-facts/

eLife. (2018, January 18). Touching: Skin cell to nerve cell communication uncovered [Webpage]. Retrieved from https://www.technologynetworks.com/neuroscience/news/how-we-sense-touch-skin-cells-communicate-with-nerve-cells-296464/

Chapter 8

Clark, R.E., & Martin, S.J. (Eds.). (2018). *Behavioral neuroscience of learning and memory*. New York, NY: Springer International Publishing.

Springen, K. (2010, January 1). Recall in utero. *Scientific American Mind, 20*(7), 15.

Northrup, C. (2016). *Goddesses never age: The secret prescription for radiance, vitality, and well-being*. Carlsbad, CA: Hay House.

Bennett, D.A., Schneider, J.A., Buchman, A.S., Barnes, L.L., Boyle, P.A., & Wilson, R.S. (2012, July 1). Overview and findings from the Rush Memory and Aging Project. *Current Alzheimer Research, 9*(6), 646-663.

Wilson, R.S., Boyle, P.A., Yu, L., Barnes, L.L., Schneider, J.A., & Bennett, D.A. (2013, July 23). Life-span cognitive activity, neuropathologic burden, and cognitive aging. *Neurology, 81*(4), 314-321.

Simpson, M. (2011, October 30). A sister's eulogy for Steve Jobs. *The New York Times*.

Chapter 9

Reber, P. (2010, May 1). What is the memory capacity of the human brain? *Scientific American*. Retrieved from https://www.scientificamerican.com

Ebbinghaus, H. (1885). *Memory: A contribution to experimental psychology* (Ruger H. A. & Bussenius C. E., Trans.). In *Classics in the History of Psychology*. Retrieved from http://psychclassics.yorku.ca/Ebbinghaus/index.htm/

Bjork, R., & Bjork, E. (1992). A new theory of disuse and an old theory of stimulus fluctuation. In Healy, A., Kossly, S., & Shiffrin, R. (Eds.), *From learning processes to cognitive processes: Essays in honor of William K. Estes* (Vol. 2, pp. 35-67). Hillsdale, NJ: Earlbaum.

Burnett, M. (Creator) & Weiner, D. (Director). (2007-2019). *Are you smarter than a 5th grader?* [TV series]. CBS Television City, CA: Mark Burnett Productions.

Corkin, S. (2013). *Permanent present tense: The unforgettable life of the amnesic patient H. M.* New York, NY: Basic Books.

MacKay, D. (2014, May/June). The engine of memory. *Scientific American, 24*(3), 30-38.

Wikipedia/Henry Molaison. (n.d.). Retrieved July 19, 2019, from Wikipedia: https://en.wikipedia.org/wiki/Henry_Molaison

Carey, B. (2015). *How we learn: The surprising truth about when, where, and why it happens*. New York, NY: Random House.

Carey, B. (2010, December 6). No memory, but he filled in the blanks. *The New York Times*.

Oteyza, M. (Producer), & Cowperthwaite, G. (Producer & Director). (2013). *Blackfish* [Motion picture]. New York, NY: Magnolia Pictures.

Chapter 10

Rawson, K.A., & Dunlosky, J. (2011). Optimizing schedules of retrieval practice for durable and efficient learning: How much is enough? *Journal of Experimental Psychology: General, 140*(3), 283-302.

Rohrer, D., & Taylor, K. (2006). The effects of overlearning and distributed practice on the retention of mathematics knowledge. *Applied Cognitive Psychology, 20*, 1209–1224.

Carpenter, S.K., Cepeda, N.J., Rohrer, D., Kang, S.H.K., & Pashler, H. (2012). Using spacing to enhance diverse forms of learning: Review of recent research and implications for instruction. *Educational Psychology Review, 24*(3), 369-378.

Roediger, H.L., III, & Karpicke, J.D. (2018, March 29). Reflections on the resurgence of interest in the testing effect. *Perspectives on Psychological Science, 13*(2), 236-241.

Doctor, P. (Director), & Rivera, J. (Producer). (2015). *Inside out* [Animated film]. Burbank, CA: Disney, & Emeryville, CA: Pixar.

Bell, M.C., Kawadri, N., Simone, P.M., & Wiseheart, M. (2013, March 22). Long-term memory, sleep, and the spacing effect. *Memory, 22*(3), 276-283.

Roizen, M. & Oz, M. (2019, February 10). Sleep soundly and safely. *Houston Chronicle.* Retrieved from https://www.houstonchronicle.com

Huffington, A. (2014). *Thrive: The third metric to redefining success and creating a life of well-being, wisdom, and wonder.* New York, NY: Harmony.

Bagnall, V. (2017, April 21). The best ways to revise—what does the evidence say? [Webpage]. Retrieved from https://connectionsinmind.co.uk

Putnam, A.L., Sungkhasettee, V.W., & Roediger, H.L., III. (2016, September 29). Optimizing learning in college: Tips from cognitive psychology. *Perspectives on Psychological Science, 11*(5), 652-660.

Putnam, A.L., Sungkhasettee, V.W., & Roediger, H.L., III. (2016, November 22). When misinformation improves memory: The effects of recollecting change. *Psychological Science, 28*(1), 36-46.

Chapter 11

Tse, D., Langston, R.F., Kakeyama, M., Bethus, I., Spooner, P.A., Wood, E.R., . . . Morris, R.G.M. (2007, April 6). Schemas and memory consolidation. *Science, 316*(5821), 76-82.

Clement, J. (2019, May 14). Daily time spent on social networking by internet users worldwide from 2012 to 2018 (in minutes). Retrieved from https://www.statista.com

Nielsen (2018, July 31). Time flies: US adults now spend nearly half a day interacting with media [Webpage]. Retrieved from: https://www.nielsen.com/us/en/insights

Smith, K. (2019, June 13). 126 amazing social media statistics and facts [Blog]. Retrieved from https://www.brandwatch.com

Pew Research Center. (n.d.). *State of the news media.* Retrieved July 19, 2019, from https://www.pewresearch.org/topics/state-of-the-news-media/

Digital around the world in 2018: Key statistical indicators for the world's internet, mobile, and social media users [Graphic]. (2018, January). Retrieved from https://www.smartinsights.com

Chapter 12

Brown, P.C., Roediger, H.L., III, & McDaniel, M.A. (2014). *Make it stick: The science of successful learning.* Cambridge, MA: Belknap Press.

Whitney, D., Trosten-Bloom, A., & Rader, K. (2010). *Appreciative leadership: Focus on what works to drive winning performance and build a thriving organization.* New York, NY: McGraw-Hill Education.

Hill, W.E. (1915). My wife and my mother-in-law [Illustration]. Retrieved July 19, 2019, from Wikipedia: https://en.wikipedia.org/wiki/My_Wife_and_My_Mother-in-Law

Davachi, L., Kiefer, T., Rock, D., & Rock, L. (2010). Learning that lasts through AGES. *NeuroLeadership Journal, 3*, 1-10.

Jung-Beeman, M., Bowden, E.M., Haberman, J., Frymiare, J.L., Arambel-Liu, S., Greenblatt, R., . . . Kounios, J. (2004, April 13). Neural activity when people solve verbal problems with insight. *PLoS Biology 2*(4).

Newman, T. (2018, April 30). What happens in the brain during a 'eureka' moment? Retrieved from https://www.medicalnewstoday.com

Tik, M., Sladky, R., Luft, C.D.B., Willinger, D., Hoffmann, A., Banissy, M. J., . . . Windischberger, C. (2018, August). Ultra-high-field fMRI insights on insight: Neural correlates of the aha!-moment. *Human Brain Mapping, 39*(8), 3241-3252.

Davis, J. (2014, May 18). *The neuroscience of learning* [Presentation]. American Society for Training and Development International Conference and Exposition. Washington, DC.

Chapter 13

Andreatta, B. (2018). *Wired to connect: The brain science of teams and a new model for creating collaboration and inclusion.* Santa Barbara, CA: 7th Mind Publishing.

Moser, M-B., & Moser, E.I. (2016, January). Where am I? Where am I going? *Scientific American, 314*(1), 26-33.

Maguire, E.A., Woollett, K., & Spiers, H.J. (2006). London taxi drivers and bus drivers: A structural MRI and neuropsychological analysis. *Hippocampus, 16*(12), 1091-1101.

Jabr, F. (2011, December 8). Cache cab: Taxi drivers' brains grow to navigate London's streets. *Scientific American.* Retrieved from https://www.scientificamerican.com

Caruso, C. (2017, July/August). Don't forget: You, too, can acquire a super memory. *Scientific American, 28*(4), 10-12.

Handwerk, B. (2017, March 13). Neuroscientists unlock the secrets of memory champions [Webpage]. *Smithsonian.* Retrieved from https://www.smithsonianmag.com/science-nature

Dresler, M., Shirer, W.R., Konrad, B.N., Muller, N.C.J., Wagner, I.C., Fernandez, G.,…Greicius, M.D. (2017, March 8). Mnemonic training reshapes brain networks to support superior memory. *Neuron, 93*(5), 1227-1235.

Chapter 14

Dorough, B., Ahrens, L., Newall, G., Frishberg, D., Yohe, T., Mendoza, R (Composers). (2002). *Schoolhouse rock!* [DVD]. Burbank, CA: Buena Vista Home Entertainment.

The Daily Show with Trevor Noah (Producer). (2016, November 29). *Exclusive—Mahershala Ali extended interview* [Video]. Retrieved from http://www.cc.com/video-clips

Word Science Festival (Producer). (2009, July 23). *Bobby McFerrin demonstrates the power of the pentatonic scale* [Video]. Retrieved from https://www.youtube.com/watch?v=ne6tB2KiZuk/

Word Science Festival (Producer). (2014, July 29). *Notes and neurons: In search of the common chorus* [Video]. Retrieved from https://www.youtube.com/watch?v=S0kCUss0g9Q/

Bell, C.L. (2004). Update on community choirs and singing in the United States. *International Journal of Research in Choral Singing, 2*(1). Retrieved from https://acda.org

Menehan, K. (2014, April 6). How to get the whole room singing [Webpage]. Retrieved from https://www.chorusamerica.org

Rossato-Bennett, M. (Producer & Director), McDougald, A. (Producer), & Scully R. (Producer). (2014). *Alive inside: A story of music and memory* [Motion picture]. United States: Projector Media.

Top 11 health benefits of singing. (2019, February 11). Retrieved from https://www.healthfitnessrevolution.com/top-11-health-benefits-of-singing/

Moisse, K., Woodruff, B., Hill, J., & Zak, L. (2011, November 14). Gabby Giffords: Finding words through song. *ABC News.* Retrieved from https://abcnews.go.com

Wearing, D. (2005). *Forever today: A memoir of love and amnesia.* London, England: Corgi.

Thompson, W.F., & Schlaug, G. (2015, March/April). The healing power of music. *Scientific American, 26*(2), 32-41.

Chapter 15

Roediger, H.L., III, & Karpicke, J.D. (2006, September). The power of testing memory: Basic research and implications for education practice. *Perspectives on Psychological Science, 1*(3).

III. DO: BUILDING SKILLS + DESIGNING HABITS

Branson, R. (2012). *Like a virgin: Secrets they won't teach you at business school.* New York, NY: Penguin.

Chapter 16

Skill [Webpage] and Habit [Webpage]. (n.d.). *Wordnik.* Retrieved from https://www.wordnik.com

Clark, R.E., & Martin, S.J. (Eds.). (2018). *Behavioral neuroscience of learning and memory.* New York, NY: Springer International Publishing.

Suchan, B. (2018, November 15). Why don't we forget how to ride a bike? *Scientific American.* Retrieved from https://www.scientificamerican.com

MacKay, D. (2014, May/June). The engine of memory. *Scientific American, 25*(3), 30-38.

Gratton, L., & Scott, A. (2017). *The 100-year life: Living and working in an age of longevity.* London, England: Bloomsbury Business.

Barrett, H. (2017, September 4). Plan for five careers in a lifetime. *Financial Times.* Retrieved from https://www.ft.com

Csikszentmihalyi, M. (2008). *Flow: The psychology of optimal experience.* New York, NY: Harper Perennial Modern Classics.

Dietrich, A. (2003, June 1). Functional neuroanatomy of altered states of consciousness: The transient hypofrontality hypothesis. *Consciousness and Cognition, 12*(2), 231-256.

Dietrich, A. (2004, December 1). Neurocognitive mechanisms underlying the experience of flow. *Consciousness and Cognition, 13*(4), 746-761.

Gruber, M.J., Gelman, B.D., & Ranganath, C. (2014, October 22). States of curiosity modulate hippocampus-dependent learning via the dopaminergic circuit. *Neuron, 82*(2), 486-496.

Duhigg, C. (2012). *The power of habit: Why we do what we do in life and business.* New York, NY: Random House.

Chapter 17

Andreatta, B. (2016, December 9). *The best way to change habits through workforce learning* [Blog]. Retrieved from https://learning.linkedin.com/blog

Track and field [Webpage]. (n.d.). Retrieved from https://tagteach.com/TAGteach_track_and_field/

Keysers, C., & Gazzola, V. (2014, April). Hebbian learning and predictive mirror neurons for actions, sensations and emotions. *Philosophical Transactions of the Royal Society B: Biological Sciences, 369*(1644), 20130175.

Gardner, B., Lally, P., & Wardle, J. (2012, December). Making health habitual: The psychology of 'habit-formation' and general practice. *The British Journal of General Practice, 62*(605), 664–666.

Lally, P., van Jaarsveld, C.H.M., Potts, H. W. W., & Wardle, J. (2010, October). How are habits formed: Modelling habit formation in the real world. *European Journal of Social Psychology, 40*(6), 998-1009.

Del Giudice, M., Manera, V., & Keysers, C. (2009, March). Programmed to learn? The ontogeny of mirror neurons. *Developmental Science, 12*(2), 350-363.

Dohle, C.I., Rykman, A., Chang, J., & Volpe, B.T. (2013, August 5). Pilot study of a robotic protocol to treat shoulder subluxation in patients with chronic stroke. *Journal of Neuroengineering and Rehabilitation, 10.*

Krebs, H.I., Dipietro, L., Levy-Tzedek, S., Fasoli, S., Rykman, A., Zipse, J.,...Hogan, N. (2008). A paradigm shift for rehabilitation robots. *IEEE-EMBS Magazine, 27*(4), 61-70.

Bionik (n.d.). *Published research: Neuorecovery within reach* [Webpage]. Retrieved from https://www.bioniklabs.com/published-research

Andreatta, B. (2018). *Brain-based Manager Training* [Presentation]. Retrieved from www.Britt Andreatta.com/Training

Nohria, N., & Beer, M. (2000, May-June). Cracking the code of change. *Harvard Business Review.*

Leonard, D., & Coltea, C. (2013, May 24). Most change initiatives fail—but they don't have to. *Gallup Business Journal.* Retrieved from https://news.gallup.com/businessjournal/162707/change-initiatives-fail-don.aspx

Andreatta, B. (2017). *Wired to resist: The brain science of why change fails and a new model for driving success.* Santa Barbara, CA: 7th Mind Publishing.

Chapter 18

Bavelier, D., & Green, C.S. (2016, July). The brain-boosting power of video games. *Scientific American, 315*(1), 26-31.

The Medical Futurist. (2018, June 7). The Swedish speed camera lottery and healthy living. Retrieved from https://medicalfuturist.com/swedish-speed-camera-lottery-healthy-living

Duhigg, C. (2012). *The power of habit: Why we do what we do in life and business.* New York, NY: Random House.

Kapp, K. (2012). *The gamification of learning and instruction: Game-based methods and strategies for training and education.* San Francisco, CA: Pfeiffer.

Kazdin, A., & Rotella, C. (2014). *The everyday parenting toolkit*. New York, NY: Mariner Books.

Yale Parenting Center [Website]. (n.d.). Retrieved from https://yaleparentingcenter.yale.edu/

Chapter 19

Hikosaka, O. (2010, July). The habenula: From stress evasion to value-based decision-making. *Nature Reviews Neuroscience, 11*(7), 503-513.

Ullsperger, M., & von Cramon, D. (2003). Error monitoring using external feedback: Specific roles of the habenular complex, the reward system, and the cingulate motor area revealed by functional magnetic resonance imaging. *Journal of Neuroscience, 23*(10), 4308-4314.

Seligman, M. (1972). Learned helplessness. *Annual Review of Medicine, 23*(1), 407-412.

Peterson, C., Maier, S., & Seligman, M. (1995). *Learned helplessness: A theory for the age of personal control*. Oxford, England: Oxford University Press.

Brown, B. (2012). *Daring greatly: How the courage to be vulnerable transforms the way we live, love, parent, and lead*. New York, NY: Gotham Books.

Chapter 20

Edmondson, A. (1999). Psychological safety and learning behavior in work teams. *Administrative Science Quarterly, 44*(2), 350-383.

Edmondson, A., & Zhike, L. (2014). Psychological safety: The history, renaissance, and future of an interpersonal construct. *Annual Review of Organizational Psychology and Organizational Behavior, 1*, 23-43.

Edmondson, A. (2012). *Teaming: How organizations learn, innovate, and compete in the knowledge economy*. San Francisco, CA: Jossey-Bass.

Costly conversations: Why the way employees communicate will make or break your bottom line [Press release]. (2016, December 6). Retrieved from https://www.vitalsmarts.com.press/2016/12/costly-conversations-why-the-way-employees-communicate-will-make-or-break-your-bottom-line/

Duhigg, C. (2016, February 25). What Google learned from its quest to build the perfect team. *New York Times*. Retrieved from https://www.nytimes.com

Chapter 21

Bobinet, K. (2016, January/February). The power of process. *Experience Life*. Retrieved from https://experiencelife.com

Dweck, C. (2008). *Mindset: The new psychology of success*. New York, NY: Random House.

McChesney, C., Covey, S., & Huling, J. (2012). *The four disciplines of execution: Achieving your wildly important goals*. New York, NY: Free Press.

Chapter 22

Rizzolatti, G., & Craighero, L. (2004). The mirror-neuron system. *Annual Review of Neuroscience, 27*, 169-192.

Winerman, L. (2005). The mind's mirror. *American Psychological Association, 36*(9), 48.

Iacoboni, M., Molnar-Szakacs, I., Gallese, V., Buccino, G., Mazziotta, J.C., & Rizzolatti, G. (2005). Grasping the intentions of others with one's own mirror neuron system. *PLoS Biology, 3*(3), E79.

Iacoboni, M. (2008). *Mirroring people: The science of empathy and how we connect with others*. New York, NY: Picador.

Model mugging [Website]. (n.d.). Retrieved from http://modelmugging.org/

Chapter 23

Practice [Webpage]. (n.d.). Retrieved from https://www.instructure.com/bridge/products/practice

Mursion [Website]. (n.d.). Retrieved from https://www.mursion.com/

Cubic [Website]. (n.d.). Retrieved from https://www.cubic.com/

Strivr [Website]. (n.d.). Retrieved from https://strivr.com/

Academy925 [Website]. (n.d.). Retrieved from https://academy925.com/

Amplifire [Website]. (n.d.). Retrieved from https://amplifire.com/

Area9 [Website]. (n.d.). Retrieved from https://area9lyceum.com/

Maise, E. (2015, September 24). 890—Oil rig learning, curators and connectors, trip to Asia [Blog]. *Elliott Masie's Learning Trends*. Retrieved from http://trends.masie.com/archives/2015/9/24/890-oil-rig-learning-curators-and-connectors-trip-to-asia.html

Pixvana [Website]. (n.d.). Retrieved from https://pixvana.com/

SilVR Thread [Website]. (n.d.). Retrieved from https://www.silvrthread.com/

Thomas, D., & Brown, J.S. (2011). *A new culture of learning: Cultivating the imagination for a world of constant change*. Scotts Valley, CA: CreateSpace Independent Publishing Platform.

Ericsson, A., & Pool, R. (2017). *Peak: Secrets from the new science of expertise*. New York, NY: Mariner Books.

Gladwell, M. (2008). *Outliers: The story of success*. New York, NY: Little, Brown and Company.

IV. LEARN: WHERE IT ALL STARTS

Rohn, J. (1985). *7 strategies for wealth and happiness*. New York, NY: Three Rivers Press.

Chapter 25

Kandel, E., Kupfermann, I., & Iversen, S. (2000). Learning and memory. In *Principles of Neural Science* (4th ed.). E. Kandel, J. Schwartz, & T. Jessell (Eds.). New York, NY: Elsevier.

Clark, R.E., & Martin, S.J. (Eds.). (2018). *Behavioral neuroscience of learning and memory*. New York, NY: Springer International Publishing.

Andreatta, B. (2019, May). *Wired to grow 2.0* [Presentation]. Association for Talent Development (ATD) International Conference and Exposition. Washington, DC.

Dirix, C.E.H., Nijhuis, J.G., Jongsma, H.W., & Hornstra, G. (2009, July 15). Aspects of fetal learning and memory. *Child Development, 80*(4).

Morokuma, S., Fukushima, K., Kawai, N., Tomonaga, M., Satoh, S., & Nakano, H. (2004). Fetal habituation correlates with functional brain development. *Behavioural Brain Research, 153*, 459–463.

Welch, M.G., & Ludwig, R.J. (2017). Mother/infant emotional communication through the lens of visceral/autonomic learning. *Early Vocal Contact and Preterm Infant Brain Development*, 271-294.

Sousa, D.A. (2017). *How the brain learns* (5th ed.). Thousand Oaks, CA: Corwin.

Brown, P.C., Roediger, H.L., III, & McDaniel, M.A. (2014). *Make it stick: The science of successful learning*. Cambridge, MA: Belknap Press.

Carey, B. (2015). *How we learn: The surprising truth about when, where, and why it happens*. New York, NY: Random House.

Siegal, D., & Bryson, T. P. (2011). *The whole-brain child: 12 revolutionary strategies to nurture your child's developing mind*. New York, NY: Bantam.

Merriam, S.B., & Bierema, L.L. (2014). *Adult learning: Linking theory and practice*. San Francisco, CA: Jossey-Bass.

Chapter 26

Bloom, B. (1956). *Taxonomy of educational objectives: The classification of educational goals*. New York, NY: Longman.

Andreatta, B. (2011). *Navigating the research university: A guide for first year students*. Boston, MA: Cengage Learning.

Kolb, D.A. (1983). *Experiential learning: Experience as the source of learning and development*. Upper Saddle River, NJ: Prentice Hall.

Chapter 27

Gardner, H. (2011). *Frames of mind: The theory of multiple intelligences* (3rd ed.). New York, NY: Basic Books.

Armstrong, T. (2017). *Multiple intelligences in the classroom* (4th ed.). Alexandria, VA: ASCD.

Shearer, C.B., & Karanian, J.M. (2017). The neuroscience of intelligence: Empirical support for the theory of multiple intelligences? *Trends in Neuroscience and Education, 6*, 211-223.

Davis, K., Christodoulou, J., Seider, S., & Gardner, H. (2011). The theory of multiple intelligences. In R.J. Sternberg & S.B. Kaufman (Eds.), *Cambridge Handbook of Intelligence* (pp. 485-503). Cambridge, England: Cambridge University Press.

Dweck, C. (2008). *Mindset: The new psychology of success.* New York, NY: Random House.

Butler, R. (2006). Are mastery and ability goals both adaptive? *British Journal of Educational Psychology, 76*(3), 595-611.

Bronson, P., & Merryman, A. *NurtureShock: New thinking about children.* New York, NY: Twelve.

Andreatta, B. (2015, March 17). *Create a growth mindset culture and unlock your talent's potential* [Webinar]. Retrieved from https://learning.linkedin.com/en-us/webinars/17/05/creating-a-growth-mindset/watch-recording?

Dweck, C., & Hogan, K. (2016, October 7). How Microsoft uses a growth mindset to develop leaders. *Harvard Business Review.*

Vander Ark, T. (2018, April 18). Hit refresh: How a growth mindset culture tripled Microsoft's value. *Forbes.*

Hagel, J., III, & Brown, J.S. (2010, November 23). Do you have a growth mindset? *Harvard Business Review.*

Dweck, C. (2015, September 22). Carol Dweck revisits the 'growth mindset.' *Education Week.*

O'Keefe, P.A., Dweck, C.S., & Walton, G.M. (2018, September 6). Implicit theories of interest: Finding your passion or developing it? *Psychological Science, 29*(10).

O'Keefe, P.A., Dweck, C., & Walton, G. (2018, September 10). Having a growth mindset makes it easier to develop new interests. *Harvard Business Review.*

Chapter 28

Hudson, F. (1999). *The adult years: Mastering the art of self-renewal.* Hoboken, NY: Jossey-Bass.

Slavid, L. (2019). [Personal communication with author].

McLean, P.D., & Hudson, F.M. (2011). *Life launch: A passionate guide to the rest of your life* (5th ed.). Santa Barbara, CA: The Hudson Institute of Santa Barbara.

Chapter 29

Bloom, F.E. (2007). *Best of the brain from Scientific American: Mind, matter, and tomorrow's brain.* Washington, DC: Dana Press.

Brown, P.C., Roediger, H.L., III, & McDaniel, M.A. (2014). *Make it stick: The science of successful learning.* Cambridge, MA: Belknap Press.

Hanson, R. (2013). *Hardwiring happiness.* New York, NY: Harmony Books.

Brown, B. (2015). *Rising strong: How the ability to reset transforms the way we live, love, parent, and lead.* New York, NY: Random House.

Achor, S. (2010). *The happiness advantage: How a positive brain fuels success in work and life.* New York, NY: Currency.

University of Queensland. (n.d.) What is neurogenesis? [Webpage]. Retrieved from https://qbi.uq.edu.au/brain-basics/brain-physiology/what-neurogenesis

Sousa, D. A. (2017). *How the brain learns* (5th ed.). Thousand Oaks, CA: Corwin.

Moser, M., & Moser, E. (2016). Where am I? Where am I going? *Scientific American, 313*(1), 26-33.

Tavares, R., Mendelsohn, A., Grossman, Y., Williams, C., Shapiro, M., Trope, Y., & Schiller, D. (2015). A map for social navigation in the human brain. *Neuron, 87*(1).

Hikosaka, O. (2010, July). The habenula: From stress evasion to value-based decision-making. *Nature Reviews Neuroscience, 11*(7), 503-513.

Ullsperger, M., & von Cramon, D. (2003). Error monitoring using external feedback: Specific roles of the habenular complex, the reward system, and the cingulate motor area revealed by functional magnetic resonance imaging. *Journal of Neuroscience, 23*(10), 4308-4314.

Rizzolatti, G., & Craighero, L. (2004). The mirror-neuron system. *Annual Review of Neuroscience, 27*, 169-192.

Chapter 30

Goleman, D. (2013). *Focus: The hidden driver of excellence.* New York, NY: Harper.

Johnstone, A.H., & Percival, F. (1976). Attention breaks in lectures. *Education in Chemistry, 13*, 49-50.

Ackerman, C. (2018, November 13). What is Kaplan's Attention Restoration Theory (ART)? *Positive Psychology.*

Burns, R.A. (1985 May). Information impact and factors affecting recall. *ERIC.* Retrieved from https://eric.ed.gov/?id=ED258639

Middendorf, J. (1996). The "change-up" in lectures. *National Teaching and Learning Forum 5*, 1-5.

Stuart, J., & Rutherford, R.J. (1978, September 2). Medical student concentration during lectures. *Lancet, 312*(8088), 514-516.

McLeish, J. (1968). *The lecture method.* Cambridge, England: Cambridge Institute of Education.

Chapter 31

Andreatta, B. (2014). *The neuroscience of learning* [Video]. Carpinteria, CA: LinkedIn Learning.

MacLean, P.D. (1990). *The triune brain in evolution: Role in paleocerebral functions.* New York, NY: Plenum Press.

Maslow, A. (1943). A theory of human motivation. *Psychological Review, 50*(4), 370-396.

Korb, A. (2012, November 20). The grateful brain: The neuroscience of giving thanks. *Psychology Today.*

Kinne, A. (2019, March 27). Gratitude–The ultimate performance-enhancing substance. *Workhuman.* Retrieved from https://resources.globoforce.com/globoforce-blog/gratitude-the-ultimate-performance-enhancing-substance

Hölzel, B., Carmody, J., Vangel, M., Congleton, C., Yerramsetti, S., Gard, T., & Lazara, S. (2011). Mindfulness practice leads to increases in regional brain gray matter density. *Psychiatry Research, 191*(1), 36-43.

Ricard, M., Lutz, A., & Davidson, R. (2014). Neuroscience reveals the secrets of meditation's benefits. *Scientific American, 311*(5), 38-45.

Davidson, R., & Begley, S. (2012). *The emotional life of your brain: How its unique patterns affect the way you think, feel, and live—and how you can change them.* New York, NY: Hudson Street Press.

Broderick, P. (2013). *Mindfulness curriculum for adolescents to cultivate emotion regulation, attention, and performance.* Oakland, CA: New Harbinger Publications.

Association for Mindfulness in Education [Website]. (n.d.). Retrieved from http://www.mindfuleducation.org/

Flook, L., Goldberg, S.B., Pinger, L.J., & Davidson, R.J. (2015). Promoting prosocial behavior and self-regulatory skills in preschool children through a mindfulness-based kindness curriculum. *Developmental Psychology, 51*(1), 44–51.

Goleman, D., & Davidson, R.J. (2017). *Altered traits: Science reveals how mediation changes your mind, brain, and body.* New York, NY: Avery.

Chopra, D., & Tanzi, R.E. (2012). *Super brain: Unleashing the explosive power of your mind to maximize health, happiness, and spiritual well-being* [Audiobook]. New York, NY: Random House Audio.

Gladding, R. (2013, May 22). This is your brain on meditation. *Psychology Today.*

Schwarts, J., & Gladding, R. (2011). *You are not your brain: The 4-step solution for changing bad habits, ending unhealthy thinking, and taking control of your life.* New York, NY: Penguin.

Zabletal, K. (2017, June 26). Neuroscience of mindfulness: What happens to your brain when you meditate. *Observer.*

Chapter 32

Carey, B. (2015). *How we learn: The surprising truth about when, where, and why it happens.* New York, NY: Random House.

Brown, B. (2019). The call to courage [Documentary]. *Netflix.* Retrieved from https://www.netflix.com/title/81010166.

Brown, B. (2012). *Listening to shame* [Video]. *TED.* Retrieved from www.ted.com

Brown, B. (2010). *The power of vulnerability* [Video]. *TED.* Retrieved from www.ted.com

Katie, B. (1994). *Loving what is: Four questions that can change your life.* New York, NY: Three Rivers Press.

Chapter 33

Clark, R.E., & Martin, S.J. (Eds.). (2018). *Behavioral neuroscience of learning and memory.* New York, NY: Springer International Publishing.

Roediger, H.L.III, & Karpicke, J.D. (2006, September). The power of testing memory: Basic research and implications for education practice. *Perspectives on Psychological Science, 1*(3).

Hartley, J., & Davies, I.K. (1986). Note-taking: A critical review. *Programmed Learning and Educational Technology, 15*, 207.

May, C. (2014, June 3). A learning secret: Don't take notes with a laptop. *Scientific American.* Retrieved from https://www.scientificamerican.com

Brown, S. (2014). *The doodle revolution: Unlock the power to think differently.* New York, NY: Portfolio.

Miller, J. (2014, August 14). Here's why, how, and what you should doodle to boost your memory and creativity. *Fast Company.*

Wakhlu, N. (2012, February 12). *Graphic recording* [Video]. Retrieved from https://www.youtube.com/watch?v=4AthvSWmMlw

Pink, D. (2010). *Drive: The surprising truth about what motivates us* [Video]. Retrieved from https://www.thersa.org/discover/videos

Brown, B. (2103). *Empathy* [Video]. Retrieved from www.thersa.org/discover/videos

Rifkin, J. (2010). *The empathic civilization* [Video]. Retrieved from https://www.thersa.org/discover/videos

Crowley, D. (2018, November 5). Dan Pink: Evidenced-based approach [Graphic]. Annandale, VA: Crowley & Co. Retrieved from https://www.learning2019.com/l18-graphic-illustrations/07-danpink

Pink, D. (2018). *When: The scientific secrets of perfect timing.* New York, NY: Riverhead Books.

Chapter 34

Andreatta, B. (2016). *Organizational learning and development* [Video]. Carpinteria, CA: LinkedIn Learning.

Andreatta, B. (2014). *The neuroscience of learning* [Video]. Carpinteria, CA: LinkedIn Learning.

Goleman, D. (2015). *Focus: The hidden driver of excellence.* New York, NY: Harper.

V: DESIGN + DELIVER LEARNING

Franklin, B. (2007). *Poor Richard's almanack.* New York, NY: Skyhorse Publishing.

Chapter 35

Andreatta, B. (2016). *Organizational learning and development* [Video]. Carpinteria, CA: LinkedIn Learning.

Andreatta, B. (2017). *Workshop facilitation* [Video]. Carpinteria, CA: LinkedIn Learning.

Ericsson, A., & Pool, R. (2017). *Peak: Secrets from the new science of expertise.* New York, NY: Mariner Books.

Chapter 36

Andreatta, B. (2016). *Organizational learning and development* [Video]. Carpinteria, CA: LinkedIn Learning.

Andreatta, B. (2014). *The neuroscience of learning* [Video]. Carpinteria, CA: LinkedIn Learning.

Andreatta, B. (2015, June 2). *Creating a transformative culture of learning: The benefits of developing employee potential* [Webinar]. Retrieved from http://w.on24.com/r.htm?e=992131&s=1&k=EB 9841B132019EB6627CD26E023E4684

Chapter 37

Andreatta, B. (2016). *Organizational learning and development* [Video]. Carpinteria, CA: LinkedIn Learning.

Andreatta, B., Thomson, L., Pate, D., Schnidman, Lu, L., & Dewett, T. (2017). *Workplace learning report: How modern L&D pros are tackling top challenges.* Carpinteria, CA: LinkedIn Learning.

Andreatta, B., & Petrone, P. (2016, November 18). L+D pros—Here's how to ensure you're seen as a strategic partner [Blog]. Retrieved from: https://learning.linkedin.com/blog

Chapter 38

Andreatta, B. (2016). *Organizational learning and development* [Video]. Carpinteria, CA: LinkedIn Learning.

Andreatta, B. (2017). *Workshop facilitation* [Video]. Carpinteria, CA: LinkedIn Learning.

Andreatta, B. (2017). *Wired to resist: The brain science of why change fails and a new model for driving success.* Santa Barbara, CA: 7th Mind Publishing.

Chapter 39

Andreatta, B. (2016). *Organizational learning and development* [Video]. Carpinteria, CA: LinkedIn Learning.

Andreatta, B. (2015, September 24). *Best practices for corporate online learning* [Webinar]. Retrieved from http://learn.gototraining.com

Gates, L. (2019). *Coaching and developing employees* [Video]. Carpinteria, CA: LinkedIn Learning.

Kaye, B., & Giulioni, J.W. (2019). *Help them grow or watch them go* (2nd ed.). San Francisco, CA: Berrett-Koehler Publishers.

Andreatta, B. (2018). *Change Quest™ facilitator training* [Video]. Retrieved from www.Britt Andreatta.com/Training

Knapp, J. (2016). *Sprint: How to solve big problems and test new ideas in just five days.* New York, NY: Simon & Schuster.

Chapter 40

Andreatta, B., & Petrone, P. (2017, July 17). Want to build a culture of learning? You need to embrace failure [Blog]. Retrieved from: https://learning.linkedin.com/blog

Andreatta, B. (2017). *Workshop facilitation* [Video]. Carpinteria, CA: LinkedIn Learning.

Andreatta, B. (2018). *Wired to connect: The brain science of teams and a new model for creating collaboration and inclusion.* Santa Barbara, CA: 7th Mind Publishing.

Chapter 41

Andreatta, B. (2017). *Workshop facilitation* [Video]. Carpinteria, CA: LinkedIn Learning.

Andreatta, B. (2010). *Instructor's manual for freshman success course* [Unpublished manuscript]. University of California, Santa Barbara.

Andreatta, B. (2018). Andreatta, B. (2018). *Change Quest™ facilitator training.* Retrieved from https://BrittAndreatta.com/Training

Andreatta, B. (2019). *Four Gates to Peak Team Performance™ facilitator training.* Retrieved from https://BrittAndreatta.com/Training

Chapter 42

Andreatta, B. (2017). *Workshop facilitation* [Video]. Carpinteria, CA: LinkedIn Learning.

Andreatta, B. (2015, March 17). *Flip your management training: Inspire your employees with blended learning* [Webinar]. Retrieved from http://www.lynda.com

Chapter 43

Kirkpatrick, D.L., & Kirkpatrick, J.D. (2007). *Implementing the four levels.* San Francisco, CA: Berrett-Koehler Publishers.

Phillips, J., & Phillips, P.P. (2016). *Handbook of training and evaluation measurement methods* (4th ed.). London, England: Routledge.

Phillips, J., & Phillips, P.P. (2015). *Measuring the success of leadership development.* Alexandria, VA: ATD Press.

Andreatta, B. (2015, April 22). *Demonstrating the ROI of learning: Calculating and demonstrating success* [Webinar]. Retrieved from http://www.lynda.com

Andreatta, B. (2018, July 25). *How to make talent a c-suite issue* [Webinar]. Degreed. Retrieved from https://www.youtube.com/watch?v=Ysn4zjj3vcA

Andreatta, B., & Petrone, P. (2017, March 24). How to calculate the cost of employee disengagement [Blog]. Retrieved from https://learning.linkedin.com/blog

VI. CREATE A GROWTH CULTURE OF LEARNING

Soehren, M. (2014). [Keynote address]. *Masie Learning Conference.* Orlando, FL. Retrieved from http://new.learningtalks.com/learning-2014/martha-soehren/

Chapter 44

Andreatta, B. (2015, March 17). *Create a growth mindset culture and unlock your talent's potential* [Webinar]. Retrieved from https://learning.linkedin.com/en-us/webinars/17/05/creating-a-growth-mindset/watch-recording?

Andreatta, B. (2017). *Creating a culture of learning* [Video]. Carpinteria, CA: LinkedIn Learning.

Andreatta, B. (2015, June 2). *Creating a transformative culture of learning: The benefits of developing employee potential* [Webinar]. LinkedIn Learning. Retrieved from http://w.on24.com/r.htm?e=992131&s=1&k=EB9841B132019EB6627CD26E023E4684

Grossman, R. (2015, May 1). How to create a learning culture. *HR Magazine.*

Association for Talent Development Research. (2016). *Building a culture of learning: The foundation of a successful organization.* Alexandria, VA: ATD Press.

Bersin, J. (2016). *Research report: Predictions for 2016.* Deloitte.

Corporate Executive Board. (2011). *L&D team capabilities survey.* Retrieved at https://www.cebglobal.com/

Chapter 45

Andreatta, B. (2017). *Creating a culture of learning* [Video]. Carpinteria, CA: LinkedIn Learning.

Bersin by Deloitte. (2017). *High-impact learning culture organization: Maturity model and top findings.* Deloitte University Press.

Association for Talent Development Research. (2016). *Building a culture of learning: The foundation of a successful organization.* Alexandria, VA: ATD Press.

Wells, J. (2017). *10 Ways to build a culture of continuous learning. Talent development.* Alexandria, VA: ATD Press.

Gallup. (2017). *State of the American workplace.* Retrieved from https://www.gallup.com/workplace/238085/state-american-workplace-report-2017.aspx

Gallup. (2017). *State of the global workplace.* Retrieved from https://www.gallup.com/workplace/238079/state-global-workplace-2017.aspx

McLean & Company. (2015). *Formalize a learning and development strategy* [Proprietary PDF].

Deloitte. (2019, May). *2019 Global human capital trends: Leading the social enterprise* [PDF]. Retrieved from https://www2.deloitte.com/insights/us/en/focus/human-capital-trends.html

Deloitte. (2017, May). *2017 Global human capital trends: Rewriting the rules for the digital age.* Retrieved from https://www2.deloitte.com/insights/us/en/focus/human-capital-trends/2017.html

World Economic Forum. (2018, September 17). *The future of jobs report 2018.* Retrieved from https://www.weforum.org/reports/the-future-of-jobs-report-2018

Society for Human Resource Management. (n.d.). *Placing dollar cost on turnover* [Webpage]. Retrieved from https://www.shrm.org/resourcesandtools/hr-topics/behavioral-competencies/critical-evaluation/pages/placing-dollar-costs-on-turnover.aspx

LinkedIn Learning. (2019). *2019 Workplace learning report: Key findings* [PDF]. Retrieved from https://learning.linkedin.com/content/dam/me/business/en-us/amp/learning-solutions/images/workplace-learning-report-2019/pdf/workplace-learning-report-2019.pdf

Chapter 46

Greiner, L. (1998, May). Evolution and revolution as organizations grow. *Harvard Business Review.*

Andreatta, B. (2018). *Change Quest™ model facilitator training* [Video]. Retrieved from Retrieved from www.BrittAndreatta.com/Training

Andreatta, B. (2016). *Organizational learning and development* [Video]. Carpinteria, CA: LinkedIn Learning.

Andreatta, B., & Petrone, P. (2016, December 2). The 6 stages every organization goes through as it matures [Blog]. Retrieved from https://learning.linkedin.com/blog

Andreatta, B. (2017). *Cracking the code: How organizational growth and consciousness shape talent development* [Presentation]. Society for Human Resource Management International Conference and Exposition. New Orleans, LA.

Laloux, F. (2014). *Reinventing organizations.* Millis, MA: Nelson Parker.

Chapter 47

Andreatta, B. (2017). *Creating a culture of learning* [Video]. Carpinteria, CA: LinkedIn Learning.

Andreatta, B. (2016). *Organizational learning and development* [Video]. Carpinteria, CA: LinkedIn Learning.

Degreed [Website]. (n.d.). Retrieved from https://degreed.com/

PathGather [Website]. (n.d.). Retrieved from https://www.pathgather.com/

LinkedIn Learning [Website]. (n.d.). Retrieved from https://www.linkedin.com/learning/

eLearning Industry [Website]. (n.d.). Retrieved from https://elearningindustry.com/
Masie Center [Website]. (n.d.). Retrieved from https://masie.com/

Chapter 48
Andreatta, B. (2016). *Organizational learning and development* [Video]. Carpinteria, CA: LinkedIn Learning.
Andreatta, B. (2017). *Creating a culture of learning* [Video]. Carpinteria, CA: LinkedIn Learning.
TED [Website]. (n.d.). Retrieved from https://www.ted.com/

Chapter 49
Andreatta, B. (2016). *Organizational learning and development* [Video]. Carpinteria, CA: LinkedIn Learning.
Andreatta, B. (2017). *Creating a culture of learning* [Video]. Carpinteria, CA: LinkedIn Learning.
Corporate Executive Board (2011). *L&D team capabilities survey*. Retrieved at https://www.ceb-global.com/
Andreatta, B. (2014, September). *Building L&D programs that maximize employee potential* [Webinar]. Retrieved from https://www.shrm.org/Pages/Custom404.aspx?requestUrl=https://www.shrm.org/multimedia/webcasts/pages/0914lynda.aspx
Association for Talent Development [Website]. (n.d.). Retrieved from https://www.td.org
Phillips, J., & Phillips, P.P. (2017). *The business case for learning*. Alexandria, VA: ATD Press.
Deloitte. (2019, May). *2019 Global human capital trends: Leading the social enterprise*. Retrieved from https://www2.deloitte.com/insights/us/en/focus/human-capital-trends.html
Andreatta, B., & Petrone, P. (2017, July 24). The most common challenges to building a learning culture (and how to overcome them) [Blog]. Retrieved from https://learning.linkedin.com/blog
Society for Human Resource Management [Website]. (n.d.). Retrieved from https://www.shrm.org

Chapter 50
Andreatta, B. (2017). *Creating a culture of learning* [Video]. Carpinteria, CA: LinkedIn Learning.
Brown, B. (2016, May 24). [Keynote address]. *Association of Talent Development (ATD) International Conference and Exposition*. Denver, CO.
Carter-Scott, C. (1991). *The corporate negaholic: How to deal successfully with negative colleagues, managers, and corporations*. New York, NY: Villard.
Wikipedia/Conway's law. (n.d.). Retrieved July 19, 2019, from Wikipedia: https://en.wikipedia.org/wiki/Conway%27s_law
Soehren, M. (2014). [Keynote address]. *Masie Learning Conference*. Orlando, FL. Retrieved from: http://new.learningtalks.com/learning-2014/martha-soehren/

Books by Dr. Britt Andreatta

 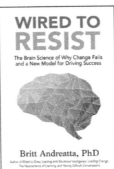 

Available at Amazon, Barnes&Noble, iBooks, and Google.
Learn more at www.BrittAndreatta.com/books

ACKNOWLEDGMENTS: PRACTICING GRATITUDE

This edition has been an intense journey. Because of some health issues in my family (everyone is good now), the project timeline got pushed back again and again. I'd set new, and what I hoped were realistic deadlines, only to blow past them to set new ones. It was an ongoing lesson in letting go of control, something that I am not great at...yet. As a result, my team shouldered this project in ways they did not sign up for and still, God bless them!, they came through for me on every level. At the end, we did a marathon push of late nights and weekends, which meant they were reading about how important breaks are for learning and creativity while not getting to take any. The irony is not lost on me and I am forever grateful for their support and flexibility.

My amazing book team includes: Jenefer Angell (Passionfruit Projects.com) whose skill at editing makes writing books easy and rewarding; Teresa Fanucchi, my incredible executive assistant who also happens to be a citation ninja; Claudia Arnett (BeTheMarkets.com) who does an amazing job with all my marketing, social media, and training programs, and Leah Young (Leah-Young.com) who directs and produces my videos as well as designs my website and platform.

A special shout out to my fabulous colleagues who brought their expertise to reviewing the book: Lisa Slavid, Director of Organizational and Performance Management at the University of California at Santa Barbara, and LV Hanson, Senior Culture Strategist at Procore.

My gratitude also goes to the teams of neuroscientists and researchers who shared their work with me. Your insatiable curiosity and willingness to dig deeper benefit us all. A special thanks to Michael Pollan, Brian Clark, Frederic Laloux, Elliott Masie, and Jamani Caillet for giving me permission to use their wonderful graphic images.

I'd also like to thank my wonderful husband Chris and my daughter Kiana who support and love me all of the time, even when I am deep in my research and writing. My kitties and chameleon also lent their support by being my audience as I talked through ideas. And of course, my family and friends.

Finally, to my tribe of leadership and learning professionals who work hard to bring out the best in their people and organizations through the power of learning. I am honored to share this important work with you and hope that it helps you help others.

Here's to the power of yet!

ABOUT THE AUTHOR

Dr. Britt Andreatta is an internationally recognized thought leader who creates brain science–based solutions for today's challenges. As CEO and President of 7th Mind, Inc., Britt Andreatta draws on her unique background in leadership, neuroscience, psychology, and learning to unlock the best in people and organizations.

Britt has published several titles including *Wired to Connect: The Brain Science of Teams and a New Model for Creating Collaboration and Inclusion*, and *Wired to Resist: The Brain Science of Why Change Fails and a New Model for Driving Success.* Upcoming books focus on the neuroscience of purpose and the conscious evolution of organizations.

Formerly Chief Learning Officer for Lynda.com and Senior Learning Consultant for Global Leadership and Talent Development at LinkedIn, Britt is a seasoned professional with more than 25 years of experience. She regularly consults with businesses, universities, and nonprofit organizations on leadership development and learning strategy. Corporate clients include Fortune 100 companies like Comcast and Apple, and also Ernst & Young, Microsoft, Domino's, LinkedIn, Franklin Covey, TransUnion, Avvo, Rust-Oleum, Alter Eco Foods, and Zillow.

Dr. Andreatta has worked with major educational institutions like the University of California, Dartmouth University, and the University of New Mexico, and nonprofit organizations like the YMCA and Prison Fellowship's Warden Exchange Program. Dr. Andreatta has served as professor and dean at the University of California, Antioch University, and several graduate schools.

She has received over 10 million views worldwide of her courses on Lynda.com and LinkedIn Learning. Other titles include *The Neuroscience of Learning, Creating a Culture of Learning, Organizational Learning & Development, Leading Change, Having Difficult Conversations*, and *Leading with Emotional Intelligence.*

A highly sought-after and engaging speaker, Britt delivered a TEDx talk called "How Your Past Hijacks Your Future." She regularly speaks at corporate events and international conferences, receiving rave reviews like "best speaker of the conference" and "best keynote I've ever heard."

Britt's industry accolades include several prestigious awards, such as the 2016 Global Training & Development Leadership Award from the World Training & Development Congress. She won the Gold Medal for *Chief Learning Officer* magazine's Trailblazer Award, and was also nominated for the CLO Strategy Award for her work in designing a performance management program based on growth mindset principles. *Talent Development* magazine identified her as an "outstanding thought leader and pioneer" featured in the June 2017 issue.

Dr. Andreatta regularly consults with executives and organizations on how to maximize their full potential. To learn more, visit her website and social channels:

Website: www.BrittAndreatta.com

LinkedIn: www.linkedin.com/in/brittandreatta/

Twitter: @BrittAndreatta

Take These Ideas Beyond the Page

Britt Andreatta has created a range of engaging and robust training materials based on the brain science of success. Become a certified trainer or take online ecourses. Learn more at:

BrittAndreatta.com/Training

The Change Quest™ Model training teaches vital skills for anyone leading or going through change. Become a certified trainer or take the individual ecourse for managers and employees.

The Four Gates to Peak Team Performance™ training focuses on how to consistently create high-performing teams. Discover the secrets of collaboration and why inclusion is vital. Become a certified trainer.

Materials include hands-on activities that drive real behavior change, videos of Britt teaching the content, content for a range of audiences, and a copy of the related book (*Wired to Resist* or *Wired to Connect*). It's online and self-paced. More topics coming soon. Learn more at:

BrittAndreatta.com/Training

PRAISE

"You were not only the best keynote we have had for this annual conference, you were the best keynote I have seen, EVER."

Mark Walker, Board Member, Technology Affinity Group

"Britt taught her unique science-based approach to change management. The material was easily understandable and thought-provoking; it allowed participants to immediately apply the lessons and framework to how they lead change and initiatives. Top managers from a variety of offices found it extremely valuable."

Lisa Slavid, Organization and Performance Management,
University of California, Santa Barbara

"I've done the 'required' management and leadership training at a number of companies from small startups to giants in the enterprise space—including Microsoft and Cisco—and, without a doubt, the training that Britt Andreatta has created has been the most engaging and useful of all. The way she combines scientific research, first-hand experience, and practical advice has been incredibly valuable."

Tim Ahlers, Director of Product Management, Avvo

"The top two sessions were Britt Andreatta and Barack Obama" + "Your research/presentations are THE BEST! Thank you for pouring your passion and curiosity into your work and sharing it with us."

Attendees, Association for Talent Development's (ATD)
International Conference and Expo 2018

"Britt, sending a ton of thanks for your support of the Leader meeting last week—a TERRIFIC experience. The talk you gave spirited people in such a positive way AND your delivery was flawless. Thank you for helping us to get our leaders into the "think differently" space. Loved it!"

Martha Soehren, Chief Talent Officer and SVP, Comcast

"When a company has a major culture shift, you can rarely look to one person. Britt was an exception to this. What looked like company-wide management training became the foundation for the conversations, relationships, and plans to positively impact the culture. She was the rock star in the organization making sure the culture was solid."

Hilary Miller Headlee, VP of Global Sales, Alteryx

"You have powerful influence in our field and a whole generation of Learning & Development professionals is hungry for your message. People are better because of what you do."

Cory Kreeck, Executive Director for Training and
Development, Beachbody

CPSIA information can be obtained
at www.ICGtesting.com
Printed in the USA
LVHW022252260819
628943LV00022B/1530/P